19·99

Working with Men in Health and Social Care

Working with Men in Health and Social Care

Brid Featherstone
Mark Rivett
and
Jonathan Scourfield

SAGE Publications
Los Angeles • London • New Delhi • Singapore

First published 2007

SAGE Publications Ltd
1 Oliver's Yard
55 City Road
London EC1Y 1SP

SAGE Publications Inc.
2455 Teller Road
Thousand Oaks, California 91320

SAGE Publications India Pvt Ltd
B 1/I 1 Mohan Cooperative Industrial Area
Mathura Road
New Delhi 110 044

SAGE Publications Asia-Pacific Pte Ltd
33 Pekin Street #02-01
Far East Square
Singapore 048763

Library of Congress Control Number: 2006939013

British Library Cataloguing in Publication data

A catalogue record for this book is available from the British Library

ISBN 978-1-4129-1849-7
ISBN 978-1-4129-1850-3 (pbk)

Typeset by C&M Digitals (P) Ltd., Chennai, India
Printed on paper from sustainable resources
Printed in India by Replika Press Pvt. Ltd

Contents

Acknowledgements

The practice example on pages 35–36 ('Expansion of positive masculine qualities in men with depression') is reprinted with permission of the World Publishing for Men's Health GmbH, from Kilmartin, C. (2005) 'Depression in men: communication, diagnosis and therapy', *Journal of Men's Health and Gender*, 29(1): 95–99. Copyright © 2005.

The practice example on pages 144–147 ('Cognitive therapy for men') is reprinted with permission of John Wiley & Sons, Inc., from Mahalik, J.R. (2005) 'Cognitive therapy for men', in G.E. Good and G.R. Brooks (eds) *The New Handbook of Psychotherapy and Counseling with Men*. San Francisco: Jossey Bass, pp. 217–233. Copyright © 2005.

We are also grateful for permission from the Domestic Abuse Intervention Project, 202 East Superior Street, Duluth, Minnesota 55802 (www.duluthmodel.org) to reproduce the Power and Control Wheel, the Equality Wheel and the Lesbian/Gay Power and Control Wheel (pages 102, 103 and 110, respectivity).

Thanks to James Rowlands for the practice example on page 111.

1 Introduction

A book such as this would not have been written twenty years ago. An awareness of men as gendered is fairly new in health and social welfare. It took some years after the early development of social scientific interest in the social construction of masculinity for academics and practitioners to show an interest in practical engagement with men as gendered – that is, in engaging with men in such a way as to recognise how their identities and conduct are shaped by the way they are raised as men. A very early example of academic literature on the topic was Bowl's *The Changing Nature of Masculinity* in 1985. Around this time, small numbers of workers were trying out innovative work with particular groups of men – mostly offenders of various kinds for whom masculine socialisation had most starkly contributed to the problems they caused for others and themselves (see, for example, Senior and Woodhead, 1992). There were also around this time small groups of men working on masculinity through activist roots in various breeds of men's group that had arisen in the wake of feminism, either in support of or opposition to it. By the mid-to-late 1990s there was more dedicated interest and a small raft of books from mainstream publishers on working with men in probation, social work, counselling and community education (Pringle, 1995; Cavanagh and Cree, 1996; Newburn and Mair, 1996; McLean et al., 1996; Wild, 1999; Christie, 2001; Pease and Camilleri, 2001). By the time this book is being written the number of publications on men's health has mushroomed. In some areas of practice – e.g., family support, some aspects of health promotion, some work with abusers – it is now fairly mainstream to encounter explicit interest in work with men. However, in other fields of practice, for example social care for adults, the profile of explicit engagement with 'men's issues' is very rare.

Who is the book for?

We are aiming for breadth of appeal, beyond those who will most immediately identify with the tag 'health and social care'. The book should be relevant to social workers, youth and community workers and also to nurses and other health care professionals. We would also see it as relevant to work with offenders and to counselling. Our own professional backgrounds are as practitioners in child and family social work, probation and family therapy and also in training practitioners in these fields and in conducting related research.

Fundamentally, the book is about interventions in social contexts. These are likely to be 'psycho-social' interventions. It is often individual patients, clients or service users that workers encounter, and there is inevitably a psychological and therapeutic dimension to this work in addition to help with social functioning and social networks. The term 'social interventions' is used, in places, to clarify the scope of the discussion. We also refer in places and where appropriate to 'therapy' and 'psycho-social' interventions.

The book is inevitably about problematic aspects of masculinity. Social workers, nurses, counsellors and probation officers do not spend much of their time with men who are problem-free. They are there to arrange care for or to intervene in some way with men who are in some kind of need or whose behaviour is causing problems for others. Despite the macro-level global picture of continuing male privilege (Oakley, 2003), we are not dealing in this book with men who *enjoy* privilege but with men who are troubled and troublesome.

The scope of the book

One of the main messages of this book is that there are choices to be made in work with men; choices of a theoretical nature with important implications for practice. We should not assume that by declaring an interest in masculinity practitioners in health and social welfare will necessarily agree with each other. Even if they do apparently agree on a key idea, agreement in one area may well mask profound differences about other aspects of the work. These are the key issues that repeatedly surface in the book and that concern theoretical choices with implications for practice:

- How do we understand the nature of masculinity? Is our understanding more biological, sociological, political or psychological?
- How do we understand processes of change? On which theories of therapeutic and social intervention is our work based?
- What are our gender politics? For example, do we focus more on men's pain, or on attacking privilege, or on the differences between men?
- Are we more idealistic or pragmatic in our interventions? Do we seek transformation of men or more humble goals? Do we reinforce aspects of mainstream masculinity in order to engage with men, or should that be avoided?

We cannot, as authors, of course stand outside these debates. We have particular slants on the chapters we write and inevitably there are slight differences between the three of us. Our main pitch is for theoretical breadth rather than narrowness. We do not think it is helpful to close our thinking and our practices to traditions we know little about or do not like the look of. We do not think it is helpful to attempt ideological purity in this kind of work. The world is too complex a place for theoretical rigidity or political correctness in how we intervene with people's lives.

Our general stance is that men are not all the same but neither are they all different. There is considerable diversity of men in the client base of social workers, nurses, probation officers, counsellors and so on. But while there is diversity, psychological, sociological and political generalisations can inform our work. Men can cause problems for others and they themselves can also experience problems. We should not therefore approach work with men on the assumption that we are dealing with men either as a risk or a resource, a perpetrator or a victim. Either/or should be replaced with both/and (Goldner, 1991). This might – to some readers – seem like fence-sitting. We would argue that our stance is a principled position. Furthermore, at this point we should say a few words about how we understand the relationship between theory and practice.

This relationship is a contested one. It is beyond the remit of this chapter to do justice to the debates that are ongoing. Suffice to say that, as Fook (2002) notes, the idea of a linear relationship between acquiring knowledge in the academy and applying it in practice is problematic at a range of levels. The critique of 'grand theories' associated with the post-modern turn in the social sciences has had an impact here, although developments in relation to valuing and validating 'practice wisdom' precede this turn. Moreover, varying strands in the social sciences often subsumed within the umbrella term 'discourse analysis' (this term covers a very diverse and internally differentiated set of approaches), have contributed to a growth that has proved highly influential with those seeking to develop 'theories' *of* practice (rather than theories *for* practice) (see, for example, Taylor and White, 2000). A central issue is that practices with people in a variety of settings in health and social welfare involve people talking to each other about what troubles them, what might help and so on. There is, therefore, an increasing interest in understanding the function of talk in terms of establishing moral worth and discursive constructions.

We have sought to outline a variety of approaches because this offers the opportunity to consider differing ways of understanding men's lives and practices and to consider the value or otherwise of differing theoretical tools. As Chapter 3 addresses more fully, we think that there are important political choices and consequences involved in adopting particular theoretical perspectives. However, our approach is wide-ranging. Tackling the misery and injustice of our world, particularly in relation to the changes needed in and by men, requires as many tools as possible. We simply cannot afford the comfort zone which a comfortable theoretical purity would leave us in.

The final point to be made about the scope of the book is that we attempt some kind of international coverage, but have to admit our limitations in this regard. We are UK-based (Wales and England) and this location does to an extent limit the book's reflection of global diversity in terms of culture and policy development. We have intentionally not attempted to discuss the organisational context in which practice with men takes place, for fear this would limit the international focus of the book as well as the professional disciplines. Where we use practice examples, organisational culture does come through, however. Most of our practice examples are from the UK but we have also tried to incorporate some internationalism in this regard.

The structure of the book

The book is divided into three parts. The two crucial variables in approaches to working with men determine the organisation of the first two parts of the book: that is, gender politics (Part I – Chapters 2 and 3) and practice theories (Part II – Chapters 4 and 5). Part I sets the context for practice with men in gender theory, social policy and the occupational culture of relevant organisations. Part II provides a summary of practice models. Part III (Chapters 6–11) is organised according to specific groups of service users and includes chapters on fathers, abusive men, physical and mental health, boys and older men. Chapters 6–11 foreground broader issues for each theme and also offer some specific practice examples. Each of these chapters also includes suggestions of key reading. Unavoidably, there is some overlap of content, so the practice examples and discussions of particular practice issues could potentially have featured in more than one chapter. We have had to make some pragmatic decisions about organisation.

We begin the book with, in the next chapter, an overview of some key sociological and psychoanalytical theories of masculinity.

PART I

The Theory and Politics of Masculinity

2 Understanding Masculinities

Introduction

The last decades have seen an explosion in the study of gender relations. The key impetus for this was the re-emergence of feminism at the end of the 1960s. While the study of women and women's experiences was at the heart of this enterprise, understanding men's power and behaviour was, in complex ways, integral to the overall project. Through revealing the dynamics of gender relations, men and masculinity became visible in new and hitherto hidden ways. As Connell et al. (2005) note, however, those who became involved in understanding and working around issues to do with men and masculinity (in effect a 'new' field of study) took diverse positions – particularly in relation to questions of gendered power relations. In this chapter we offer an overview of some of the theoretical debates while the political implications are explored more fully in Chapter 3.

Language: debates and definitions

Debates and disagreements about language recur in the literature. The term 'men's studies' (as a reaction or counterpart to women's studies) has been rejected by many scholars in this field on the grounds that such a symmetrical approach is misleading (and politically problematic) in the context of the asymmetry of gender relations which rendered women's studies a project borne out of the process of subordination and oppression. Connell et al. (2005) suggest that terms such as 'studies of men and masculinities' or 'critical studies of men' are more accurate, as they reflect the inspiration from feminism, but do not imply a simple parallel with such research. Hearn (2004) appears to favour the term 'critical studies of men' and raises doubts about the usefulness of the concept of masculinities, pointing out the diverse and, to some degree, incompatible positions that have been adopted by theorists using such terms (see also Hearn, 1996). Connell (2000), who has been most associated with developing work around masculinities and with the term itself, has acknowledged that there are real difficulties in defining masculinity and masculinities. He also notes concerns that the varying definitions of masculinity and masculinities deployed in the literature are vague, circular and inconsistent. While agreeing with Hearn that the real object of concern is something called men, and that talk of masculinities can muddy the field, Connell does argue, however, that to talk about a group called men presupposes a distinction from and relation with another group called women, in effect presupposing an account of gender. It, therefore, presupposes what needs to be theorised and accounted for – the domain of gender.

> We need some way of naming conduct which is oriented to or shaped by that domain, as distinct from conduct related to other patterns in social life. Unless we subside into defining masculinity as equivalent to men, we must acknowledge that sometimes masculine conduct or masculine identity goes together with a female body. It is actually very common for a (biological) man to have elements of 'feminine' identity, desire and patterns of conduct. (Connell, 2000: 16–17)

We agree with Connell in relation to the above observations, but would also like to align ourselves with the political sharpness of the charge carried by the term *critical*, as in 'critical studies of men'. We also align ourselves with both Hearn and Connell's concern to actively repudiate those who wish to reclaim masculinity as an essence and/or return to a particular age of men's power. A possible reformulation is that of 'critical studies of masculinities'.

Theorising within the field of men and masculinities: overview and background

The field is complex and diverse. Like feminists, theorists have mined pre-existing bodies of thought such as psychoanalysis in order to identify their potential for critical and emancipatory purposes as well as for their role in normalising and regulating (Segal, 1990; Connell, 1995). History and anthropology have provided important disciplinary spaces to displace and destabilise taken-for-granted normalising prescriptions about what men are or have been 'really' or essentially, and have contributed to strands of thought within the social sciences, which increasingly support the recognition of men and masculinities as socially constructed and produced, varying over time and space. Feminist and gay scholarship have provided crucial contributions at a range of levels; particularly in relation to emphasising how power relations work to construct and reproduce particular gender regimes.

The following sections, which outline key influences and themes in the study of men and masculinities, draw very strongly from the work of Connell (1995, 2000) and, to a lesser extent Segal (1990), who have provided highly accessible and detailed accounts.

The 'making' of men psychically

For Connell it all begins, perhaps surprisingly, with Freud: 'It was Freud, more than anyone else who let the cat out of the bag. He disrupted the apparently natural object 'masculinity', and made an enquiry into its natural composition both possible, and in a political sense, necessary' (Connell, 1995: 8). Engagement with Freud by feminists and critical gender theorists is often seen as surprising and, indeed, Connell's observation that he opened more doors than he himself walked through and than many of his more conservative followers felt able to, is an apt reflection on his complex and contradictory legacy for those who seek to challenge oppressive gender orders and practices (see Segal, 1990).

Although attempting to summarise the key tenets of Freud's work is very problematic, not least because his views shifted and changed over the course of his work, the following gives a flavour of why he is often invoked by some contemporary theorists as helpful. For Freud, children are not born with a ready-made social and cultural identity. This offers a rejoinder to those who wish to make claims in relation to essential or biological differences between the sexes. Rather such identities are formed and acquired crucially through their relationships with their mothers and fathers. Through observing their parents, they come to recognise their own biological sex, but this is a tension- and conflict-ridden process. The boy comes to learn to be a man, through learning to submit himself to the power of the father and suppressing his love for his mother. Freud saw the process as complex and central to his sense of adult masculinity as fragile and based upon the tragic encounter between desire and culture.

> The point he most insistently made about masculinity is that it never exists in a pure state. Layers of emotion co-exist and contradict each other. … Though his theoretical language changed, Freud remained convinced of the empirical complexity of gender and the ways in which femininity is always part of a man's character. (Connell, 1995: 10)

As is well known, and has already been alluded to, Freud's work and legacy has carried both conservative and radical potential and a range of writers offer helpful summaries of subsequent developments (see, for example, Frosh,

1987). It is beyond the scope of this chapter to address such scholarship in detail but rather our aim is to signpost some key developments in psycho-analytic theory in relation to theorising masculinity and in particular those which inform contemporary analyses (see also Chapter 4).

Connell (1995) suggests that the work of Karl Jung is of interest not least because of the way it has been used by contemporary activists and theorists in the US such as Bly (1990) to explore the sources of and solutions to contem-porary male discontents. Jung distinguished between the self that is con-structed in transactions with the social environment – the persona – and the self which is formed in the unconscious from repressed elements – the anima. These tended to be opposites and this was, to a large extent, a gendered oppo-sition. He gradually came to focus not on the repression of femininity within men (he did recognise its presence within men), but on the resulting *balance* between a masculine persona and a feminine anima. He came to argue that the feminine interior of masculine men was shaped not only by individual men's life histories but also by inherited archetypal images of women. According to Connell (1995) he developed an interesting and progressive (in the context of the 1920s) theory of the emotional dynamics of patriarchal marriage, using the idea of a masculine/feminine polarity to call for a gender balance in mental and social life. However, while Freud was struggling to over-come the masculine/feminine polarity, Jung not only settled for it, but pre-sented the opposition as rooted in universal and timeless truths about the human psyche. Moreover, the notion of the need for an appropriate 'balance' rooted in these truths has been used by those such as Bly to suggest that mod-ern feminism has tilted the balance 'too far' and that 'soft' men, by caving into feminism, have lost the 'deep masculine' (Connell, 1995).

Bly and his followers (primarily in the US) not only developed a politics of 'me-too-ism' (Gutmann and Vigoya, 2005), which focused attention in a reac-tive way on male discontents, but, according to many writers, also led to a reac-tionary politics. This was not only the case in relation to feminism, but, with its advocacy of a return to a patriarchal order, Edwards (2005) argues Bly's approach was implicitly, if not explicitly, homophobic. It is important to note that Seidler (2006) dissents from readings of Bly and the movement he inspired which see it as straightforwardly reactionary (see also Chapter 4 in this book).

Within the emergence of very wide-ranging feminist challenges to the gen-dered order at the end of the 1960s, feminists, after decades of little interaction, began to engage with psychoanalysis again (Segal, 1990). This engagement had, and continues to have, a considerable impact upon scholarship into men and masculinities (often controversially, see McMahon, 1999, and discussion below).

There were two main strands of engagement. Juliet Mitchell (1974) in the UK and Irigaray (1982) in France, using the work of Lacan, were concerned more with theorising femininity than with masculinity, although there was an implicit account of masculinity (see Segal, 1990, for a summary). Lacanian theory focuses on symbolic processes and constitutes an outright rejection of the biological in the study of human consciousness. Masculinity is not an empirical fact or an external archetype, but rather the occupant of a place in symbolic and social relations (Connell, 1995). According to this approach, the 'Law of the Father' constitutes culture. Oedipal repression creates a system of symbolic order in which the possessor of the phallus, a symbol distinct from an empirical penis, is central. Gender is a system of symbolic relationships, not fixed facts about persons:

> The subject ... can only assume its identity through the adoption of a sexed identity, and the subject can only take up a sexed identity with reference to the phallus, for the phallus is the privileged signifier. (Segal, 1990: 85)

Although influential for many feminists and those interested generally in exploring the complexities of gendered power relationships, there are clear limits to the utility of Lacan's work. He is seen as indifferent to particular historical processes, material constraints and realities. Moreover, given the primacy afforded language in the theory, he gives an ahistorical account of how meanings and identities are produced in language. Indeed, it is argued that the primacy he affords to language is in itself unconvincing and too determinist, although, as Segal notes, this is not to deny the importance of language. A key point for many is that Lacanian analysis does not address the possibility of the transformation of masculinity, rather 'the identification of the problem is as far as we can get' (Segal, 1990: 90).

Others, such as Chodorow (1978), have turned to what happens in families. In classical psychoanalysis the drama centred on the Oedipal entry into masculinity. However, for Chodorow the drama centres on the pre-oedipal period and crucially on the separation from femininity. In *The Reproduction of Mothering* Chodorow argued that the gendered division of care-taking in which mothers were exclusively responsible for children, both boys and girls, was a key factor in the creation and perpetuation of male dominance. The key to understanding why men and women develop as they do, as well as to why men continue to dominate women, lies in the fact that women, not men, mother. In a society where women are devalued, women's relations with their sons and daughters cannot but develop in contrasting ways. Mothers experience their daughters as less separate from themselves and girls in turn retain their early and intense identification and attachment to their mothers. Moreover, they grow up with a weaker sense of boundaries, although with a greater capacity for empathy and sensitivity towards others. Boys, by contrast, are pushed to disrupt their primary identification with the mother. They must repress and deny the intimacy, tenderness and dependence of the early bond with the mother, if they are to assume a masculine identity. McMahon (1999: 182) summarises: 'As a result men are overly concerned with maintaining interpersonal boundaries, do not define themselves in relational terms and have diminished relationship capacities. The same processes also explain the contempt men express towards women'.

Chodorow argued that being mothered by women generates conflicts in men about their masculinity, conflicts which are heightened because of men's absence from child care. They have to develop their identity in the absence of their father, and this is fraught with anxiety, because masculinity remains abstract in such a context.

> Given the remoteness of the model of masculinity provided by the father, the boy's masculine identity is largely defined negatively, in terms of what the mother is not. Consequently masculine identity remains doubly uncertain, based upon rejection of the concrete feminine identity represented by the mother and the uncertain adoption of an abstract masculine identity represented by the idealised father. (McMahon, 1999: 183)

Many feminists over the years have criticised this early work of Chodorow, particularly because of its universalism and its apparent privileging of the site of caretaking as *the* locus of producing and reproducing male domination and female subordination. Chodorow, it is argued, was guilty of generalising inappropriately and of not situating key categories such as mothering within specific cultural historical contexts. Engagement with such criticisms is beyond the remit of this chapter (for examples, see Segal, 1987, 1990). However, as we shall see below, compatible theoretical criticisms have also been levelled at theorists in the field of men and masculinities.

Of interest in the context of the concerns of this book is that Chodorow's work and object relations theories generally have become influential among theorists of masculinity (see Chapter 4 for discussions in relation to practice models). According to McMahon (1999) this is because it permits analyses which are critical of, but at the same time sympathetic to, men. McMahon's work will be returned to in more detail in the discussion below on materialist feminist approaches to men.

For writers such as Connell, whatever the merits and demerits of particular analyses that engage with it, the worth of psychoanalysis in understanding masculinity lies in its help in grasping the structuring of personality and the complexities of desire at the same time as the structuring of social relations with their contradictions and dynamism (see also Jefferson, 1994). It is also worth noting here that for many feminists this too would appear to be the case, which is why psychoanalytic understandings have been considered crucial as part of understanding the complexities of gender relations (Hollway, 1997, is one example). As will become apparent throughout this book, currently psychoanalytic ideas also inform some research on areas such as fathers (see Chapter 6) and the making of young masculinities (see Chapter 10). We will return to psychoanalytic approaches when exploring some of the more contemporary trends in theorising. But now we move on to exploring key moments in the social sciences which have contributed towards the field of men and masculinities in terms of scholarship and research.

The making of men socially

The first attempt to create a 'social science' of masculinity was concerned with the notion of the male sex role. The idea of a male sex role is now seriously critiqued and not considered useful by many contemporary theorists (although as we shall see in Chapter 6 it has informed research and popular ideas on fathers) but this work will be explored briefly in order to build up a picture of what has led to contemporary developments.

According to Connell (1995), sex role research has its origins in nineteenth-century debates about differences between the sexes. In a project which was founded on resistance to demands by women for emancipation, a 'scientific' doctrine of innate sex differences stimulated research into such differences. This gave way to sex role research. The use of the concept of 'role' provided a way of linking the idea of a place in the social structure with the idea of cultural norms. This work dated from the 1930s and through the efforts of anthropologists, sociologists and psychologists, the concept had, by the end of the 1950s, become a key term in the social sciences. According to Connell (1995) there are two ways in which the role concept can be applied to gender; firstly where the roles are seen as specific to definite social situations, and secondly, the more common approach, in which being a man or a woman means enacting a general set of expectations attached to one's sex. In this approach there are always two sex roles in any cultural context. Masculinity and femininity are interpreted as internalised sex roles, the products of social-isation or social learning. This concept mapped smoothly onto the idea of sex differences and the two notions have been consistently conflated. Although sex roles can be seen as the cultural enactment of biological sex differences, this does not have to be so. In the work of Talcott Parsons, the very influential sociologist writing in the 1950s, the distinction made between male and female roles is treated as a distinction between instrumental roles and expressive roles in the family. Instrumental roles are those played by men, expressive by women, and in Parsons' functionalist theory, in order for families to work well, it was important that the respective roles are adhered to.

This does allow for change, in that the agencies of socialisation can transmit different expectations, and indeed sex role theory blossomed within second-wave feminism and sex role research became a political tool to demonstrate how key agencies of socialisation socialised men and women into stereotypical and oppressive roles. Some of those who became involved in Men's Liberation too saw sex role research as helpful in demonstrating the oppressiveness of sex roles.

Connell's critique of sex role theory is widely shared by contemporary theorists in the field of men and masculinities (see Whitehead, 2002). Connell argues that role theory is logically vague and is used to describe too many different things: occupation, hobby, stage in life and so on. It is also incoherent insofar as it exaggerates prescription (that is, how strongly adherence to correct roles is insisted upon by key agents of socialisation) but at the same time it assumes that prescriptions are reciprocal (between men and women); it underplays power relations and inequalities. Furthermore, the difficulty with power is seen as part of a wider difficulty with social dynamics. The male sex role literature constantly sees change as impinging on the role from elsewhere, for example, changes that take place as a result of technological change. It does not have a way of understanding change as a dialectic within gender relations. For Connell, male sex role theory is reactive. He suggests that this is why those men who had worked hard for changes in sex roles in the 1970s could not generate an effective resistance to those in the 1980s, such as Bly and the mythopoetic movement, who rejected them as 'soft' and instituted a cult of an imaginary past. As already indicated, Connell's reading of Bly is not shared by other theorists of masculinity such as Seidler (2006). Indeed, this is part of a broader critique by Seidler of Connell's work, explored further below.

The arrival of masculinity and masculinities

If much of the first wave of critical writings by men in the social sciences was 'power blind' (Whitehead, 2002), this situation changed with the publication in *Theory and Society* of an article by Carrigan et al. (1985). They argued for an understanding of masculinity that recognised dominant interpretations and definitions of masculinity as embedded in and sustained by a range of male-dominated institutions such as the state, education, the family, the workplace and so on. This was neither a product of functional sex roles nor a psychological property. Masculinity was a vital tool in the armoury of male dominance, informing the gender system while legitimising and reinforcing male power and the institutional aspects of male power connected with the individual and collective practices of men. Drawing on the work of the Italian Marxist Gramsci on 'hegemony', they argued that there was a dominant form of masculinity called 'hegemonic masculinity'.

Connell developed this analysis further in his book *Masculinities*. This defined masculinity as 'simultaneously a place in gender relations, the practices through which men and women engage that place in gender, and the effects of these practices in bodily experience, personality and culture' (1995: 71). Connell argued that hegemonic masculinity can be defined as the configuration of gender practice that embodies the currently accepted answer to the problem of the legitimacy of patriarchy, which guarantees or is taken to guarantee the dominant positions of men and the subordination of women. Hegemonic masculinity is, therefore, not a fixed character type, always and everywhere the same: 'It is, rather, the masculinity that occupies the hegemonic position in a given pattern of gender relations, a position always contestable' (1995: 76). This is not to say that the most visible bearers of hegemonic masculinity are always the most powerful people – they may be exemplars such as film actors or even fantasy figures. Individual holders of institutional power or great wealth may be far from the hegemonic position in their personal lives. Nevertheless, hegemony is likely to be established only if there is some correspondence between cultural ideals and institutional power, collective if not individual. It is also the successful claim to authority, more than direct violence, which is the mark of hegemony, although violence often underpins or supports authority.

Connell noted the importance of recognising multiple masculinities in the context of the interplay between gender and other social divisions. However, to recognise more than one kind of masculinity was only a first step, the relations between different kinds of masculinities needed to be understood, as did the relations within them. Connell develops the following categories: subordinated, complicit and marginalised masculinities. Gay men represent the most conspicuous form of subordinated masculinities, though not the only one; those who are characterised as 'wimps' also come within this category. In terms of complicit masculinities, he argues that just as normative definitions of masculinity face the problem that not many men actually meet the normative standard, this also applies to hegemonic masculinity. The number of men rigorously practising the hegemonic pattern in its entirety may be quite small. Yet, the majority of men gain from its hegemony, since they benefit from the 'patriarchal dividend' – the advantage that men in general gain from the overall subordination of women (p. 79). Masculinities that are constructed in ways that realise the patriarchal dividend, without the tensions or risks of being at the frontline of patriarchy, are complicit in this sense. A great many men who draw the patriarchal dividend respect their wives and mothers, are never violent towards women, do their allotted share of the housework, bring home the family wage and can easily convince themselves that feminists are unreasonable extremists. Basically they collude with the existing gender order and do not challenge its inequities.

While hegemony, subordination and complicity are relations internal to the gender order, the interplay of gender with other structures such as class and race creates further interplay between masculinities. Marginalisation is always relative to the authorisation of the hegemonic masculinity of the dominant group. Connell points out, for example, that in the US particular black athletes may be exemplars for hegemonic masculinity, but the fame and wealth of individual stars has no trickle-down effect. It does not yield social authority to black men in general. Marginalised masculinity is also a relevant concept for understanding the gender identities and gender practices of white working-class men.

Connell argues that in order to engage with and analyse what is going on more precisely it is necessary to explore three structures of gender relations: power relations, production relations and cathexis. Power relations concern the overall subordination of women and dominance of men. This general structure persists despite local reversals such as women-headed households and resistance of many kinds. This resistance does mean there is a problem of legitimacy, which has great importance for the politics of masculinity. For example, Connell sees the scale of contemporary male violence as pointing to crisis tendencies in the modern gender order. Furthermore, as we shall see in the chapter on working with fathers, the rise of women-headed households is intimately bound up in very complex ways with the emergence of a renewed politics around fathers and fatherhood, a politics which is being engaged with in very diverse ways by feminists and pro-feminists alike. Connell seems to construct production relations within the public realm of paid work where there has been a clear if complex gender division of labour. He points to the growth in women's participation in the paid labour force as an indicator of potential change here. Finally, cathexis refers to desire and he notes the change in patterns of cathexis with the growth in visibility of gay and lesbian sexuality.

For Connell, understanding gender relations in all their depth and complexity requires concrete studies, not *a priori* theorising. *Masculinities* includes life story research with a range of men including environmentalists, unemployed young men and gay men and, further, Connell's work since (e.g., Connell, 2000) has engaged with the politics of boys' education and men's health. A key theme, continued by others (Watson, 2000), is the exploration of 'bodily practices'. As we shall see (particularly in Chapter 8), a rich research literature now exists on men, masculinities and bodies that 'work', 'fail', are redundant or idealised. Connell's work and in particular the concept of 'hegemonic masculinity' has been massively influential, if not without its critics over the years (see Connell and Messerschmidt, 2005, for a review of the criticisms of 'hegemonic masculinity' and a re-statement of its utility). An outline of some of these debates is offered below.

Rethinking masculinities today

Contemporary analyses/critiques appear to have emerged from a number of sources: post-structuralists (for example, Whitehead, 2002) and the work of Seidler (2006), which cannot be clearly categorised theoretically, but which is fundamentally concerned with exploring diversity and context, the work of those influenced by materialist feminists such as McMahon (1999) and psychoanalytically-influenced approaches such as that of Jefferson (1994, 2002). Given the complexity of the field what follows can only be a brief overview.

According to Whitehead (2002) the concept of hegemonic masculinity shifted the debate on patriarchy forward at a time when much of feminism was drawing on notions of patriarchy. He argues that the concept of hegemonic masculinity achieved what the concept of patriarchy failed to do. It offered a nuanced account of processes and practices while staying loyal to notions of gender, sexual ideology and male dominance. It signalled the multiple, contested character of male practices in the context of larger formations of gender structure. Thus, it provided feminist and pro-feminist scholarship with a complex yet accessible theory from which to critique and interrogate men's practices in multiple settings, while recognising that such practices do not go uncontested and, at the same time, maintaining adherence to the concept of male power as structural.

Whitehead (2002), as a post-structuralist, however, criticises the debt to Gramsci and critical structuralism. The concept of 'hegemonic' masculinity assumes power is fundamentally contested between social groups, men and women. He argues that in the final analysis all that is being offered is a fine tuning of conflict theory. Moreover, and this is a persuasive insight, actually pinning down a strict definition of hegemony in Connell's work is not easy; it is a very slippery concept. Connell is trying to provide an overarching explanation alongside the need to look at institutional and everyday practices. For example, recent work by Messerschmidt (2005) has used the concept of hegemonic masculinity to explore adolescent boys' use of sexually violent behaviour in American high schools. This provides very helpful insights into what is valued in particular locales or gender regimes, but the same concept seems over-stretched if then used to explore what happens in, for example, a cabinet meeting of the UK government. As Whitehead notes, hegemonic masculinity is a useful shorthand descriptor of dominant masculinities, but over-use can result in obfuscation.

Furthermore, hegemonic masculinity takes great care not to predict men's behaviour and indeed it is often suggested that only a minority of men express and perform its pattern – although is that a minority of men in each institution, country or worldwide? Just what it is is never actually illuminated and yet Whitehead notes that somehow this unclear and slippery model of masculinity serves to stabilise a structure of dominance and oppression in the gender order. Whitehead argues that there is little of substance in the notion and yet it is used to explain an extraordinarily powerful social order. Whitehead further argues that there is a fundamental inconsistency, in that while Connell attempts to recognise difference and resistance, his primary underpinning is a fixed male structure. It is not surprising then, when confronted with the circularity of the agency–structure dualism, that many theorists within this tradition resort to locating hegemonic masculinity within a wider patriarchal state. In his defence, Connell (2002) asserts that in fact hegemony is not fixed but is historically concrete and he insists that 'like class relations, gender relations change historically, and the pattern and depth of hegemony changes also' (p. 89). Connell also notes that 'Hegemony in gender relations can be contested and may break down' (p. 89).

Jefferson (1994, see also 2002) has also engaged with Connell's work. He starts by asking why particular men adopt the particular masculine positions they do and suggests the need to theorise the individual subject. He argues for the need to address society, structures, discourses and the subject and personality in non-dualistic and non-determinist ways. Theoretically, this means weaving together discourse-based and psychoanalytic theories. Life history research is promoted as the best means of capturing how and why men take up particular positions. In the 1990s this approach chimed with concerns within the social sciences and feminism about how and whether 'big stories', in the form of overarching explanations about male domination and female oppression, repress and exclude the local and the 'different' and silence those who do not fit. Fraser and Nicholson (1990), reviewing such debates in the context of a range of critiques particularly from those influenced by postmodernism, argue for theorising which is explicitly historical and thus less easily inviting of false generalisations. However, they also note the dangers here:

> Of course, the process of framing a phenomenon within a context is always one than can be further extended. Therefore, one could, theoretically, invoke this ideal to such an extent that all that is left viable are descriptions of particular events at particular points in time. (Fraser and Nicholson, 1990: 9)

Jefferson is, of course, arguing for more than engaging with particular events at particular points in time but actually for engaging with specific men with their own particular psychic and social biographies in specific contexts. Interestingly, Messerschmidt (2005), who also advocates life history research, is deeply critical of Jefferson's engagement with psychoanalysis, arguing that specific boys (in his research) made conscious choices 'to pursue hegemonic masculinity (defined by the practices in their milieu of home and school) as their project, or the fundamental mode by which they chose to relate to the world and express themselves in it' (p. 208). The materiality of bodies often matters in the pursuit of a project, according to Messerschmidt, but emphatically not the unconscious.

Seidler (2006), a leading writer on masculinity, in his recent work has avoided alignment with a particular theoretical approach but his arguments have resonance with Whitehead's concerns. In a critique of what he sees as a dominant tendency within the men and masculinities literature, exemplified in the work of Connell, he argues against universalist assumptions that masculinities can be understood exclusively as relations of power. He argues that men's power has to be understood in relation to specific cultures and traditions and that transformations in gender relations across generations mean we have to think in new ways about men, masculinities, cultures, bodies, sexualities and emotional life. He challenges, in particular, what he sees as the universal applicability of Western models of hegemonic masculinity and suggests we need to think differently about diverse cultural masculinities and recognise that men have to engage differently with their own cultural traditions. He also directs attention to the importance of looking at 'generational' differences between groups of men and the differing implications of growing up with mothers who work, are feminists and so on (this echoes the issues raised by many feminists in more recent years). He suggests the need to abandon thinking about hegemonic masculinities and explore 'culturally dominant masculinities'. This may seem little different from the idea of hegemonic masculinity as culturally authoritative in a given context (Connell, 1995, 2000, 2002) and it still does beg the age-old question that Seidler does not satisfactorily address, which is whether such dominant cultural masculinities can only be understood discretely or whether there are patterns across cultures embedded in particular structures. Furthermore, there is rather a 'straw man' quality to many of his critiques. For example, Seidler's own work, and that of many of the contributors to the Connell et al. collection (2005) showcases the global reach of scholarship around men and masculinities. Such work is being carried out now in a very diverse range of countries but also operates variously within an engagement with the implications of globalisation and the apparent growth in 'powerful global men', whose reach via the control of technology, corporations and so on is unparalleled historically (Connell, 2000).

It does appear to us that theorists such as Connell et al., while differing on how to understand crucial notions such as power, do share an interest in understanding the local and the contextual to varying degrees and to charting plurality among men, resistance and instability in gender relations. In contrast, McMahon (1999) unapologetically argues from a materialist feminist perspective that it is in the material interests of men as a group to resist women's demands for change in power relations. While he confines his analysis to the domestic division of labour within the home, he does base it on a more general theoretical approach, which has over the years been variously influential in feminist thought (Delphy, 1984). This approach differs significantly from most of those offered above in that he treats men as a category with interests that they consciously seek to advance or protect, and such interests lie within their concern to keep their existing privileges, which in McMahon's specific analysis correlate with continuing to have women take care of them and their children. As McMahon himself fully acknowledges, his is not an approach currently much in favour theoretically in the social sciences. It falls too much within a 'grand theory' approach which treats men as an undifferentiated category and it assumes that interests are pre-given 'facts' rather than discursively constituted.

Conclusion

As we outlined in our introductory chapter, our approach to this book and its subject matter is rooted in our concern to stay open and inquiring rather than prescriptive and dogmatic. In engaging with the theories outlined we inevitably find some more persuasive than others. For example, we see psychoanalytic insights as helpful in exploring the complexities of men, masculinities and gender relations, though not if they are used in a reductive and one-dimensional way. We do not find grand theories that base themselves on one 'cause' – such as the pursuit of men's interests or the male drive to power – all that persuasive. We find that we can situate ourselves fairly broadly within the approach outlined by Connell et al. (2005) in their introduction to the *Handbook of Studies on Men and Masculinities*. This can be summarised as follows: men and masculinities are socially constructed, produced and reproduced, variable and changing across time and space, within societies and through life courses and biographies, men have a relationship, albeit differentially, with gendered power. Both material and discursive aspects need to be analysed in the context of how gender and other social divisions intersect in their construction. A specific rather than an implicit or incidental focus on the topic of men and masculinities is required in the context of recognising them as explicitly gendered. Finally, feminist, gay and other critical scholarships offer crucial insights in understanding men and masculinities. A note of caution, however, is in order before closing this chapter. As will become readily apparent, some aspects of the approach above are much more clearly engaged with in this book than others, for many reasons including our own limitations and that of the materials available to us.

Key texts

Connell, R.W. (2005) *Masculinities*, second edition, Cambridge: Polity.

This is the same as the seminal first edition (1995), but with a new preface which gives an overview of men's studies in more recent years. The first half of the book deals with theory. The second half is based on life history interviews and is very readable.

Kimmel, M.S., Hearn, J. and Connell, R.W. (eds) (2005) *Handbook of Studies on Men and Masculinities*, London: Sage.

The best source for overviews of research on just about every topic you could think of where social scientists have studied men and masculinities.

Whitehead, S. (2002) *Men and Masculinities*, Cambridge: Polity.

A good overview of theories in the field, from a post-structuralist perspective.

3 The Politics of Masculinity

We often come across practitioners in the fields of health care, social care or criminal justice who say they are interested in 'working with men' or 'masculinity'. These phrases have some currency in practice culture, hence our use of 'working with men' in the title of this book. They do not, however, in themselves tell us much about what people do in their contact with men as clients or patients and they do not tell us anything about the underlying principles. Why name men at all? What does that mean for the purpose of your intervention? What are you trying to achieve? How does your intervention fit into the bigger picture of the gender order?

One of this book's main arguments is that we need to be able to identify the aims and underlying philosophy of our work with men. There are competing approaches out there. There is a world of difference between, for example, consciously engaging with men as fathers because you think they generally avoid responsibility for child care and doing so because you believe fathers are unfairly demonised and their needs and 'rights' are often ignored. Counselling men with the aim of uncovering their deep-rooted emotional trauma has profoundly different implications from individual therapy that aims to change patterns of thinking so that men do not behave so abusively.

Approaches to working with men tend to be polarised. To give an example, Scourfield and Dobash's (1999) research highlights debates about the politics of masculinity within and between projects working with violent men. One agency said they had been criticised by other men's groups for being 'men bashers'. Another said it had been criticised for 'letting men off the hook'. The strength of feeling that can be found was illustrated by one worker's comments about an agency perceived as having a different ideology. He said 'they probably think I'm scum' and 'I wouldn't refer anyone to them if my life depended on it'. In the light of this contested terrain, we have to acknowledge that readers of this book with existing interests and experience in the field of work with men are bound to bristle at bits of the book with which they do not agree. The field of men's work is particularly fraught with various kinds of political correctness – the fear of being either too nice to men or too critical of them, depending on what your gender politics are.

To some extent, however, apparent differences can also mask common ground. It should be noted that practitioners working within contrasting gender ideologies may nonetheless use some rather similar means to achieve different ends – for example some very similar pragmatic ways of initially engaging with men. Our own position on the politics of masculinity, which we will make clear throughout the book, is that a victim–perpetrator dualism is unhelpful. Approaches that crudely characterise men either as dominant and enjoying undue social privilege or as marginalised and experiencing suffering, without acknowledging how these two aspects interact, do not capture the complexity of the lives of real men and do not respond to the multi-layered psycho-social terrain of gender relations.

The chapter consists of four sections:

- First, we describe the political, social and cultural context in which health and social care interventions with men have to be located. We give an overview of how social policies are developing in response to what has come to be seen as the 'problem of men'.
- Second, we discuss various different ways of mapping different ideological orientations towards masculinity. We refer to how theorists have categorised different approaches within pressure groups and men's organisations and we relate these to politics of health and social care interventions.
- In the third section, we discuss the politics of masculinity in the culture of frontline practice, with reference to research on child protection, probation and young people's mental health.
- In the fourth section, we discuss the issue of pragmatism and idealism in work with men. That is, we explore some tensions between interventions that aim to transform masculinities and those which have more modest reformist aims.

We end the chapter by summarising some key questions that need to be asked about interventions – both those that make masculinity explicit and those that do not.

The political, social and cultural climate

Chapter 2 referred to some aspects of the contemporary social and cultural climate of gender relations. In this section we outline the ways in which some men and certain aspects of masculinity have come to be identified as a deliberate and conscious target of social policies in recent years.

The socio-cultural climate has certainly changed in relation to men in perhaps the last three decades. Second-wave feminism has obviously had a huge impact on how we view men. In an era that has been characterised as 'reflexive modernity' (Giddens, 1991) it can be argued that we no longer take for granted our place in the gender order. While recognising this shifting ground, we should not of course exaggerate the extent of social change. Delamont (2001) and Oakley (2003), among others, have argued that many material gender inequalities are enduring, despite what could be seen as changing discourses of gender in the West. An example of where we can see change in our ideas about gender – what we could perhaps call the rhetoric of gender equality – but continuity in actual practices, can be seen in the research on new fathers undertaken by Lupton and Barclay (1997). These researchers describe the fathers they studied as talking about the importance of them 'being there' for their children in a way that their own fathers were not for them. However, despite their best intentions, the men could retreat into traditional male behaviour, particularly at times of difficulty and anxiety (as indeed could the women).

Not surprisingly, in this climate of changing ideas about men (if not significant change in actual behaviour) we can see a developing interest in questioning dominant ideas about masculinity from practitioners in a variety of fields – health care, social care, counselling and criminal justice work – as well as some initiatives from government that aim to respond to particular issues concerning men. In the UK, for example, policy attention has been paid to the education of boys, to fathering and to men's health. These are consciously masculinised social policies. These developments are not restricted to the English-speaking West. The United Nations Commission on the Status of Women has turned its attention to the role of boys and men in achieving gender equality (DAW, 2004). To some extent masculinity has been problematised in policy debates in and about the developing world. We can see this, for example, in academic and NGO discourse on masculinity and development that includes the perspectives of Westerners but also those involved in development within the world's poorest countries (Jackson, 2001; Sweetman, 2001; Cleaver, 2002; Ruxton, 2004).

In order to properly analyse masculinity policy we need to consider these developments as a whole, making international comparisons and considering them in relation to policies that directly address women. We cannot hope to do a thorough job here, but simply make some initial overview comment insofar as these policies are relevant in context to the politics of working with men. We do so briefly in this section and again in the section that follows it. Here we consider briefly the questions of 'why masculinity' and 'why now'?

When considering why Western governments in particular are consciously targeting policies on men in the 2000s, we obviously have to note the influence of second-wave feminism. Without activists and politicians calling for policies directed at women, we would not have seen the subsequent focus on men. The idea that one of the impacts of second-wave feminism has been a so-called 'crisis' of masculinity has arguably become a common sense assumption for very many people – a lay sociological theory that we see rehearsed in the media (Coyle and Morgan-Sykes, 1998). Popular ideas include the notion that men are 'losing out' in the wake of feminism and that they do not know quite how to conduct themselves because traditional identities are being called into question. Working-class men in particular are seen within this discourse as struggling to find their way in the context of a rapidly changing labour market (see Faludi, 1999).

A popular aspect or variation of the 'crisis' discourse is the notion of the 'masculine deficit'. This is the idea that men in a socially marginal position – perhaps working class men or black men – cannot fulfil the masculine dominance they have grown up to expect, because of the structural limitations imposed by their marginal social status, and this deficit will often lead to some kind of damaging behaviour – perhaps violence or other offending. This is also well established as a lay theory, but in fact has found more nuanced expression in the social scientific writings of authors such as Segal (1990), Messerschmidt (1993) and Connell (1995).

The masculine deficit idea described above is often associated within social science and indeed even within lay discourse with a pro-feminist position, insofar as it recognises the historical dominance of men. In addition, and not from a feminist perspective, there is also a global preoccupation with the erosion of men's power. This is the idea that improvements in women's quality of life must necessarily mean loss of status and power for men. Various commentators have set out what Lingard (2003), with reference to the so-called 'underachievement' of boys, has called 'recuperative masculinity politics', which is based on an attempt to reclaim traditional privileges for men. The currency of these arguments also goes some way to explaining the policy attention to men and masculinity. While various commentators have criticised the zero-sum argument about social power on which recuperative masculinity politics are based, up to a point we have to acknowledge that some changes in the gendered division of labour will mean men doing more domestic work and some gains for women will inevitably mean some losses in the traditional privileges of men. Of course pro-feminist activists (and some therapists and nurses and social workers) would argue that this kind of change is good for men and that, in fact, men's well-being will be enhanced by gender equality. If patriarchy is bad for men's health, for example (see Chapter 9 of this book), then change can be good for men. As New (2001) puts it, changes in gender relations may not be in men's *conservative* interests, but could be seen to be in their *emancipatory* interests.

Categorising the politics of masculinity

Next we move on to consider how different approaches to the politics of masculinity can be categorised. The first thing to note is that various scholars have attempted to construct typologies of masculinity politics as expressed in social movements. Clatterbaugh (1990) identifies various distinct approaches: the conservative legacy of those arguing for continuity with traditional models of masculinity; men's rights approaches which clearly see men as having lost out post-second wave feminism; pro-feminist men (both liberal and radical versions); men in search of spiritual growth – that is, what are often called 'mythopoetic' men's groups; socialist men who insist on the equal relevance of class and sex inequality (mirroring socialist feminism) and finally the various responses of gay and black men that emphasise inequalities between men. Connell (1996) comes up with alternative labels. His categories are masculinity therapy (mythopoetic groups, sometimes referred to as the 'men's movement'), the defence of patriarchy, queer politics and transformative politics (anti-sexist men). Finally, Messner (1997) has constructed a useful model of the 'terrain of the politics of masculinity'. Although he does this initially with reference to social movements in the USA, ranging from the Promise Keepers to the Million Man March, he argues that such a model can be used as a tool for analysing the politics of masculinity more generally. It has certainly been applied to government policies (Scourfield and Drakeford, 2002) and we would argue it is useful for mapping the politics of interventions.

Messner's 'terrain' model (see Figure 3.1) is a neat and accessible way of visually locating the ideological orientation of any given approach to working with men and we refer to it at various points during the book. We should be able to identify whether practice approaches are more focused on the institutional privileges of men, the costs of masculinity or on differences between men. So, for example, if an intervention is primarily designed to reduce men's violence towards women, with an emphasis on domestic authority, then its focus is on men's privileges. If a worker aims to advocate for separated fathers in disputes over custody then he is concerned with the costs of masculinity. If a project engages black young men and has a consciously anti-racist agenda then it could be seen to be focusing on differences between men.

There have been some interesting attempts at cross-national analyses of government policies on masculinity. Hobson's (2002) interesting collection analyses the politics of fatherhood in five countries in Europe and America. Hearn et al. (2002a) provide a broad overview of law and policy in relation to men and men's practices across Europe. They make some broad distinctions between the different countries' approaches to policy development, observing that the Nordic countries have paid some specific policy attention to men

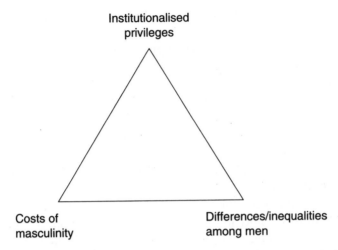

Figure 3.1   The terrain of the politics of masculinities (Messner, 1997: 12)

since the 1980s, the established EU member nations have limited specific focus on men and the former Soviet nations have very limited specific emphasis on men (see Chapter 6 for more details). Despite these broad distinctions, Hearn and Pringle (2006) also acknowledge that there are some apparent contradictions. For example, policies on violence against women are more developed in the UK than in the Nordic countries, despite the general trend of more proactive policies towards gender equality in Scandinavia.

As an example of how the politics of masculinity can be analysed, Scourfield and Drakeford (2002) have attempted to analyse the politics of masculinity under New Labour in the UK. Their overall argument is that New Labour proceeds with policy optimism about men in the home and pessimism about men outside the home. In contrast, there has been policy pessimism about women in the home and optimism about women outside the home. Furthermore, where New Labour is optimistic, it tends to produce policies that are encouraging and facilitative, and where New Labour is pessimistic, it can produce policies that are authoritarian.

To flesh out this argument, we first summarise their arguments about family policy. They point to some limited advances in policies for work–life balance, such as statutory paternity leave and rights to part-time work for men. These could of course be seen as challenging the traditional privileges of men insofar as they are encouraging men to spend more time on care for children rather than on economic provision. Government rhetoric tends to be more geared towards men's *rights* to involvement in child care, however. There seems to be a fundamental optimism with regard to fathering. There are perhaps assumptions that we live in an era of the 'democratic family' (Giddens, 1998) in which men are increasingly keen to be intimately involved in the care of children. Certainly there is a new emphasis under New Labour on men's involvement with care, as opposed to the previous Conservative administration, whose main intervention was the setting up of the Child Support Agency to enforce the *financial* responsibility of absent parents (most often fathers). In contrast, Scourfield and Drakeford argue, New Labour could be seen to be pessimistic about mothering. There have been authoritarian moves to 'encourage' lone mothers out of the home and into work and parenting interventions within the criminal justice system that have disproportionally affected mothers (Ghate and Ramalla, 2002).

To move on to policies concerning the public sphere, we can see attention being paid to masculinity in the fields of health, education, criminal justice and employment. Scourfield and Drakeford argue that there is negativity towards men outside the home in the rhetoric of New Labour, particularly in the blaming of working-class young men for the wider social problems of crime, bad health and laddish culture. In Messner's terms, there are indications within this rhetoric of challenge to aspects of the privileges of masculinity – men's privilege of irresponsibility, for example. In terms of actual policies, there are some areas where New Labour could be seen as attempting to shore up traditional working-class masculinity based on manly work and manly leisure. The New Deal and action on underachievement of boys can be seen as a concerted effort to shore up young men's positions in society, and maintain their social advantage over women – what Lingard calls recuperative masculinity politics or Messner a response to the perceived costs of masculinity in the aftermath of second-wave feminism. There are other areas, criminal justice in particular, where some poor working-class men are encountering overt social control. In fact, the policy priorities in terms of spending on men have been employment and control. To a limited extent, within the home New Labour has an optimistic role-broadening view of men. Outside the home, however, Scourfield and Drakeford argue it has a more pessimistic view that relies upon role-narrowing and a punitive and authoritarian reaction to those who stray beyond it.

The politics of practice

It is important to consider how the politics of masculinity work out in practice and how particular ideas about men as clients and patients become taken for granted in specific occupational contexts. Therefore, in this section, we discuss examples of gendered occupational culture in welfare professions. We refer to qualitative research in three different contexts: the Probation Service, child protection work and professionals in health, education and social care who encounter young people in distress.

The picture of gendered organisational culture is a complex one. As Lupton and Barclay (1997: 9) write, 'within … institutions there may be a number of competing discourses around a particular phenomenon'. The concept of *discourse* is particularly useful for any discussion of organisational culture. It conveys the idea of a body of concepts, values and beliefs within which people operate, which become accepted as knowledge. We do not propose however that this characterisation of different trends and approaches as separate discourses implies these are unassailable categories. To borrow the term Connell (1995) uses in relation to his hierarchy of masculinities, these are 'configurations of practice' (p. 81), rather than tightly bounded approaches.

Probation

The Probation Service in South Wales was the setting for research by Holland and Scourfield (2000). These authors identified three distinct discourses of masculinity within the culture of the service, as revealed in interviews with staff and analysis of case records and court reports. They found that most probation officers in their study appeared to be negotiating more than one of these discourses in their professional lives. The three discourses of masculinity were characterised as traditional (boys will be boys), new (explicitly challenging masculinity) and mainstream (implicitly challenging masculinity).

The traditional discourse involved an ostensibly non-gendered approach of emphasising the marginalisation of men who offend rather than their masculinity, i.e., their powerlessness rather than their use of power. There was little sense of agency here, with non-gendered offenders being seen as victims of deep-rooted social and personal problems. This discourse involved a great deal of mitigation of men's damaging behaviour in terms of simple (and often single) explanatory factors, such as drug or alcohol use. Holland and Scourfield speculate that behind this simple connection there is perhaps an assumption that the disinhibiting effects of alcohol or drugs allow the natural aggressive social character of men to come out. Boys will be boys, when the mask slips.

Most of the officers interviewed showed some familiarity with the attention given in feminist-inspired academic and practitioner probation literature to the masculinity–crime connection and its implications for probation work. They referred to the influences in men's upbringing, including family, peers, community and media, that encouraged a desire to dominate and to be seen to perform appropriately aggressive, independent masculinity. They talked about using these insights into the making of men in their work, sometimes explicitly. Holland and Scourfield characterised this as a new discourse of explicitly challenging masculinity. This discourse has a rather different view of men's agency from the traditional discourse. Men are seen as responsible for their actions in the sense that part of socially constructed masculinity is a desire to control, to get their own way, although some of the respondents' talk of damaging models of masculinity tended to see men as imprisoned by upbringing.

The dominance of cognitive-behavioural approaches is reflected in many of the accounts of working with men in this study. Holland and Scourfield argue that a significant amount of the accounts of practice in both files and interviews could be seen as implicitly challenging masculinities (the third discourse) through practice that can broadly be labelled cognitive-behavioural (see Chapter 4 of this book). Much of the practice described in the probation officers' accounts in interviews and case file recording drew on cognitive-behavioural ideas in some way; particularly in linking clients' beliefs with their actions, challenging the logic of those beliefs, and tracing the consequences of particular ways of thinking. This practice is ostensibly gender neutral in the sense that the therapeutic methods are intended for men and women alike. However, the data reveal that there are often-mentioned examples of methods linked to cognitive-behavioural approaches that serve to question a masculinity based on rigid thinking and internalised beliefs in the right to dominate others.

Each of these discourses of masculinity can be seen to have strengths and weaknesses. Of course, the traditional discourse is open to criticism from feminists for failing to deconstruct masculinities, thus reinforcing traditional justifications for abusive behaviour. Conversely, there is a risk that the new discourse of explicitly challenging masculinity may not recognise that probation officers are in the business of working specifically with marginalised men, not men in general and that the marginalised status of the clientele should have implications for methods of intervention. The traditional discourse does take account of the very real welfare needs of men who offend. Whereas an extreme adoption of the traditional discourse would mean only helping men with these welfare needs, thus helping change marginalised masculinities into hegemonic ones, a caricature of the new discourse might involve treating all male clients as uniformly powerful, as if they make completely free choices, unaffected by other social factors, to abuse and dominate women, children and other men.

Child protection

Scourfield's (2003) ethnographic research with statutory social workers in a child care team reveals discourses of masculinity in the context of child abuse and neglect. He identified mostly pejorative discourses of client masculinity – men as a threat, men as no use, men as absent, men as irrelevant. However, there were also certain types of cases and certain aspects of professional 'values' talk where a discourse of 'men as no different from women' could be detected. There were also cases where a mother was seen as failing in her expected role of servicing children and the father was constructed as (surprisingly) capable in contrast.

Discourses of femininity are also very important in understanding the problems of engaging men in the child protection process. Scourfield found social workers – both men and women equally – talking of women as profoundly oppressed in the families they worked with, oppressed by poverty but especially by men. Despite this feminist consciousness, when it came to decisions about children's welfare in practice, the social workers saw women as ultimately responsible for children, in a way that men were simply not expected to be. The social workers did ascribe to an ideal of gender equality in families, but the families they worked with were seen as being so far from equal that it was women who had to be expected to make changes and indeed, despite being oppressed by social forces, were seen as ultimately making free choices to stay with abusive men or leave them.

An interesting diversity of construction of social problems emerges when we break down the discourse of men as a threat. There were markedly different constructions of men who were sexually abusive to children and men who were violent towards women. Sex offenders were regarded as understandable according to a predictable template of behaviour and attitudes: we should assume that multiple offences will have been committed; these offences are deliberate and planned and involve the 'grooming' of children; abusers will minimise and deny their abuse, so are generally not to be believed, whereas children are always to be believed if they apparently disclose abuse; you should not expect abusers to change their behaviour, at least not without intensive specialist therapy. In contrast to this homogenising discourse, men's physical violence towards women was subject to a wide range of different interpretations, including both the mainstream feminist account of violence based on men's coercion of women over disputed domestic authority and also more traditional pre-feminist accounts of domestic violence such as mutual hostility in a couple or alcohol as the primary cause.

We could speculate about the roots of this diversity in constructing men's abusiveness, perhaps with reference to ambivalence about women clients and the unassailable category of childhood innocence, but this would be beyond the scope of this chapter. What we can note here, as with the probation research above, is that there are – potentially – lessons to be learned from both the construction of sexually abusive men and of violent men. So, for example, the social workers' theories of sex offending emphasise the need for constant awareness of the possibility that men will minimise the severity of behaviour and the intent behind it. This may be a useful insight into other types of behaviour, such as physical violence or avoidance of domestic work. Equally, the more case- and context-specific approach to men's behaviour we see in cases of domestic violence could be seen as a challenge to the blanket assumptions made about men who sexually abuse.

Young people in distress

As part of a mixed-method study on help-seeking which aimed to inform suicide prevention, Scourfield and colleagues conducted qualitative interviews in the UK with health, social care and education professionals who might encounter young people in distress and focus groups with a range of young people, most of whom were in population groups that might be considered to be at a greater risk of suicide according to epidemiological research. Unlike the studies of probation and child protection above, then, these data provide an insight into both lay and professional discourse. The findings summarised below have not been previously published, although other aspects of the research have been written up for publication (see Smalley et al., 2004; Greenland et al., 2007).

It should be acknowledged that the young people who took part in the focus groups were not straightforwardly representative of the general youth population. These were patients, clients of social workers and youth workers and some were trainee social care workers, so their expressed opinions reflect both lay and professional formulations of gender and mental health. Many of these young people were in fact actively negotiating the boundaries of lay and professional discourse, moving in and out of both domains. In two groups, the young people we spoke to were both recent 'clients' and were also now in some kind of staff role.

Above all both groups – professionals and lay people – talked about men not talking. There are several different reasons given for this, but the issue of talking really did dominate the discussion about gender in the interviews and focus groups. Of course most suicide prevention, at least as it is popularly understood, is talking therapy, but also talking therapy as a good thing arguably has a strong hold on the public consciousness.

There was also talk about masculinity in crisis: some aspects of traditional masculinity are bad for men but things have gone too far and men do not know how to be men these days. This kind of talk came particularly from some of the groups of 'clients', in particular care leavers, a peer-education youth group and some former drug users. These were in many ways the young people within the sample who had experienced the most obvious difficulties and had been in most contact with health and social welfare professionals.

This kind of talk also came particularly from the men in the groups. It is worth noting that these two issues – men as not talking and men as confused by social change – are also the two dominant strains in the very limited media discourse on gendered suicide (Coyle and Morgan-Sykes, 1998).

To consider for a minute the differences between the two types of qualitative data, the professionals were more likely to focus on problems men cause (many of these professionals are engaged in some kind of social problems work so this is in a sense their job) and general socio-economic problems of young people – poverty, unemployment and so on. The lay people focused much more on the limitations of gender roles and the difficulties of finding your way in a changing world. Of course these differences could be due to methodological effects. The fact that the lay people spoke more of the challenge of knowing how to be a man these days could be to do with the conversation having taken place in a group setting. It could also be to do with the construction of youth as a time of exploration and also confusion.

It could be argued that an exclusive emphasis on the importance of just talking about problems underplays the importance of attitudinal change and also the material political change that could potentially prevent some suicides (see Smalley et al., 2005). However, in the focus groups with young people in particular, aspects of hegemonic masculinity were being questioned. Some aspects were rejected and some others that were seen as no longer acceptable in the wake of feminism were mourned. Although there is ambivalence here, we can perhaps see potential for committed professionals to capitalise on this questioning in work with men.

General observations about practice culture

The various pieces of qualitative research summarised above reveal diverse and contradictory discourses of masculinity in practice culture. Although there are some traditions (for example in the Probation Service) of ignoring masculinity and not 'naming' men as men, the general tendency in the practice settings studied is to see contemporary masculinity as problematic. Across the various analyses presented by Scourfield and colleagues we can see this emerging both in terms of the problems men cause and the problems they experience, but we do not often see a balance between these two insights. So men with mental health problems are more straightforwardly seen as social victims whereas in the context of child protection there is a general tendency to see men as victimisers. There is arguably a certain victim–perpetrator polarisation evident here. This may be appropriate in some specific circumstances; for example there is evidence that men are rightly labelled as 'perpetrators' of most domestic violence. However, as a general worldview in relation to men, to exclusively emphasise either pole – victim or perpetrator – is both inaccurate and unhelpful. The world is a rather more complex place than this simplistic criminal justice categorisation allows. To pick up one of the main messages of the previous chapter, what is needed is gender theorising that encompasses the material reality of the relative power of most men over most women and also the nuances of gender relations and gender identities, and the complications of multiple and sometimes contradictory discursive practices.

Pragmatism and idealism

Where health and social welfare practitioners focus on men and aspects of masculinity as conscious targets of interventions, there are a wide range of approaches taken, as we have noted several times in this chapter already. A wide range of different approaches are taken to the question of how pragmatic or idealist an intervention should be. When we refer to pragmatism and idealism, we mean the practice dilemma of how much change we should expect. This will most typically mean how much we should expect men themselves to change, though for some interventions the primary target of change may be health and social welfare services rather than men as clients or patients. We dwell here on the question of change in men. There are perhaps two main issues:

1 what level of change constitutes success or progress and
2 is it acceptable to use traditional aspects of masculinity which could potentially be seen as harmful to men and women as a means for intervention or as a pragmatic way of initially engaging with men?

We deal with each of these in turn.

To first take the question of what level of change is desirable, some programmes are undoubtedly quite ambitious and set out to profoundly change men's behaviour. Examples would include therapeutic and educational work with men who physically or sexually abuse others; transformative psychotherapy, which aims to profoundly disrupt dominant masculine patterns of processing emotions; and pro-feminist groupwork based around anti-sexist organisations, which aims towards the ideal of symmetrical equality in relationships between men and women. In contrast, some interventions have more modest aims, either because they are realistic about the limitations of what they can achieve or because in a particular context, changes in men that might seem to some as quite small and limited could nonetheless be seen as a major achievement. An example of the latter would be work with men who are severely marginalised economically. The collection on fatherhood in South Africa by Richter and Morrell (2006) provides some examples here. Morrell (2006) notes that in the context of ongoing poverty and the legacy of apartheid, it may be that for some South African fathers, owning responsibility for paternity, trying to be a 'good role model' and materially providing for their families are worthy aims. This stops some way short of a radical transformation of traditional gender roles, but it takes account both of how political and economic marginalisation can have an impact on relationships (see Hunter's chapter in Richter and Morrell, 2006) and also of a cultural context where 'a "big man" only commands respect when he is able to provide' (Morrell, 2006: 21).

The second issue of pragmatism/idealism is the dilemma of whether it is justifiable or counter-productive to use some traditional aspects of masculinity as a means to challenge others. To use an example fairly relevant to health and social welfare issues, Morrell (2005) raises the issue of whether sport necessarily reinforces traditional gendered patterns of behaviour or can provide a means to subtly challenge damaging behaviours. He notes that the culture of sport is conventionally seen within critical men's studies as encouraging misogyny, violence, aggression, homophobia and competitiveness. However, Morrell argues that in some contexts (e.g, football in South Africa) sport affirms historically marginal racial and ethnic identities, can help men to lead more healthy lives and can even be the context for gender equality work. Fitzclarence and Hickey (2001) describe with reference to Australian Rules Football how coaching can be a means of engaging young men in social responsibility and offering pastoral support. We discuss the use of sport in health and social welfare interventions at various points during the book and in Chapter 10 in particular.

There are examples of where aspects of hegemonic masculinity are re-worked (but not fundamentally disrupted) in a mental health context (see also Chapter 9). Kilmartin (2005) recommends strategies for working with depressed men, which are reproduced in the practice example below – the first of many we use in the book. He addresses psychotherapy, but his ideas for practice could equally be used in any health or social welfare role where individual men are being engaged. His is a pragmatic approach, working with some aspects of hegemonic masculinity rather than overtly opposing them and aiming to 'expand' his clients' conceptions of what it is to be a (fairly traditional) man.

Practice Example – Expansion of positive masculine qualities in men with depression

- *Courage* is masculine. It is courageous to take a psychological risk by expressing your feelings, asking for what you want and talking about masculinity in the face of the cultural pressure to deny your feelings, get what you want through domination and uncritically accept the culturally dominant definition of masculinity.

- *Independence* is masculine. Men can be independent by not always doing what other men do when there is good reason to resist.
- *Leadership* is masculine. Men can be leaders by showing other men healthier visions of masculinity and more effective ways of dealing with their emotional lives.
- *Assertiveness* is masculine. Men can be assertive by claiming their rights as dignified human beings. Men can assert their rights to have feelings, to express those feelings, to behave outside of dominant definitions of gender and to ask for what they want in relationships.
- *Facing a challenge* is masculine. Men can see a challenge as getting something done despite difficulty. The challenge can be faced by building the skills that they have not acquired because cultural masculinity conspires against them. They can accept the challenge to learn how to better relate to others, respect women, take care of their health, and deal effectively with their emotions.

From Kilmartin (2005: 99).

Kilmartin is deliberately using aspects of hegemonic masculinity to help men get better. We can see how some people would object to this strategy as effectively perpetuating and reinforcing dualistic gender identities that are fundamentally bad for men and women. This is, however, a pragmatic approach which is more likely to succeed with some (though not all) men than a more radical transformative approach that sets out to reconstruct gender identities. We should end this section by acknowledging that the more idealistic approaches are often more about rhetoric than actual practice. The reality of what actually is achieved in interventions with men is in fact often more mundane and considerably less radical than grand ideological aims would claim.

Conclusion

We conclude this chapter by briefly summarising some key issues to consider when analysing the politics of interventions with men. We list some questions that should be asked about interventions so that the implications for gender relations can be as clear as possible. We would argue that these questions are relevant both to interventions that make masculinity explicit, such as a father's group, and to those that do not, such as general primary health care. These issues arise throughout the book in different guises and as such lead us into the chapters that follow, with their focus first on generic practice models and then on specific health and social welfare issues for men.

What assumptions are revealed about the nature of sex and gender? Is the practice approach based on essentialist assumptions about biological sex – for example that men's social cognition is different from women's or that men are more interested in sex or more inclined to aggression? Conversely are there assumptions that gender identities and gendered practices are entirely socially constructed? If so, what level of change is expected? Can masculinities be deconstructed or does socially constructed gender lock men into particular practices via a deep-rooted and enduring socialisation?

What are the discourses of masculinity?   What are the key messages and beliefs about men as clients or as workers that circulate in the culture of the organisation? Is there a general tendency to view men as oppressive, or downtrodden, or difficult to work with or vulnerable? Are there in fact diverse and even contradictory discourses of masculinity around? What are the implications of these different discourses for the way the work gets done? How do mainstream professional ideologies fit with a particular focus on men? For example, should 'empowerment' necessarily be a goal, even if you are aiming to challenge an aspect of men's privileges?

What are the practical results of policies?   What actual initiatives get funded or supported? What do they set out to do? What are their aims, either stated or unstated? What are the outcomes for girls and women as well as for boys and men? How do clients and workers of both sexes experience interventions? What differences, if any, do they make to their lives? Do they 'work', either in the terms in which they set out to be effective or in terms of some unintended knock-on effect?

What happens between policy and implementation?   What differences emerge between the stated intentions of politicians or managers and implementation in street-level bureaucracy? How does the political rhetoric of, for example, promoting men's health through self-examination to monitor testicular cancer actually relate to what advice frontline staff give to men as patients? How does talk of the importance of engaging more fathers in family support services actually materialise in targeted interventions? What actually goes on between staff and men as service users?

The bigger picture   Although these questions might seem to be of more academic interest, they have a place in the toolbox of the reflective practitioner: Why have these particular social problems come to be seen as masculinised at this particular point in time? How do policies and practices in relation to men connect with the wider ideological climate in each local and national context? How can they be explained in terms of social basis of each country? How do they relate to models of welfare state and gender regime? How do claims about the 'problem of men' spread? What does the development of masculinity policy and social interventions with men tell us about the process of policy transfer and the global circulation of policy?

This chapter has introduced some themes in the politics of masculinity that recur throughout the book in different ways. We now follow it with an overview of generic practice models for work with men, starting with engaging men as individuals.

Key texts

Clatterbaugh, K. (1997) *Contemporary Perspectives on Masculinity,* second edition, Boulder, CO: Westview Press.

The updated second edition of Clatterbaugh's 1990 book, which gives a readable overview of the range of different men's groups and political positions on masculinity, with reference to the USA.

Hobson, B. (ed.) (2002) *Making Men into Fathers. Men, Masculinities and the Social Politics of Fatherhood,* Cambridge: Cambridge University Press.

An impressive collection of papers on the politics of fatherhood in several Western countries.

Messner, M. (1997) *The Politics of Masculinity*, Newbury Park: Sage.

Rather similar in scope to the Clatterbaugh book and also about the USA, but includes a useful map of the 'terrain' of the politics of masculinity (see Figure 3.1).

PART II
Practice Models

4 Practice Models 1: Working with Men as Individuals

Introduction

In this chapter we explore practice approaches to direct work with individual men. Although the discussion will lean towards situations where men ask for psychological help (which represents the bulk of the literature), the principles of these approaches are relevant to all situations in which a worker in a health or social care setting is working with a male client/patient. We demonstrate this generality by giving a variety of practice examples. We hope that by doing so, we can show that many of these approaches are full of useful, pragmatic and applicable techniques for working with men. Because of the diverse ideas covered in this and the following chapter, there are more frequent practice illustrations in these two chapters than there are from Chapter 6 onwards.

After an exploration of some common themes that underpin all of these approaches, we will delineate the value of psycho-dynamic, cognitive-behavioural and counselling approaches to men's work. We will end the chapter with an extended case discussion of the work undertaken with a man who had been sexually abused as a child. This case is presented as a summary of the themes in the chapter and as a vivid example of direct work with a man informed by the theories and practices described earlier in the chapter.

Although we try to highlight commonalities between different practice models, there are also important differences. Most of the models that have been described for working with men aim to *ameliorate* men's pain/distress and change aspects of their behaviour that cause problems for others. In other words, they seek to improve the lives of men (and women and children) by effecting change in a presenting problem. These models want to change, predominantly, the man himself. However, there are other models that seek a *transformation* of the man and may have a wider social change perspective (e.g., Rowan, 1997). The approaches to direct work with individual men therefore replicate the terrain of the politics of masculinities described in Chapter 3: some focus on the costs of masculinity, some seek to alter institutional privileges while some emphasise the specific needs of minority men.

Common theories shared by practice models

Chapter 2 explained that there are many theories proposed that explain the 'unique' aspects of male psychology. Chapter 2 also described some cogent criticisms of these theories. We do not want to repeat these theories here, but it is important to acknowledge that, critiqued or not, they inform all the interventions with individual men that we outline in this chapter.

Thus many writers who describe models for working with individual men assume that men are 'psychically made' (Chapter 2) in a psychological process which differentiates them from their mothers (Greenson, 1993; Jukes, 1993). These writers and practitioners further assume that this process is psychologically painful for men and explains their suppression of (or inability to 'feel') emotion. Some see it as explaining both some men's hostility to feminine ways of relating and also something called 'father hunger' (Bly, 1991), i.e., longing to get support and respect from their fathers.

While recognising that sociologists of gender such as Connell (1995) find the idea of sex role socialisation unhelpful in various ways (for example, it does not allow for men's agency and it assumes one sex role rather than multiple masculinities), it is nonetheless true that most practitioners and writers in men's work assume that men are 'socially made' (Chapter 2). This process leads to them being expected to behave in certain ways and to perform certain roles. These practitioners generally see this socialisation as having psychological costs for men (Levant and Pollack, 1995; Faludi, 1999). Some understanding of male socialisation and its costs is generally regarded as a prerequisite for successful work with men.

Clearly, these theories and knowledges are contested. Within some fields of direct work, it has been proposed (Pocock, 1995) that if the theory has some usefulness in the moment to moment process of therapy, then it has some value. This acceptance of its value, however, does not invest the theory with 'truth' but rather recognises its 'story-like' quality. Something similar to this sceptical pragmatism is perhaps necessary in working with men.

Wanting to work with men

For practitioners who are working with men there is one issue in which sceptical pragmatism will not be enough. We would argue that practitioners have to *want* to work with men for the process to be helpful. This may seem an obvious statement, but clearly it is frequently not the case that practitioners are allowed to choose with whom they work. For instance, a female community psychiatric nurse may have to work with male and female substance misusers in a community team. But it may also be good practice for teams to account for men's work to be allocated to those workers who are keen to undertake it. Team members may not wish to work with men for a number of reasons. They may have personal memories/influences. For instance, a male worker who experienced an authoritarian father as a child, may find himself unable to think clearly when working with a man accused of abusing his own child (*counter-transference*: see section on psycho-dynamic approaches). Alternatively, a worker may ascribe *otherness* to certain men and be over-affected by social stereotypes. An example would be a female probation officer who found herself unable to work with a black British man accused of pimping because she became too angry at his alleged offences.

Practice Example

A team that worked with domestically violent men and with children who had witnessed domestic violence aimed to ensure that in all their work both male and female staff were involved (to model respectful relationships to men, women and children). It also aimed to mix the kinds of work undertaken so that no one team member became 'stuck' in one aspect of the work. However, the team had to rethink its assumptions when first one member of staff and then another became pregnant. After much discussion, it was agreed that women who were pregnant may feel more exposed to the misogyny of the abusive men and that this was not in their best interest. It was agreed that although pregnancy was not an 'illness' it did constitute a 'special case' in work in which gender and abuse were integral. The team therefore 're-formed' to allow some women to specialise in children's work and others to specialise in men's work.

Of course, this dynamic can equally work the other way: some workers may be motivated too strongly by a 'mission' to change men and this may complicate their working relationships with their clients. This zeal may again originate in personal experiences or it may be a deeply held political commitment.

Many commentators make the point that if workers frequently find that they have to help male clients, then they should be aware of their own prejudices. In short, if the worker does not actually like men, then their work with men will probably reflect this. In some training courses in health and social care, workers will be encouraged to analyse their own gender beliefs (Wilkins, 1997), and to understand how these will affect the way they work with men. Erickson phrases this in this way for women workers:

> We must not abandon the elements that make us women, such as warmth and nurturing, in an attempt to gain acceptance by becoming honorary men ... we must learn to do what traditionally has been considered the man's prerogative and responsibility. We must exercise leadership and operate with a task focus. (1993: 25)

Erickson's work demonstrates in some detail the pitfalls that might befall a female worker who works with men. Other authors show that men also can bring to this work a competitiveness and a focus that may be unhelpful (Freudenburger, 1990). Indeed, Freudenburger comments that many male therapists may reflect dominant aspects of male socialisation in their work and allow male clients to 'hide' and not face their struggles fully. In this sense, male workers might collude and 'let men off' from working on the painful issues that need to be addressed.

It is impossible for practitioners to not be affected by their own experiences and they bring these into their work with men. The literature demonstrates that an awareness of their motivation is crucial. Essentially, moreover, men's work needs to have at its core a respect for men as people.

Clients' choice of gender of worker

Similarly, practitioners need to respect the views of a male client with whom he wishes to work. Practitioners will know that men who ask for help will often come with a view about whether they would like to see a man or a woman. The reasons for these preferences may often be to do with the client's own stereotyped view of gender. Thus, one client may want to speak to a woman because he assumes women are 'better' at helping people through problems. But another client may prefer to speak to a man because a man will 'understand' and, perhaps more importantly, will not expect him to be too emotional!

In these examples, the male clients have a different view on how they want the worker to 'contain' their anxieties. In cases of trauma such as sexual abuse, this dynamic may require considerable thought and discussion. Again, for instance, if a man was abused by another man as a child, he may prefer not to talk about this to a male in a private therapeutic space. On the other hand, if this were to happen, then the worker would need to be aware that complex processes may develop in which a similar pattern of 'feeling abused' may be evoked if the client felt unheard (Gartner, 1999).

The unconscious effects of gender socialisation also influence the process of working with men. Various studies (for example, Werner-Wilson et al., 1997) have shown that workers will often respond in gendered ways to comments by clients. In this dynamic, sometimes the assumption that men do not want to talk about emotional difficulties will motivate a worker to avoid these difficulties. For instance, if a male client were to speak about feeling hopeless, a male worker might immediately respond with a problem-solving question such as 'What have you tried to do about this?' With a female client, it is more likely that the worker will take time exploring the depth of the hopelessness before moving on to trying to collaborate on strategies of solution. Typically, such a process may be played out in a GP surgery, which will affect the type of treatment offered.

These points function to highlight the role of gender in any direct work with men. They also highlight how complex the balance can be between accepting stereotypes (e.g., 'men don't talk about feelings'), challenging stereotypes (e.g., not letting men only work with men because this may lead to them feeling safe in not talking about feelings) and working through stereotypes (e.g., using male workers to help clients expand their emotional language). They also highlight the role of unconscious processes which are well described in much of the psycho-dynamic literature about working with men.

Psycho-dynamic approaches to working with men as individuals

All psycho-dynamic practice rests on the assumption that the therapy replicates troubled past relationships and therefore provides a space from which these troubled experiences can be repaired. In classic terms this is called the transference (Jacobs, 1988). In later understandings of this process, therapists have used attachment theory to explain that in therapy a safe space is created from which the client can explore and transform past and present pain (Evans, 2006). In many renditions of this process, therapists have talked about the primary childhood relationship with parents as being the predominant process within the therapy room. Thus Jacobs in his analysis of therapy with a female client, notes that 'the difficulty she had already expressed, about seeing a male counsellor, was also present in her current relationships with other men apart from myself' (1988: 12).

He goes on to suggest that this woman's difficulty in seeing a male therapist had its origins in her relationship with her father. Evans (2006) also notes that the gender of the worker, in this case in genetic counselling practice, inevitably evokes memories of the parent of the same gender from the client's birth family. This dynamic should be kept in mind by all health and social care workers who work with male clients.

This concept highlights for any worker that there is an inter-relationship between the helper, the client and the client's unresolved conflicts with his parents.

Practice Example

Paul presented at his local Citizens' Advice Bureau asking for help with his debts. He was allocated a male debt counsellor who helped him work out how to consolidate his debts and indeed made a number of telephone calls to various banks and loan companies on his behalf. After over half an hour of collaborating, the counsellor happened to mention that it was very important for Paul to pay the contributions required on the date that was specified every month. The way he spoke reminded Paul of times when his father had humiliated him when he was a child. He already felt shamed and out of control and he began to get angry. On this occasion, the counsellor did not comment on what he had done that might have triggered old memories. But he did work hard to repair the working relationship by saying 'I am sorry if I have said something that upsets you, I am here to help you sort this problem out. Let's go back and sort out what arrangements would work for you'.

From a psycho-dynamic perspective, therefore, the worker should always ask themselves how their representation of gender may be unconsciously triggering memories in the client. It is crucial to remember that this triggering is not to be regarded as a handicap. Rather, it is a therapeutic tool, which both orientates the helper and can be used directly in the work. It is also important to recognise that *transference* goes both ways. Thus some male clients may evoke experiences within the worker which may 'get in the way' of helping that client. In psycho-dynamic terms, this is called *counter-transference*.

Psycho-dynamic theories also contribute an understanding about men's embodiment and how this affects their psyches and psychological functioning. We will not elaborate on this theme here as it has been mentioned in Chapter 2 and will be further explored in Chapter 8. It is important to end this section with the observation that psycho-dynamic ideas about working with men are often fundamental in other interventions and can provide significant insights into the work.

Cognitive-behavioural models for working with men

Cognitive-behavioural therapy (CBT) has become the most researched and promoted way of helping individuals within the mental health field (Roth and Fonagy, 2005). These approaches have also been applied to a wide range of situations, including depression, pain management, violence and offending in general, parenting and recovery after major operations. CBT intervention centres upon the cognitions that lead to individuals feeling or behaving in certain ways. Treatment seeks to change these 'maladaptive cognitions' by teaching alternative ways of thinking and by challenging the unhelpful thoughts. Despite their common use, few CBT applications routinely incorporate a gender analysis into their application. For instance, in the field of depression (Padesky, 1995), the specific aspects of male socialisation and development that may contribute to depression and which may manifest in male-specific cognitions, are not generally highlighted (Real, 1997, though see the Kilmartin intervention in Chapter 3).

However, there are a number of counsellors who have argued that CBT is an ideal form of intervention for men. It has become a primary intervention tool in work with abusive men and its application with offenders in general could be seen as implicity challenging masculinities (see Chapter 3). Since we discuss CBT in this context in some detail in Chapter 7, we do not deal with the model in great depth at this point.

Practice Example

Delwyn came to an emergency social service desk asking for advice about how to deal with his daughter, who was staying out late and missing school. The worker took a detailed description of the problem but was disconcerted because it did not sound as if Delwyn really cared about what would be done. The worker decided not to see this as an 'attitude' issue towards social service involvement, but chose to ask Delwyn why he was giving this impression, when he clearly did care and had come in to ask for help. Delwyn was then able to say that he had never asked for help before and didn't think anything could be done, nor that 'talking about it would help'. The worker was then able to talk with Delwyn about these thoughts and to show him how they were a self-fulfilling prophesy. This conversation interested Delwyn and he began to see how his thoughts towards his daughter contributed both to her behaviour and his own depression about life.

Mahalik (2005) makes the point that male socialisation makes cognitive therapy especially appropriate for men. He argues that cognitive approaches would be classed as 'treatments of choice' in terms of men's lack of emotional language (in contemporary parlance we have termed this 'emotional literacy' [Killick, 2006]) and their lack of empathy. Mahalik (2005) draws on David and Brannon's (1976) snappy descriptions of the dominant male role to highlight the kind of cognitions that can be seen as unhelpful and incorrect. These authors have said that hegemonic masculinity (not the term they use) means 'no sissy stuff', 'being a sturdy oak', being a 'big wheel' and in times of trouble 'giving them hell'. All these cognitions, which might be contributing to an individual man's distress, should be challenged. Mahalik (2005) gives more appropriate cognitive responses to some of these cognitions (see Chapter 9). Thus, the cognition that a man should achieve no matter what, can be countered by realistic thoughts about other sides of life. The cognition that emotions are 'sissy' can be countered with the alternative view that sharing feelings helps maintain close relationships that give great joy and significance to life. This alternative can be tried out as an experiment to see if it does lead to negative or positive consequences.

In many ways, cognitive techniques are more often integrated into other intervention approaches. It would seem that further work needs to be undertaken, however, to elicit any specific cognitive techniques that would be applicable to diverse male populations such as gay men and men from minority ethnic cultures.

Counselling approaches to working with men

The variety of approaches that could be classed as 'counselling' within the field of working with men is myriad (see Scher et al., 1987; Kupers, 1993; Wild, 1999; Good and Brooks, 2005). Some of these approaches seek to help men in general to 'change' (Wild, 1999); some seek to use therapy as a 'transformational process' for individual men (Rowan, 1997); and some seek the more modest aim of ameliorating the pain that some men cause others or experience in their lives. Most of these approaches share a view that workers in health and social care often fail to take account of the aspects of masculinity that both make getting help difficult and contribute to the problems that men present. Good and Brooks (2005: 12), for instance, note that 'the mental health community is poorly prepared to meet the needs of many men' and they therefore want to educate workers and to describe better ways of engaging and helping men.

Practice Example

Gwyn, aged 27, came to a counsellor after his relationship with his partner came to an end. In the first session, he could only talk about how angry and let down he felt. He was especially angry that he had disclosed to his parents that he was gay and he and his partner had moved in together after a period of intense hostility from both sets of families. Gwyn felt angry and embittered. The counsellor gently asked if he felt any other emotions and if he felt he had done anything to contribute to this break-up. Gwyn initially thought the counsellor was being biased and had a prejudice against gay relationships. However, when he came back to the second session, he had begun to feel the pain and hurt rather than the anger which had protected him initially. As these feelings were expressed, Gwyn was able to accept his own part in the breakdown and begin the task of building his self-esteem up again.

Most of the counselling approaches mentioned share a view that one of the first tasks of the worker is to help the man feel comfortable with the situation of receiving help. Good and Brooks state that: 'For some time, mental health professionals have recognized that men are reluctant to take on the client role' (2005: 8).

This leads them to argue that counsellors require a model of working that does not rely on 'feminine modes of intervention' but rather newer '"masculine" styles must be developed' (p. 8). By this is meant a therapeutic engagement that has a practical focus rather than an initial emotional focus. There has been some research evidence to substantiate that men prefer problem-solving therapeutic interventions at least at the start of the therapy (Bennun, 1989). Along with this understanding goes a belief that therapy with men may take patience on behalf of the counsellor because the man needs to be gently invited into the process.

Furrow (2001) writes about this most coherently. He states that workers should structure their early sessions with men so that the session does not appear to be loose and dangerously open. He says that many men like to know what they are going to talk about rather than harbour fears that intimate details will be discussed without warning. Furrow then observes that workers should not expect emotional vulnerability but accept the limited vulnerability often offered as sufficient until the man wants to offer more (e.g., feels safe in the setting). Moreover the worker should attend to the man's feelings of relevance. Thus, the topics of conversation should match as closely as possible the man's stated goals in the session.

Practice Example

Karl, a young father, initially came to his local family centre to collect discounted nappies for his child. In these exchanges he began to talk to the staff there about the fact that his partner was struggling to get out at all and had sent him to help out. Staff at the family centre encouraged Karl to talk a little more every time he came. He stopped for a cup of tea and was pleased to see toddlers playing with parents in the play room. Only after a few visits did he finally ask for help with teaching his child to sleep through the night. After this advice, he began to come to the centre with his baby to 'give his partner a rest'. He also began to come down when job advisors held advice sessions at the centre and only then seemed to accept the centre as a place where he could get advice and help.

The second common feature of most counselling approaches to work with men is that one of the primary focuses of the work should be to increase men's emotional repertoire. Real (1997), who has written a self-help book for depressed men, comments that 'few things about men and women seem more dissimilar than the way we tend to handle our feelings' (p. 23). Therefore, like many counsellors, he argues that help must include the expression and wider understanding of emotions. Perhaps the form of counselling that has taken this perspective most to heart is that of the mythopoetic men's movement. Some of the controversies about this movement have been described in Chapter 2. At this point it is useful to note that followers of this approach encourage men to retreat to wild places, express their pain and repressed emotions and thus become more fully human. The writers in this tradition have drawn extensively on storytelling as a medium to draw men into the process of 'healing' (Bly, 1991; Meade, 1993).

A third common feature of counselling perspectives in working with men is an emphasis on *responsibility building*. In some approaches this is typified by helping the man see how he contributes to the relationship problems, mental health problems or situational problems he finds himself struggling with. In others, it transcends individual responsibility and encourages the man to act to help others: indeed to transcend his own socialisation (Rowan, 1997).

Working with boys and men who have been sexually abused

In a number of ways, working with men who have been sexually abused provides an example and summary of the issues involved in working with men as individuals. Therefore, in this section, we wish to discuss this area more fully. First, the history of working with sexually abused men demonstrates the slow pace at which a need for help for men has come to be acknowledged. Etherington (1995) has argued that this was partly because the field of sexual abuse interventions initially could not accept that men could be victims of such abuse. Second, the sexual abuse of men (as boys) demonstrates how dominant male socialisation conflicts with help-seeking (see Chapter 9 of this book). Etherington (1995) comments that because sexual abuse makes boys into victims, dominant gender socialisation makes it less possible for them to admit the experience. Hence only as it has become more acceptable for men to accept their vulnerability have men come forward and acknowledged what happened to them as children. Third, even then, helping services are more likely to be provided to boys who have been abused than to men (Christopherson et al., 1989; Nyman and Svensson, 1995; Spiegal, 2003). Last, because of all these factors, many men who were abused as children often present other difficulties to services (e.g., depression, aggression) rather than the trauma of abuse.

Etherington provides a summary of how sexual abuse contravenes specific male gender roles and poses specific psychological difficulties for men.

> When boys are sexually abused, gender and sexual issues include those related to fears about being homosexual; gender and sexual identity confusion; feelings of inadequacy as a male and fears about being effeminate; sexual compulsion, sexual addiction, and hyper-sexuality; and avoidance of sexual activity. (1995: 7)

Etherington also notes that many men fear that they also will become abusers as they have internalised a view of masculinity that it is inherently abusive. It is important to acknowledge that many of these fears and symptoms may also occur for sexually abused girls and, indeed, some abused children will exhibit a great resilience despite abuse. However, Etherington's analysis demonstrates that practitioners working with sexually abused men should be able to work with a range of specific difficulties associated with men's gender concepts as well as work with the trauma.

In work with such men, the initial discussion with them must relate to the gender of the worker. Some men would prefer to work with a practitioner who was not the same gender as the abuser: be that male or female. Here again it is impossible to avoid gender expectations. Some men would rather not disclose what has happened to them to a woman. This may be partly because they feel that admitting to being a victim would make the woman worker think less of them (they are 'less than a man'). Others feel more comfortable disclosing personal problems with women. This again would conform to the gender expectation that women are the 'best' gender to help with emotional problems.

Helping men who have been sexually abused, as in other abuse counselling, often requires patience and time from the helper. Cabe states that:

> For sexually abused boys, boundaries have been horribly violated. Trusting others again and talking about the trauma tends to be very difficult. Consequently, counsellors must be very patient, avoiding forcing the client to self-disclose, and wait until the client is ready to talk. (1999: 213)

Once this self-disclosure has begun, the worker may have to contain the emotional *catharsis* so that the client can control the resulting emotional experience. However, once the disclosure begins it is crucial that the client is heard, understood and his pain acknowledged. Workers can expect to find that the man has 'cut himself' off from the experience for many years and may have adopted a form of dissociation in order to cope with it. As the man tells the story of his abuse, intense feelings of shame may emerge. It is not uncommon for the man to feel that in some way he 'asked' to be abused. In terms of sexual arousal, clearly this complicates the man's perception of what happened: it is difficult to accept that the boy was powerless when he experienced sexual feelings and physically responded to the abuse.

A number of texts outline approaches to work with sexually abused men (Grubman-Black, 1990; Crowder, 1995; Gartner, 1999; Spiegal, 2003). In the early stages of help, the worker's role is to facilitate the man in expressing his feelings and challenging the cognitions that may contribute to his struggle to deal with the consequences of the abuse in his life. In later stages, the worker needs to adopt a 'problem' focus and help the man overcome in practical and concrete ways these consequences. Thus, if the man is having sexual difficulties with his partner (male or female), he may benefit from a series of sex therapy sessions (possibly with his partner). If he is expressing anger in interpersonal relationships, he may benefit from some anger management sessions as well as communications coaching.

It is quite common for men to experience something they may call a 'breakdown' as they gradually describe what has happened to them. Many thoughts, fears and anxieties that had been suppressed for many years might emerge to haunt the man. In the following section we give an extended case example to demonstrate an intervention with a man who had been sexually abused. We will annotate this example to show the themes and processes outlined in this chapter.

Extended case example

James came to a mental health agency asking for help. His daughter had just disclosed that she had been sexually abused by a male adult leader in her after-school gym club. This had sent James into a very disturbed place: he was anxious, depressed and also agitated. He said that he was likely to kill this man and needed help.

Frequently, sexually abused men have 'buried' the abuse. A later trauma in their normal lives stimulates the re-awakening of the trauma. But at first they may not know what their 'problem' is.

A male community psychiatric nurse (Bill) met James and nego-tiated a three session contract with him to help him 'come to terms' with what had happened. The team's psychiatrist also agreed to prescribe medication if necessary.

Often workers can have a feeling that a man needs to tell them something they have not yet disclosed. Evidence for this may be that the man seems to have been more severely affected by an event in his life than would be expected. A limited commitment to counselling (a number of sessions) is often more appealing to men than a long-term arrangement. The CPN took care in constructing an agenda which made sense to James and included 'practical' intervention if necessary.

James came to the second session describing disturbing dreams. He said that he had something to say but was not ready yet. He said that he had not told his family or his wife what this was but he knew that they were worried about him.

Sometimes, a worker can help a man disclose by saying something like 'sometimes it is hard to say what we need to say', or 'do you think you need to tell me about it and if so what can I do to help you do this?'

Bill suggested that James write down what he felt he wanted to say for next time. When James came back he had not written anything down but he said he would tell Bill as long as Bill did not look at him while he talked.

Shame about being abused can be overwhelming for some men. Within the shame of 'allowing' the abuse to happen, is a fear of being judged as inadequate by the worker.

(Continued)

(Continued)

James had been sexually abused at a school camp when he was 13. James blamed himself and had spent his early adulthood compensating by playing physical team sports. Psychologically after the disclosure, James became suicidal. He could not think about anything except what had happened to him. He had clear ideas about how to kill himself.

After a few sessions talking about his pain, James began to be consumed by feelings of guilt. He blamed himself that he had not protected his daughter ('I of all people should have known'). He blamed himself that he was not strong enough to cope with what had happened. He blamed himself for being emotionally unavailable to his wife at a time when she needed his support and strength. He blamed himself for just not being able to work at present.

Only after three months of intensive support did James say that he wanted to talk through what had happened to him. He had begun to do so via a website for abused men. He expressed many of the thoughts that sexually abused people hold: that he had 'asked to be abused'; that he should have stopped it; that he was dirty; and even that he may be responsible for his daughter being abused. He was terrified that the investigating social services team knew that he had suffered abuse because 'everyone knows that if you have been abused, you will abuse others'.

Sometimes, the pain that emerges can turn into feelings of desolation. In such situations, workers need to be able to construct safety plans with the man and if possible alert their intimate network. In this case James refused this option but was willing to take medication to help him cope with the feelings.

Self-blame is closely connected to men thinking they have failed to live up to an ideal of 'maleness'. Many men feel a responsibility to protect their families. This is compounded if they are unable to 'provide' for their families through being off work. In this phase of work, counsellors may work with men's cognitions (e.g., challenge the thought that 'I am a bad man'). They also may use techniques to help the man contain the pain such as helping the man distract himself, 'practise' putting the feelings in a box, recognising that he is not alone in his pain.

Once these thoughts and feelings were expressed, Bill was able to use CBT methods to help James challenge them. He was able to teach James to hold onto a realistic understanding of what happens to 13-year-olds. He was able to get James to see his experience as a resource for his daughter and family rather than a threat. He also was able to begin to encourage James to see his own strengths that had got him through until now.

(Continued)

Four months into the work with James, he was able to see that he needed to learn how to tell his wife and, later, tell his daughter why he had been so upset in the last few months. He was also able now to talk about the poor sexual relationship he had with his wife and his fears that maybe he was gay and not hetero-sexual. Bill was able to work with him on these issues and set up a number of couple and family sessions to work on healing all the family together.	There are almost always relationship problems for men who have been abused. Counsellors need to be able to address these either with the man on his own, or in couple settings.
Only after six months' work was Bill able to help James decrease his medication and get back to work. He was able to establish 'problem-solving' sessions (e.g., how should James exert fatherly control over his daughter and not be over-controlled by fear that something would happen to her). The two agreed to regular but infrequent telephone contact to maintain the opportunity for James to ask for help if needed.	Help for sexually abused men can take time and the worker should always have in place a support system in case other life events re-awaken distress.

Conclusion

This chapter has described various practice models for working with men individually. It is important that these practice models are informed by a view about *why* working with men is valued: hence this chapter is consistent with Chapters 2 and 3. Many of the dilemmas described in these earlier chapters have been reprised in this chapter: Are the skills needed to work with men different from those needed with women? Are ideas about male socialisation/development useful to practitioners? Is the purpose of men's work to alleviate individual pain or to change men as a group? How far should workers integrate a gender understanding into their work with men? Each practitioner will respond to these questions differently and their responses may change over time and client group. What we have highlighted is how skills and concepts from three separate practice models can be adapted to work with men. Many of these skills and concepts have been demonstrated in a fuller case analysis of work with a man who was sexually abused as a child. In the next chapter, we apply a similar approach to other contexts in which practitioners in the health and social care setting work with men: in groups, families and communities.

Key texts

Good, G.E. and Brooks, G.R. (eds) (2005) *The New Handbook of Psychotherapy and Counseling with Men*, San Francisco: Jossey Bass.

This collection deals with a range of theoretical approaches and specific populations of men.

Meth, R. and Pasick, R. (eds) (1990) *Men in Therapy*, New York: Guilford.

This gives a thorough review of helping men through the life cycle and addresses social pressures affecting men in Western societies.

5 Practice Models 2: Working with Men in Groups, Families and Communities

Introduction

In this chapter we will outline some of the approaches currently used when working with men in groups, families and communities. This is a huge subject area and this chapter can only provide an overview of the literature and practice. It should by now be clear that one of this book's themes is that 'working with men' is not an easily defined pursuit: men are heterogeneous, as are the legion of possible approaches for intervening with them. This chapter will continue to reflect this diversity. However, for ease of presentation, the chapter will be divided into sections orientated to the unit of intervention: group, family, couple and community. Within the discussion that follows, it is also important to note that the interventions discussed are predicated upon theories of masculinity and ideological positions (see Chapters 2 and 3). In some instances these theories are explicit; in others they are implicit. This means that throughout the discussion a question will continually be asked: Is groupwork/family work/couple work and community work that has men as a target of intervention different, and if so what constitutes this difference?

Working with men in groups

As in the rest of this book, one of the fundamental issues to address is whether there is a specific kind of groupwork, or specific techniques that are important in working with men in groups. The answer has to be that there are specific issues that group facilitators need to be aware of and it is also true that there are generic skills that apply to all kinds of groupwork.

Engaging men in groupwork

We have already referred to the mythopoetic tradition that relies on getting men together to 'resolve men's issues'. This tradition sees itself as very much fulfilling a 'tribal' tradition in which men gathered to hunt, tell stories and plan tribal events. This idea assumes that such male gatherings were positive, 'soul-fulfilling' and not exclusive. However, feminist critics have argued that such male bonding is often exclusive, woman-blaming and centred on violent action of one sort or another (see also Gilmore, 1990). What this highlights is that for any facilitator, the gathering of men together, whether in the presence of a female facilitator or not (especially if not), can easily become a forum for men to express resentment at their partners, their limited lives, or even the world in general. This dynamic may not be unique to the gathering of men, but it is clearly one of the initial factors that must be included in any concept of group 'forming'.

Practice Example

In a mental health day centre, a social work student was asked to run a 'stress busting' group for a group of men who had been attending for a number of months. The centre staff had a view that these men seemed to complain about the lack of help they were being given and did not engage positively with other groups. When the student, who was male, convened the group, he found that rather than being interested in 'stress busting', all the men wanted to do was have another forum in which they could complain about their lives and the mental health system in general. When they described not having any financial resources, they would not look seriously at their benefit entitlements and plan how to get reviews from their benefit officers. When the student tried to teach them relaxation techniques, they said they would rather watch the TV in the centre as that was 'how they relaxed'. Only when the student asked the men if their complaining helped them cope, did they start to have a conversation with him about what they could do to improve their lives.

There has been a growing literature about the particular features of group-work with men (Rabinowitz and Cochran, 1987; Gardiner and Nesbit, 1996; Murphy, 1996; Cowburn and Pengelly, 1999; Rabinowitz, 2005). Indeed, there have even been editions of journals dedicated to the issue (Schlachet, 1994). What we will attempt here is a summary of the suggestions of these authors.

Practitioners, when they form a male-only group, often notice that it can take a considerable time for the men to begin to display comfort and spontaneity. This has been contrasted with the ease with which women typically relate in group situations (Rabinowitz, 2005) and connections have been made with dominant styles of 'male bonding'. This dynamic is explained by various writers as being due to men's assumption that they mix in all male fora competitively (either in the workplace or the sport arena) and also due to men's assumption that they look to women for emotional support, not to men. This groupwork stage has been described as 'initial ambivalence' by Rabinowitz (2005). In many ways this process is no different from the 'forming' stage of groupwork (Douglas, 2000). But it may have greater complexities because of the gendered processes involved. Often, group facilitators deal with this phase by encouraging a common agenda to emerge and by having a rather clear focus. The assumption here is that men are likely to engage better if they are clear what they are getting together to achieve.

One significant theme that emerges from the men's groupwork literature is that the groups should include a significant amount of 'action' activities and a structured format, to help reduce anxiety (Rabinowitz, 2005). An example of such a structure is that routinely undertaken in work with offenders. Newburn and Mair's (1996) book is full of such groups. Because most offenders are men, probation staff (social workers in Scotland) have a long experience of running groups with all-male participants. Such groups have a clearly defined purpose and often have very rigid curricula. Buckley and Young (1996), for instance, describe a group intervention for car crime. They explain that cars appeal to young men because they represent 'danger' and hence reinforce a masculinity based on risk taking. Buckley and Young describe their predominantly young offenders as 'hooked on speed and thrills' (p. 51). Therefore they helped devise an 18-week groupwork intervention, which involves discussion of offending behaviour, including the perceived importance of the car to youthful masculinity and also provides a practical training which centres on 'developing the knowledge and skills that are necessary in order to maintain a vehicle in a safe and roadworthy condition' (p. 51). This intervention typifies many in the field of men's work: it combines a pragmatic approach to engage men's interest with an attempt to question unhelpful ideas about masculinity. Again, the beginning of this group addresses the dynamic mentioned by Rabinowitz (2005), insofar as the group does not start with an open 'therapeutic' invitation such as 'why do you think you are all here?', but rather structures the initial meeting with tasks and activities in order to 'break the ice' and put the men at their ease. The greatest fear that some men may have is to be left to 'talk about emotions' in such a setting, so allaying this fear with an activity or direction is helpful. Many men's groups adopt the model outlined by Buckley and Young, with set tasks to be completed at set moments in the group. This approach has been extended to many probation 'problem' areas with curricula and manuals being prepared for each issue.

Most authors, however, see this 'action' focus as only the start of the men's groupwork process. Indeed, some authors seek to highlight the emotional role of the group earlier. Guarnaschelli (1994) and Rowan (1997), for instance, argue that one of the unique focuses of such groupwork is to increase the *emotional education* of men. Hence these authors, who bring a deeper therapeutic perspective into the field (a more transformational model), argue that group facilitators should encourage male support. This implies that outside structures and manuals might be unhelpful: the men in the support group need to evolve in the group in a way that meets their emotional needs. Rowan argues that the pragmatic practice of using highly structured exercises to engage men is in fact making allowances for male socialisation and is therefore *perpetuating* it. Rowan believes that too much reliance on manuals and activity after activity is actually doing a disservice to men. This critique does indeed appear relevant in some areas of practice with men (see our Chapter 7).

It is fair to say that the focus on purpose frequently dominates the gathering of men into groups. Thus there are fewer unspecified 'support groups' for men than there are groups to help them deal with alcohol, drugs and violence towards women. In the United States there is some evidence that the mythopoetic men's movement has stimulated more men's support groups, than in the UK (Guarnascelli, 1994) in the same way that women's support groups emerged in the 1960s and 1970s. It is also interesting to note that many anti-sexist men's groups, that began as general 'changing ourselves' groups, eventually became social action groups that contributed (and still do) to the campaign to stop violence against women (Christian, 1994).

There is a further concept that underpins this literature and practice: the idea that men are best engaged by *outside-in* techniques rather than *inside-out* ones. These activities and structures within groupwork typify this concept. The assumption is that men cannot immediately access levels of comfort and self-reflection within a groupwork format. What they need is to be led into this terrain gently and indirectly. An example would be the use of stories. Meade (1993) describes various stories from around the world that he tells to American soldiers who fought in Vietnam. He recounts that as the listeners get more and more emotionally involved in the story, they want to speak more and more about the traumas they have experienced. Meade (1993) says that because this is one of the functions of the stories he tells, he chooses not to edit out any violence or barbaric acts, which are often central to myths. Once the initial 'activity' or *outside-in* phase has been achieved, men's groups will inevitably begin to encourage emotional expression.

Practice Example

A male refugee worker in the UK decided that as he was working with a number of men from an African country individually, he might as well convene them as a group. Initially he was pleased to find that this idea fitted with the men's cultural expectations: they were used to gathering together both in decision-making groups and also in their religious contexts. However, it soon emerged that within the group setting, some men were seen as having a higher status and were therefore the predominant speakers while other men did not feel they had an entitlement to speak. The worker asked the higher status men individually if they would be willing to tell the group that this was not a decision-making group and so everyone had a right to speak and take part. He also met each man on his own to discuss the purpose of the group. They all agreed that the group had a role in helping them think about what they had left behind and what they needed to learn to cope with living in the UK. The worker invited a number of outside speakers into the group to talk about work opportunities, benefit entitlement, cultural resources and the British education system. The group began to 'run itself' and the worker was surprised that one day a member asked to talk about the trauma he had witnessed in the war zone. The worker knew this was dangerous as not all the men would have witnessed the same, nor would they have all been on the 'same side'. However, over the course of the next few weeks, more men talked about the ordeals of war, and of feeling unwelcome in the UK. A depth of connection built up from this group that helped sustain the members through difficult times.

Other authors comment that dominant models of masculinity can lead to two further specific issues in working with men in groups. The first relates to what might be called *resistance*, which means that many men will seek to deny that they need help and therefore refuse to seek help. This would be especially true in groups that are 'forced' into existence by some outside pressure such as the courts or child welfare system. Such resistance often poses a challenge for facilitators: men and women alike. Proposed solutions to this dynamic have been to emphasise the joint purpose of working together (Rabinowitz, 2005); naming of the resistance (Friedman, 1994); invitation to solve this together (Rivett and Rees, 2004); and techniques designed to balance positive aspects of being in the group with negative ones (Rees and Rivett, 2005).

Practice Example

In the first group session for men who have been abusive to their partners, one man who had been mandated to attend expressed ambivalence and hostility to the process. The facilitators decided to deal with this in two ways. They thanked the man for being so honest and asked him to list all the things that his current attitude to women might achieve for him in his life. He was allocated a 'buddy', who was in the group voluntarily, to help him write this list. The list demonstrated that changing his attitudes and behaviour could actually achieve a lot for him. He stated that he did not want to be a 'lonely old git' like his father was. He was then asked to talk in front of the group with his buddy about why the two of them were in the group. Gradually, he began to hear positive things about what he could gain from the group, he saw that men might volunteer for help, and he began to reflect that if only he had come to the group years ago, his life would already have turned around.

Later stages of the groupwork process

The observations in the previous section relate more to methods and techniques that may be helpful in the early stages of groupwork with men. Practitioners, however, have also commented upon features of groupwork with men in later stages. A common theme is the emergence of aggression and the managing of conflict. It is suggested that as men become more aware of the need to change, as they get closer to emotional pain, they will revert to classic forms of displacement. For many men the form of displacement most congruent with their socialisation is anger and aggression. Thus, groupwork facilitators should expect this to emerge, if not erupt. Again, there are a number of strategies to deal with this described in the literature. The one not recommended is obviously of matching aggression with further aggression. This may seem hardly worthy of note. But if a male group member expresses hostility to a male facilitator, the facilitator could react out of his own socialisation and 'rise to the challenge'. Instead, it is advisable to specify the conflict and encourage the group process to address it. This may need to be helped by facilitators reflecting what the aggression was 'trying to say' and to return to the advantages of learning how to communicate assertively, not aggressively.

This conflict stage may be followed by an acute 'sad' phase. Some authors see this phase as the moment when shame emerges and can be worked with (Friedman, 1994). Rabinowitz (2005) and Rowan (1997) see this as the realisation within the men that their usual problem-solving methods will not work any more and that there is more psychological work to do than they thought.

In counselling and groupwork literature, 'endings' are often seen as crucial. This is no less true for groupwork with men. Indeed, it is likely that endings can be even more difficult for men. During the groupwork process, the men may well have bonded with each other in a way they have never bonded with men before. They may have disclosed more to each other than ever before and they will have attended a form of help that they have never encountered before. Hence, it would not be wrong to describe the ending of the group as traumatic for some men. It may leave a gap in their lives. Practitioners therefore often assert that facilitators need to prepare for the ending well and warn the men of the gap that the end will leave in their lives. Psycho-dynamic writers have also added that the transference between group member and facilitator will also need attention at the end. Friedman (1994) notes that men may feel abandoned and rejected during this phase. In order to help men through this phase, a closing ritual is often suggested, as are 'self-help' or even 'buddy' systems to help keep the work and relationships going.

In this section we have concentrated on the particular techniques and processes involved in groupwork with men. We have chosen to emphasise generic themes in groupwork rather than isolate particular models of groupwork. Specific theoretical models are represented in the groupwork literature as much as they are in the individual work literature (e.g., psycho-dynamic, cognitive-behavioural, counselling). The one approach that has not yet been highlighted here or in the previous chapter is that of a systemic approach. It is to this that we now turn when we consider working with men in families and couples.

Working with men in families

This section needs to begin with an honest assessment of *how much* work is actually done with men within the contexts of their families and their couple relationships. Overwhelmingly, it seems that the ideology and structures of service provision collude with the absence of such work. The reality is that most family services tend to be geared to women (mothers) rather than men (fathers). It is equally true that, despite some agencies, such as Relate (relationship counselling) appearing to want to see equal numbers of men and women, attendance stills runs well below what might be expected (Bennett, 1995). That said, there is good evidence that men do attend clinics more frequently if their child is the focus of help, and there is growing evidence that more men are approaching health care agencies than in the past. Therefore, improving the skill level of social and health care workers in their delivery of services to men within the context of family relationships is crucial. This section of the chapter will therefore consider the literature with regard to working with men in families as well as providing some examples.

In terms of one intervention, family therapy, there has been a long history of therapists considering how to involve men. Berg and Rosenblum, for instance, carried out the first survey of men in family therapy in 1977. This survey suggested that 'the father was viewed as the most resistant' family member. Dougherty (1993: 77) stated that 'every woman therapist I know is privately frustrated by working with men and male therapists aren't having much better luck either'. However, these observations and the suggested solutions have raised other controversies. For instance, Berg and Rosenblum (1977: 90) argued that this evidence led to the conclusion that 'the family therapist must begin very early … to reduce resistance through a primary focus on the father'. This led others to argue that as a result family therapists were more likely to 'coddle' fathers while placing high expectation for change on mothers (Treadway, 1988). In the face of such criticisms, it is perhaps advisable to review research that might support or refute the argument that men and women require specific skills within the 'conjoint' context.

Findings from research about working with men in conjoint settings

The first place to look for this evidence is in the field of the *therapeutic alliance*. The therapeutic alliance is best described as the working relationship between the client and worker (see Friedlander et al., 2006, for a full description). Consistently, studies have demonstrated both that this relationship can be measured, and that the higher the rating (e.g., the better the therapeutic alliance), the better the outcome of the work (Friedlander et al., 2006). These studies cover all areas of helping relationships, from GP consultations to psycho-dynamic therapy (Safran and Muran, 2000). More specifically, studies into the therapeutic alliance have shown that this factor prevents the early 'dropout' of an individual from treatment (Robbins et al., 2003).

Although the research evidence on the gender variable in this alliance is not large, nevertheless there are useful findings. The first finding to note here is that the alliance with the father/man in conjoint and family therapy may have a better relationship to outcome than the alliance with the woman/ mother. For instance, Pinsof and Catherall (1986) found that women wanted the worker to engage and convince the male partner about the value of the work and therefore 'sacrificed' their own satisfaction and comfort. Symonds and Horvath (2004) studied the outcomes for 47 heterosexual couples and found that the success of the treatment was related to the alliance with the man not the woman. This finding has also been suggested in other studies (Bennun, 1989; Bourgeois et al., 1990; Johnson et al., 2002). In gay couples, however, evidence suggests that it is the openness and sexual orientation of the therapist that affects a positive outcome (Brown, 1996; Ritter and Terndrup, 2002). These findings have to be balanced by evidence that confirms that women are more positive about seeking family and relationship help and are more likely to stay in counselling despite a poorer therapeutic alliance (Cauce et al., 2002).

If we consider the role of the therapist in conjoint therapy, we also find that criticisms like those of Treadway do ring true. Various researchers have found that therapists interrupt women clients more than men (Werner-Wilson et al., 1997; Stratford, 1998); address fathers more than mothers (Postner et al., 1971); and deal with defensive men and women differently (Brown-Standridge and Piercy, 1988). When therapists are asked to explain their gender perspective they almost always reveal stereotypical biases but also deny differential treatment (Werner-Wilson, 1997).

Work has also been undertaken to understand what skills workers might need for working with men/fathers in conjoint contexts. Dienhart and Avis (1994) used a Delphi study to discover what skills family workers need in working with men in families. This study concluded that there were distinct skills needed to engage men in therapy with their families and these included being able to talk about gender socialisation with men and to construct a 'broad definition of the problem that included patterns of gender division over the whole spectrum of the family' (p. 411). This amounted to strategies to encourage men to see that their role was an essential part both of the development of difficulties and in the resolution of those difficulties. In keeping with much of what we discussed earlier in the chapter, Dienhart and Avis found that fewer family workers were confident that emotional strategies worked with men and, contrary to our discussion about structure in groupwork with men, fewer family workers felt confident about the use of active techniques, such as role play or sculpting.

Dienhart (2001) followed her original Delphi study by examining how male and female therapists differed in what they saw as important in engaging men in family work. She tentatively discovered that male workers tended to prefer to explore men's vulnerabilities and the constraints of their gender role, while female workers tended to emphasise the exploration of power and gender within the therapeutic context. Dienhart was not able to conclude that any particular strategy was 'more successful', but she was able to point to the finding that in their own largely gendered ways, both male and female workers were trying to break down 'the nuances of socialized gender differences' (p. 40).

All in all, it would therefore seem that if men are to be encouraged to engage in family contexts, practitioners do need to find distinct ways of speaking with them and helping them feel valued. This may not constitute 'coddling' but it will constitute something we might call 'taking an interest'.

Specific knowledge and skills relevant for working with men in family settings

A body of literature exists about how to work with men in family settings (Bograd, 1991; Erickson, 1993; Weingarten, 1995; Almeida, 1998; Philpot, 2005). This literature consists of literature from *family therapy* contexts and that from *fathering* contexts. Chapter 6 will outline much of the latter literature; therefore here we concentrate upon the former.

One of the themes that has continued to emerge in this book is that interventions may have an explicit *social change* (e.g., pro-feminist) emphasis or an *ameliorative* emphasis (e.g., helping men/women cope with the costs of men's socialisation). This division is true within this literature. For instance, some writers describe their practice as *pro-feminist* while others use the term *gender sensitive* for their approach (Rivett and Street, 2003). This division between practitioners is evident in how comfortable they feel adopting the description of 'feminist'. Thus, one survey of American family therapists (Dankoski et al., 1998) found that while only 10 per cent of men and 40 per cent of women agreed that the label fitted for them, in fact when practices identified by the researchers as 'pro-feminist' were listed, almost all the sample said that they adopted them.

Many writers in this field who address how to work with men will therefore use the term 'gender sensitive' when cataloguing how practitioners should work with men in family settings. Philpot's (2005) is an example of this approach. His list of helpful strategies has much in common with ones that have been proposed in individual work and groupwork. The first of these strategies is to be explicit about the differences between men's and women's perspectives in heterosexual couples. Philpot (2005) calls this 'psycho-educational'. He states that this strategy should also include references to how men are socialised and how that affects their attitudes and behaviours. The purpose is to enable the man in the family to understand that his perspective is not the only one possible and for him to understand how the rest of the family are thinking. Philpot then argues that the worker needs to centre-stage the gender differences and teach the family that these are the factors that are holding back much of the change that all family members want. This can lead to a unity between father, mother and children. Philpot believes that during the course of the therapy, the worker may need to be 'translating' the gender language of family members. Finally, Philpot sees a crucial role in asking men and women how they would like gender roles to be divided in their family/relationship. The purpose of this is to enable men and women to experiment with different roles rather than be bound by traditional or socially preferred ones.

Practice Example

Sophie's (aged 12) family came to the clinic because of fears about her anger and behaviour towards her mother and stepfather. During an early conversation with their therapist, it became evident that Sophie's stepfather (Justin) felt 'left out' of the mother–daughter relationship. As a result, when Donna (mother) asked him to help her 'calm Sophie down', he over-reacted and thereby contributed to further escalation of Sophie's temper. He was increasingly withdrawing from the family and spending more time at work. This was interpreted as him 'opting out' from both his marriage and his family responsibilities.

The male therapist carried on a conversation with Justin in front of Donna and Sophie in which some of his expectations as a father and 'provider' emerged. This helped clarify that his motivation wasn't to leave the family, but that he did not know what to do to make things work out.

This freed Donna to explain how depressed she had been feeling and that she also wanted Justin to behave in a certain way but did not know how to ask for this from him. What she said was she did not want him to 'sort' anything, but only to be with her at times.

Sophie was also able to say that though Justin was her stepfather, she saw him more as a father and she felt that he never did anything with her, nor gave her any praise or attention. What she wanted him to do was not just be the 'hard' disciplinarian but to be engaged in her life routinely: to ask her about her day and play with her on her Playstation, which was a source of escape for her.

One of the specific skills recommended for working with men in family settings is to be able to explain how men in families are constrained by their gender socialisation. Clinicians, for example, will be very conscious of the 'classic' division between the sexes when it comes to raising children. This is often played out in conflict over discipline and ways of interacting with children. One tension could be between an authoritarian (and more traditionally masculine) parenting style and a nurturing, supportive style of parenting, which may more often be associated with 'mothering'. In such a scenario, the man will criticise the woman for being 'soft', while the mother will criticise the man for being harsh and uncaring. In these situations, re-describing the interactional pattern as one that is following traditional gender socialisation can enable parents to look for alternative styles, and more collaborative gender divisions.

Another pattern frequently experienced in families with a heterosexual parent couple is that of the 'over-involved mother' and the 'peripheral father'. Papp (1988) describes this pattern when she talks about fathers' experience taking up the role of 'godfather' with all the implication of dictatorial control and threat that that implies. In such situations, Papp writes, the man's 'extreme paternalistic attitude, his avoidance of the obligations of intimacy, and his insistence on being in a one-up position in personal relationships' (p. 51) leads to misery for partner and children alike. Papp also comments that men who have internalised this model of masculinity and fatherhood find it very hard to manage adolescent children who seek independence and, in so doing, challenge the 'authority' of the father. Her method for working in such situations is to enable the man to understand how his behaviour is generating some of the problems for his family and to encourage such men to listen and hear the experience of their family members. Because Papp (1988) recognises that such men also feel constrained by their role, she seeks to show them more fulfilling alternatives by asking them both to truly receive help from their family members, and also to weigh up the costs of the role they have chosen to adopt.

Practice Example

Shane and Jenny visited a children's mental health service because their elder daughter, Nia (15), was severely depressed. As the family work proceeded, it became obvious that Jenny was herself depressed and to some degree Nia and herself appeared to form a 'supportive' sub-system within the family. Shane could not cope with his wife and daughter's depression. He constantly tried to 'persuade' them not to be unhappy and pointed out all the good things they should appreciate. In the course of the work, Jenny admitted that she had never fully recovered from post-natal depression and always felt 'not good enough' in comparison to Shane.

The counsellor decided that the first intervention to improve the resources of the family, so that they could help Nia, had to be to enable Jenny to feel stronger and less disempowered in her marriage. The counsellor, a woman, asked Shane to try to stop arguing Jenny and Nia out of their depression. She modelled a conversation between the family members in the counselling session that allowed the depth of the unhappiness to be expressed. She then asked Jenny how Shane could help her. Very quickly, Jenny described the usual pattern of asking for emotional help and being 'put down' by Shane's rational response. The counsellor asked Shane to find another way of helping. Again, he very quickly expressed his feelings of inadequacy, his sense that he could not help these women. He also connected this experience to trying to keep his mother happy when he was a child. Although Shane did not cry (unlike Jenny), he was clearly very upset and emotional. Out of this experience, he became available to try to listen to Jenny's pain, and to relate to his own unhappiness that he knew he 'blocked out'.

This session marked a moment of breakthrough. Jenny and Shane began to support each other better and Nia began to feel freer to express other feelings like anger and frustration.

Working with men in couples

We noted in an earlier section that women are more likely to seek relationship help than men (O'Brien, 1988; Bennett, 1995). Yet men also report giving a high importance to their relationships (Bennett, 1995). It is therefore crucial that workers who regularly deal with men in relationships should be aware of approaches to working with men in these contexts. These contexts can be varied. For instance, there is ample evidence that relationship distress can play a role in a number of health problems (Campbell, 2002), as it can in maintaining mental health problems (Johnson, 2002) and substance misuse difficulties (Rowe and Liddle, 2002). Thus health workers may want to intervene even if only briefly to improve men's relationships with their partners. It is equally true that the majority of family settings in which child protection services get involved will include poor couple relationships that will impact on children's welfare.

Some authors have argued that the increasing role of women in work and the growing recognition of 'companionate' relationships mean that men's roles in relationships are changing (Rampage, 2001). The suggestion is that this challenges men's traditional way of relating. At the heart of this challenge is the supposition that men need to overcome their fear of intimacy, transcend the assumption that sex equals intimacy and thus become more 'feminine'. Blackie and Clark (1987) argue that, given men's and women's typically very different expectations of partnering and marriage, it is not surprising that heterosexual relationships break down. Yet, fewer men are willing to attempt the emotional work necessary to improve their relationships. These authors suggest, in sympathy with approaches mentioned earlier in the chapter, that men in couple work require a more 'task-centred' approach or even a 'consultation' model of intervention.

Gordon and Allen (1990) comment that many men come into relationship counselling feeling pressured to be there by their partners. This may be as true for many gay men as it is for heterosexual men. However, these authors note that the risk of losing partners may make some men more aware of how dependent they are on them and that 'facing how dependent they may be is quite threatening for most men' (Gordon and Allen, 1990: 190). They suggest that workers therefore need to find a way of addressing this ambivalence and fear early on in therapy. They further suggest that the task for relationship counsellors is to both educate men about feelings and language and also to educate women to understand the nature of the separate gender 'cultures' – the reality that many men do not know the language that their partners want to hear. Gordon and Allen also comment on men's capacity to seek problem-solving solutions rather than listen to feelings: another educational task for the counsellor. Moreover, they argue that in such contexts counsellors should acknowledge that while partners may feel dominated by unexpressive men, the experience for many men in weak relationships is that they themselves feel powerless. Acknowledging this may be anathema for many who work with violent men from a pro-feminist perspective (see Chapter 7) but it is an important insight for practice nonetheless.

So far in this and the previous section we have been referring in the main to heterosexual relationships, but obviously relationship counsellors also work with men in gay relationships, and there is a growing practice literature about this subject (Davies and Neal, 1996; Halderman, 2005). Working with men in gay relationships involves not only understanding male socialisation and the variations that gay sexual orientation and gay identity may bring to this as well as relationship dynamics, but also the scarring effect of growing up in a heterosexist and at times homophobic climate. It is important that counsellors should not assume that all gay relationships function similarly, or that the map of heterosexual relationships 'fits' gay ones. It is equally important that counsellors recognise and deal with their own homophobia if they are involved in work with gay couples (Malley and Tasker, 2004). Of crucial significance in gay relationship dynamics is the degree of 'outness' (Halderman, 2005) within the couple, as well as the influence of outside influences such as family, society and work.

Johnson and Colucci (1999) suggest that gay relationships are as affected by heteronormative gender discourse as are other relationships. They state that gay and lesbian people are 'bicultural', by which they mean that the dominant sets of norms, beliefs and values have also been internalised by them. According to this argument, gay men may conform to models of masculine behaviour in intimate relationships that are similar to those seen in heterosexual men.

Practice Example

Pete and Ray visited a relationship counsellor because they had been having ongoing conflict over Ray's relationship with his parents. They had been together for two years, but while Pete's family had accepted both that he was gay and in a gay relationship, Ray had yet to tell his family about either his sexual orientation or his relationship with Pete. Ray's father in particular had very old-fashioned and homophobic attitudes. Ray had been brought up to make his father proud of his achievements and he did not want to upset him. This had led to the two men moving away from their home town when they first moved in together. Ray's father was ill and Ray saw this as a good reason not to tell him about his life but it also meant that he was keeping secrets that were very hard to keep. He and Pete came to counselling because Pete felt that Ray was ambivalent about living together. He saw Ray's resistance about

(Continued)

'coming out' to his family as evidence that the relationship was not important to Ray. And he was angry that he seemed to be second best to Ray's family.

Like many counselling situations, the couple expected the counsellor to 'change' the other partner: to convince Ray that he needed to be honest with his family; or to convince Pete that Ray did love him. Instead the counsellor helped the couple understand that their conflict was not unusual: that family loyalties often interfered with couple relationships. The counsellor helped each partner express his needs and feelings during which conversation the couple realised that their relationship mattered above these other considerations and that as a couple they had to move on with commitment. Pete accepted that when the time was right, Ray would tell his parents and Ray accepted that Pete loved him whether he was 'out' with his parents or not.

This and the previous section reviewed a number of approaches to working with men in families and couples. Now we will address the practice of working with men in communities.

Working with men in communities

Of all the areas in which workers engage with men, this is the most complex to both describe and understand. The term 'community' is used so broadly; we might say over-used. There are local geographical communities, communities of interest – men who share common characteristics or identities (e.g., sexual orientation) and online communities (an increasingly popular way for men to connect with each other), among others. We have structured this section of the chapter around three different ways in which we can conceptualise work with men in communities: first involving men in non-gender-specific community development work; second, men organising around a specific issue as men; and third, professionally-led interventions that target whole communities.

To start with the first category, there are in fact important gender issues concerning community development, which is ostensibly non-gender specific. The main issue is that in many parts of the world and in many localities, community activism is largely the responsibility of women. Beatrix Campbell's *Goliath* (1993) memorably describes housing estates in the UK where young men dominate public spaces and cause mayhem, their fathers are busy drinking in the social club and the women are campaigning for and organising better facilities for local residents. In this context it is important that men should be involved, to share the responsibility. It is also worth noting that some community development and regeneration work focuses on social problems mainly caused by men – for example, excess drinking and drug use, violence, anti-social behaviour and property crime.

The second category of work with men in communities is that of men organising around specific issues *as men*. Examples here would be as diverse as fathers' rights groups and anti-violence campaigns. A difficult issue in community development work is that of men's interests. Are men destined only to campaign in the defence of their privilege? Pease (2002) would argue that they are not. He reconceptualises men's 'interests' to include 'ideal interests that are formed by support for more abstract principles' (p. 171) such as social justice. The existence of campaigns such as the White Ribbon campaign (see below) would suggest that, indeed, it is possible for men to organise against patriarchal interests. Fathers' rights campaigns might well be seen as an example of men lobbying on behalf of their own material interests; however, the picture is rather more complex. Where men have campaigned against being made to pay maintenance for children in the context of new families, as we have seen with agitation against the Child Support Agency in the UK, the link to men's material interest is fairly clear. The case of campaigns for more access to children in the family courts is less obvious though. Many feminist commentators have been very critical of groups like Families Need Fathers and their more militant breakaway group Fathers 4 Justice, but although some of the individuals in these groups may in part be motivated by rage at their ex-partners, it has to be acknowledged that they are campaigning for the right to be involved in the *care* of children, which is hardly a traditional aspect of patriarchy.

The third approach to working with men in communities that we conceptualise here is interventions on a community level that are led by professionals. Examples would include health promotion initiatives and involving fathers in family centres (see Chapters 6 and 8). There is a certain political correctness about discussions of community work which suggests that the only 'real' community work is that which is designed and led by community members themselves – work in the community development tradition. We would argue, however, that both this model (as outlined in the first and second approaches to men in communities we described above) and professionally-led community-based interventions are needed in men's work. There are simply too many areas of social life where (some) men's behaviour is problematic for it to be sensible to leave the community action entirely up to men themselves. There need to be agendas set by men and women together, emerging from political consensus, that can steer interventions to improve everyone's quality of life. Professionally-led intervention does not have to be deficit-based, however, only focusing on the problems men cause for themselves and others. It can also build on strengths, as in the work with indigenous fathers in the Family Action Centre at the University of Newcastle, New South Wales, Australia, where an emphasis is put on affirming traditional masculine values as embodied by elders. (It should also be noted that there is a risk of reifying indigenous cultures, as a reaction to their historical oppression by colonisers, when there may be aspects that entrench gender inequalities.)

Within many communities, men will work together by default. That is, they gather for a purpose and generally it is men working together. In these settings, workers might choose to focus the work more specifically around men's issues. An example of a single focus grouping of men would be that of sports organisations. Indeed, the role of sport as a forum for the gathering of men is often underrated in the literature on men's work. There have been attempts to base men's health promotion initiatives and fathers' projects around sport (see Chapters 6 and 8 of this book). The risk, however, of placing too much store in sports clubs or any other homo-social environment is that community workers may overlook men who do not fit in with these particular masculinities.

Community work with men is of course rather more complex than our three-part model allows. Community initiatives can combine more than one approach. Family and community conferencing would be an example of this – an intervention used in the context of family problems and as a response to crime (see, for example, Braithwaite and Daly, 1994, and also Chapter 6 of this book). It has its roots in Maori communities in New Zealand, so could be seen as a grassroots initiative led by community members. However, family group conferencing has become a part of state apparatus in New Zealand and restorative justice meetings are used by statutory criminal justice agencies in several countries.

Practice Example

The White Ribbon Campaign (WRC) began in 1991 in Canada. Since then there have been WRC activities in at least 35 countries, including ones in Asia, the Middle East, Europe, Africa and North America (see www.whiteribbon.com). In Michael Kaufman's words:

> The campaign aims to mobilize the voice of men and boys. Wearing or displaying a white ribbon is a public pledge never to commit, condone, nor remain silent about violence against women. ... White Ribbon's basic philosophy is that while not all men are responsible for committing violence against women, all men and boys must take responsibility for helping to end it. (Kaufman, 2006)

What has typified the development of the White Ribbon Campaign is the local philosophy that it has adopted. It consists of local groups of men signing up to a declaration that they will not use violence against women nor will they endorse abuse of any kind against women. Each group can choose to run its own campaign materials although there are generally recognised ones that can also be used. Each group will decide how it will promulgate its message rather

(Continued)

73

(Continued)

than a central body determining this. Usually groups will organise activities on White Ribbon Day, which is the internationally recognised day to oppose violence against women. Because the WRC has a single focus, its roots in anti-sexist men's activities have become secondary to its current purpose. Hence, there is no problem with diverse men with diverse experiences and views 'signing up' to the central WRC pledge. Indeed, in the United States various male politicians from various political hues have become public supporters of the campaign. It is relevant to note that the WRC attempts to avoid much of the competitiveness evoked in gatherings of men by adopting a decentralised organisational structure, and by foregrounding the central message not the messenger. Other large-scale single focus campaigns by men may have less cohesion as a result of not adopting this structure.

Conclusion

This chapter has explored models, principles and practice in relation to work with men in groups, families, couples and communities. It has highlighted that interventions need to acknowledge that such work with men does arguably involve specific skills and knowledge. It also requires a respect for men *as men*. We have continued to emphasise that a delicate balance needs to be achieved between recognising that there are some commonalities between men and retaining an awareness of difference. This part of the book has summarised relevant practice material that can inform this delicate balance. Part III will turn to work with specific groups of men.

Key texts

Working with men in groups

Rabonowitz, F. (2005) 'Group therapy for men', in G.E. Good and G.R. Brooks (eds) *The New Handbook of Psychotherapy and Counseling with Men*, San Francisco: Jossey Bass.

This short chapter summarises relevant practice ideas for working with men in groups.

Working with men in couples and families

Bograd, M. (ed.) (1991) *Feminist Approaches for Men in Family Therapy*, New York: Harrington Press.

This text contains various chapters, written by male and female therapists, which explore how to work with men in couple and family settings from a feminist perspective.

Working with men in communities

Ruxton, S. (2002) *Men, Masculinities and Poverty in the UK*, Oxford: Oxfam GB.

Ruxton, S. (2004) *Gender Equality and Men: Learning from Practice*, Oxford: Oxfam.

The latter text contains examples from developing countries.

PART III

Working with Specific Groups of Men

6 Working with Men as Fathers

Introduction

In some Western countries men have become visible actors in a range of policy and practice arenas in relation to articulating rights or needs claims as fathers. A number of governments too have either initiated particular policy initiatives addressed to men as fathers or, as in the UK, have specifically challenged child welfare services to 'engage fathers'. In this chapter we explore these developments. First, we outline key strands of the theoretical and research literatures. We then explore policy developments in a range of countries and look at the practice issues, dilemmas and opportunities that are evident, as well as signposting possibilities for critically transformative practices in relation to gendered power relations.

First, some clarification of terms is needed. While the term 'father' is used as shorthand in this chapter, it is a rather misleading one. Increasingly there is a dispersal of fathering practices of differing kinds across households, with the emergence of a range of living situations including post-divorce parenting, step-families, lesbian/gay families and lone-mother households, where men's status in terms of biology and the law can vary in relation to different children in the same household. Some services have tried to capture this diversity by appealing to 'fathers and male carers' when advertising and developing their services. Here, however, we use the shorthand term, although we mean to imply diversity.

Researching fathers: differing theoretical approaches and key themes

Research on fathers and fatherhood in the US spans three decades in contrast, for example, to the UK where it gained momentum in the 1990s (Clarke et al., 1998). In terms of the early research from the US, much emanated from developmental psychologists concerned with exploring the influence of fathers as sex role models (see Chapter 2 for a critique of sex role theory). These studies were based upon normative assumptions, particularly about the role fathers could and should play in producing appropriately masculine sons. This research received a particular charge because of concerns about the numbers of non-resident fathers in the US and the alleged consequences for boys of growing up without appropriate male role models. There has also been a history of concern about the family structures of African-American families, which saw father absence and the prevalence of mother-headed households as a factor in the under-achievement of black children.

A significant and influential body of research contributed to a consensus that the non-residence of fathers had a negative impact upon children in terms of their intellectual and psycho-social development. However, as Johnson (1999) has argued in a comprehensive review of such research, many of the early studies were marred by poor methodological practices. For example, the role of crucial variables such as poverty and 'race' was not adequately accounted for. Moreover, Johnson notes the normative assumptions about appropriate family structures and gender roles that underlay the studies. She notes the emergence of a more recent research paradigm around 'father presence' that is less concerned with residence and more interested with the quality of relationships between all concerned.

However, as the edited collection by Daniels (1998) attests, quite fierce debates have continued in the US, with the active involvement of academics in policy debates and as cultural commentators in a range of media outlets. Stacey (1998) argues that functionalist sociologists, faced by a concerted critique of functionalism from within sociology (see Chapter 2), have turned their energies to a wider public policy arena in order to promote particular ideas about the desirability of particular family structures and focused specifically on the importance of the father in relation to fostering a variety of outcomes for children. Having noted the problematic political implications of such an insistence on fathers' roles in families and the often corresponding failure by conservatives to address the issues posed for women and children by abusive and neglectful men, Stacey does caution progressives against ignoring the faultlines that have opened up for many poor and marginalised men as a result of change in economic and gender relations. She suggests that there are clear indications that such men seem much less well equipped to deal with the hazards and opportunities posed by a changing landscape.

In the UK these types of debates became apparent in the 1990s, with a key player being the American conservative policy theorist, Charles Murray (1990), who argued that welfare systems provided incentives to women to parent without men and many men were therefore lacking the civilising influences attached to marital and paternal responsibilities. Concerns were expressed on the left of the political spectrum by Dennis and Erdos (1992) also. Specific instances of social unrest in parts of the UK in the early 1990s were read as attributable to boys growing up in fatherless households and a decline in a respectable and responsible form of masculinity (expressed and constituted through marriage and fatherhood). While such views excited much cultural comment (particularly in the media) however, the main government response at that time was child support legislation to render absent fathers financially responsible for their children.

While some of the impetus for promoting a particular model of fatherhood in the context of support for a particular family structure came from conservative sociologists in the US such as Popenoe (1998), this thinking is also underpinned by particular versions of psychoanalysis. We have already highlighted key aspects of the trajectory taken by psychoanalytic thinkers in relation to men and masculinity in Chapter 2 and noted its oppressive as well as liberatory potential. Nowhere is this more apparent than in relation to theorising about the role of the father. For Frosh (1997) there is little doubt that fathering has been preferred to mothering generally within classical psychoanalysis. Freud located fathering as something that rescues the child from the 'dangers of regressive absorption in the mother' (Frosh, 1997: 38). For Freud the father's function, particularly for boys, as boundary setter – the pointing outwards away from the closed world of the mother – is not only necessary for the mental health of the child but also for the social world. This development rests upon repudiation of the mother and associated femininity. We have already noted (Chapter 2) that more recent psychoanalytic work, influenced by feminism, opens up different possibilities for boys and girls, men and women alike. Benjamin (1995) is an influential theorist and clinician who argues against the classical psychoanalytic portrayal of the father as boundary setter. Here the father becomes more than just an oedipal prohibition. Frosh notes that for Benjamin the active presence of a loving father is something that can help a child gain 'the capacity to surmount loss and become integrated in relationships with others' (Frosh, 1997: 47).

Frosh himself develops these insights further and locates such insights in the context of contemporary social and cultural developments. He argues that men currently have difficulty in positioning themselves within any meaningful set of discourses as a result of what he sees as a crisis of masculinity intersecting with a crisis of fathering.

> Not only is it hard to become the nurturing pre-oedipal father, created *de novo* from the absence of any received model of such fathering, but it is even difficult to sustain any sense of being a prohibitive father, enforcing social values. (Frosh, 1997: 49)

Partly this is linked to the kinds of economic processes where the collapse in traditional men's work and the growth of a technological culture means that passing on work traditions between fathers and sons is no longer possible.

Furthermore, he notes the emergence of an 'administered society', where personal models of authority, located symbolically in the father, are

> replaced by bureaucratised and anonymous modes, to which the father is as much the uncomprehending subject as is his child. The father then acts in the spirit of authority, but what he communicates is primarily his impotence. (p. 48)

While Frosh may be exaggerating the extent to which many fathers actually ever were in charge in their work situations, certainly the contemporary context, fuelled by changes in women's lives, aspirations and patterns of employment would appear to bear out the persuasiveness of his observations for many fathers.

Explicitly psychoanalytically-informed research on fathers is not a significant part of the research landscape in the UK today. There is, however, one interesting small-scale qualitative study of first-time fathers from Australia (Lupton and Barclay, 1997) which uses psychoanalytic understandings within a post-structuralist frame to suggest that the men experience considerable difficulties as fathers at the social and the psychic level. The men in this study invested strongly both in being emotionally available to their children as well as in an economic provider discourse. They experienced these two discourses as being in considerable tension with one another as the demands of the workplace, particularly on young fathers, can be considerable. However, a further finding from Lupton and Barclay would suggest the need for caution about policies that fail to engage with how both men and women, at times of anxiety, can retreat into gender-differentiated discourses. This could mean, for example, that, despite their best intentions, men would absent themselves in order to cope with the anxieties thrown up by a crying baby whose needs they felt they could not meet and who disturbed their sense of being able to control their lives. From a psycho-social perspective, researching divorce, Day Sclater and Yates (1999) have suggested the importance of engaging with adult men's and women's feelings of distress at the loss of the relationship, which are often manifest in gender-differentiated ways. They argue that a professional and policy emphasis on the welfare of children can obscure adults' own needs and treat children as projections of adults' fear and anxieties. They suggest that it is possible to read the controversial calls by fathers for 'rights' in relation to their children post-divorce and separation within an understanding of men's inability to access a discourse around vulnerability. This analysis is quite sharply opposed to that of other feminists who see such calls by men as attempts to retain control over women in the context of a decline in marriage (this discussion is returned to below).

Developmental psychologists continue to be strongly represented in work on fathers and fathering in a wide range of countries (see Lamb, 2004). The diversity of the category (fathers) and the complexity of the situations in which men 'father' is explored in a wide-ranging literature. Much of the literature operates within a frame that is concerned with evaluating the implications of 'father involvement' for outcomes for children. This frame can be seen to spring from either a defensive position which suggests that fathers are important or a possibly associated desire to promote the benefits of father involvement.

What does 'father involvement' encompass? Currently, it appears to be usually explored in terms of three areas: engagement, accessibility and responsibility (Lamb and Tamis-Lemonda, 2004). The question of how much time fathers spend with their children is often crucial here and has encouraged research from a variety of disciplines. For example, there is a social policy interest particularly, but not exclusively, from feminists concerned with the gender division of labour and how much it is or is not changing. Time is but one component however. Others include what fathers actually do with their children during the time they spend with them and this links into questions about who takes responsibility for the organisation of childcare and associated tasks.

It is important to note that research on whether fathers are spending more time with their children and/or taking more responsibility points to a mixed picture across Western countries. For example, one influential piece of research in the UK on employed fathers suggested that the amount of time fathers spent with their children increased in two and a half decades – from less than 15 minutes a day in the mid-1970s to two hours by the late 1990s during the week with more at the weekend (O'Brien and Shemilt, 2003). However, there seems to be some evidence from the US to suggest that in two-parent families with employed mothers, average levels of paternal involvement in dual-earner families have increased, though by not as much as popular accounts often suggest (Lamb and Tamis-Lemonda, 2004). Overall, Lister (2003), reviewing the literature, notes the methodological difficulties in comparing different studies but suggests that the picture in the US and Europe is of some movement but without any fundamental disturbance of traditional patterns.

The most sophisticated developmental psychologists such as Lamb and Lewis (2004: 273) locate themselves within a theoretical frame that is concerned with paying attention to 'the complexity of family relationships and the patterns of influence within the family system'. Thus fathers not only influence children by interacting directly with them, but also affect maternal behaviour, just as mothers affect paternal behaviour and involvement and children influence their parents in turn. They argue, however, that paternal behaviour is more at the behest of mothers, whereas maternal behaviour is driven by more independent understandings of the maternal role. More sociologically-inclined work might suggest, however, that this description paints a rather static picture of mothers' and fathers' relationships. For example, Jane Lewis (2001), in her empirical research with mothers and fathers, suggests there is a great deal of tension and negotiation going on in individual households.

Flouri (2005) applies a process model of parenting which has a systemic framework highlighting the interacting influences of five different factors on father involvement: contextual factors, father's factors, mother's factors, quality of the co-parental relationship, and child's factors. A key point made by Flouri is that no universal claims can be made about the impact of father involvement on outcomes for children. Rather, studies show that certain aspects of father involvement in certain groups of fathers are associated with certain outcomes in certain groups of children – for example, father's interest in the child's education is related to the educational attainment of adult daughters in adult life, but not adult sons. Father involvement seems to protect against an experience of homelessness in adult sons (but not in daughters) from low, but not high socio-economic groups. One study has found no evidence to support gender differences in father involvement. Child-reported father involvement is not higher for boys than girls and fathers are as likely to be involved with their daughters as with their sons, at least in adolescence.

This is important, as the universal claim that father involvement is good for children is often made from a variety of cultural and political outlets, whereas the research generally paints a nuanced picture highlighting the importance of the parental relationship and the need for specificity. It also disrupts assumptions about either the preference of fathers for sons or their specifically positive influence upon them.

In many Western countries such as the US, Australia and the UK, there has been a great deal of concern expressed by particular men's groups about alleged inequities in their treatment as fathers in 'private' law (those referring to divorce and separation) proceedings. The research evidence, however, does not support the claims certainly in relation to an outright refusal of contact. For example, Harrison (2006) notes the worryingly low level of refusals in the context of what is known about rates of domestic violence. Bradshaw et al.'s (1999) research is of interest here. These researchers were particularly interested in exploring levels of contact between non-resident fathers and their children. They found that 47 per cent of fathers reported seeing their children at least once a week, 14 per cent at least once a fortnight and 7 per cent at least once a month. Twenty-one per cent had not seen their children in the last year and 3 per cent did not see their children at all. Only a small minority said it was due to a court order either in private or public law proceedings. Generally, however, men often expressed a great deal of anger and bitterness in relation to the system (see also Arendell, 1995).

Very little research has been carried out on the perspectives of those fathers who become involved with public law (where children are considered under child neglect/abuse procedures). Recent research carried out in the UK (Ashley et al., 2006), although quite small-scale is, therefore, important and suggests that there is a great deal to be done to meet fathers' concerns about their treatment at a range of levels. This is returned to in the section on practice (p. 88).

Feminist and pro-feminist perspectives on fathers

Differing theoretical positions have long been evident amongst feminists, often associated with different political positions. First-wave feminists were often prominent charity workers and social reformers. Lewis notes, for example, that the characteristics of the stable family favoured by charity leaders and social activists such as Helen Bosanquet required 'the firm authority of the father and the cooperative industry of all its members, the wife working at home and husband wage-earning' (Lewis, 2002: 127). Bosanquet was concerned that families at both ends of the social scale failed to conform to this model of family life, although much more concern was expressed generally about the working-class family, and as much or more about the working-class father as the working-class mother. Bosanquet was not alone in suspecting working-class fathers of unwillingness to shoulder their economic responsibilities; others, too, firmly believed that married women's employment merely provided their husbands with the opportunity to be idle (Lewis, 2002). As Lewis has noted in previous work (1992), many of the women workers and reformers were motivated by a feminist concern for the plight of working-class women and about men who were not adequately supportive of their families. She notes, however, that in the wake of World War II, there was much greater sympathy with the father than previously, with commentators deploring the decline in power of the father. Moreover, the work habits of working-class men who had proved themselves in battle were no longer regarded with suspicion. This coincided with a very explicit focus on the mother's role in securing the welfare of children.

When second-wave feminism re-emerged at the end of the 1960s a key impetus was to give voice to the concerns and needs of women. However, theorists such as Chodorow (see Chapter 2) were concerned to argue for breaking the female monopoly on caring for children. By contrast, others stressed the importance either of offering women the space to mother without men and/or to stress the dangers posed by abusive men to women and children.

Hearn and Pringle (2006) note that currently, in Sweden, there is a strand of feminist research that focuses on men as problems and as obstacles to gender equality. As already alluded to, some see demands by fathers as a means of continuing control over women through the use of children. Other research strands, however, focus on men's lives and experiences and the obstacles they may face. In the UK too there has been evidence of such 'divisions' (Featherstone, 2004), although more recently it has become apparent that certain fathers' organisations not only include feminists but are explicitly locating fathers' needs within a broader project of promoting gender equity and children's welfare (Featherstone, 2006).

The literature on the relationship between fatherhood and masculinities appears to be rather sparse (Marsigilio and Pleck, 2005). This may be partly because those concerned to elaborate a critical politics in relation to men align themselves with feminist suspicions of claims by men as fathers, seeing them as part of a project to reinforce male power over women and children. Until recently the masculinities literature could be considered 'father blind', while the fatherhood literature has engaged very little with the literature on masculinities (although see Lupton and Barclay, 1997, as a very good example of 'crossover' literature). However, this picture is changing somewhat. Moreover, the increasing visibility of gay men 'choosing' parenthood (Mallon, 2004) opens up interesting possibilities for theorising in this area.

We caution against seeing fathers as a unitary category and, therefore, recognise that there will be differing political agendas among fathers' organisations. We also suggest that, within individual fathers' subjectivities, impulses towards both supporting and undermining the mothers of their children may be evident (see also Connell, 1995, 2000). We will spell out our own position more when we talk about the premises underpinning 'good' practice in this area.

Policy developments

Comparative work that categorises differing policy regimes is well developed in the literature particularly (but not exclusively) in Europe. Feminists and pro-feminist men have taken earlier typologies (such as of Esping-Andersen, 1990) and subjected them to gendered critique and refashioning. Hearn and Pringle (2006: 370) summarise the key themes of this literature. States have been grouped into strong, modified and weak breadwinner states. They have also been categorised as follows: private patriarchy with high subordination of women, public patriarchy with high subordination of women, private patriarchy with lower subordination of women, public patriarchy with lower subordination of women.

It is beyond the remit of this chapter to discuss such typologies save to signpost the considerable diversity experienced by fathers in terms of the support offered by specific welfare regimes to facilitate their involvement with their children pre- and post-birth. Hearn and Pringle (2006), as part of the research network Critical Research on Men in Europe (CROME, 2004) involving 14 countries, have attempted to develop a typology of contemporary regimes which takes some note of this. They suggest that there are three main groupings within Europe (see also Hearn et al., 2002a):

1 The Nordic nations (Denmark, Finland, Norway and Sweden). These have either universal or relatively good childcare, relatively generous parental leave and make significant attempts to reconcile home and work. (Indeed Lister, 2006, notes the comments of the State Secretary in the Swedish Finance Ministry on the need to treat decisions on who cares for children as a structural rather than private matter).

2 The established EU-member nations (such as Ireland, Italy, Germany and the UK). These countries have variable day care provision, parental and paternity leave and variable attempts to develop home–work reconciliation policy. Other countries which might fit within this grouping in relation to these issues are stronger than Nordic countries on the availability of early childcare services (Belgium and France).

3 The former Soviet eastern bloc countries, which have relatively low levels of day care provision, parental and paternity leave and less developed home–work reconciliation policies.

Apart from policies on paternity leave and childcare, another set of developments is of interest here. Child support legislation is in place across many countries today (see Hobson's, 2002, edited collection for a review and analysis). While varying in detail and implementation it signposts a policy consensus that fathers, whatever their current marital or living arrangements, whether resident or not, must continue to contribute to the economic maintenance of their biological children.

In relation to divorce and separation a pro-contact philosophy is now almost hegemonic in many Western countries. This is in contrast with previous assumptions that a 'clean break' was best for all concerned, including children. This can pose considerable tensions in the case of 'domestically violent fathers' (Harne, 2004) and in many countries, such as Australia and the UK, services and court practices in relation to promoting contact between violent fathers and children continue to be challenged by campaigners on domestic violence (Brown, 2006; Harrison, 2006).

However, despite constant and often very visible and intimidating campaigning by some fathers' organisations, private law proceedings in the UK are not yet based upon the presumption that parenting will necessarily be shared equally post-divorce. This call is a clear marker in the battleground between feminists and those who deem themselves 'fathers' rights' activists, but it is important to note that other fathers' organisations, child welfare organisations and children's rights activists do not support such calls either. Smart (2004) argues that calls for a presumption of equal time with both parents ignore the views of children who have experienced such an arrangement and is fundamentally oriented towards the rights of adults (and not children).

It is useful in this context to note that there would appear to be clear differences between fathers' organisation in the UK. While for some the dominant, indeed only, focus is on fathers' rights and private law proceedings, there are others who locate themselves within a gender equality and child welfare project, making links with a range of organisations in the process. This seems important in terms of deconstructing assumptions that fathers' organisations are of a piece. A clear focus from one such organisation – Fathers Direct – is on transforming parental and paternity leave arrangements in the UK. This is accompanied by a further focus on supporting service providers in the childcare and child welfare arenas to 'engage fathers'.

Practice developments

Within most practice settings in child welfare, involving health and social care workers, the focus historically by workers has been on mothers in a variety of ways and for a variety of reasons. We have already noted from the historical research by Lewis (2002) that practitioners encouraged a particular gendered division of labour so it was mothers who were appealed to as the primary caretakers. Theoretical influences on social work post-World War II such as Bowlbyism provided a clear rationale for this. Ironically, perhaps, feminism – which had some impact upon social workers – fuelled a focus on women although clearly within a context of questioning how they were defined and engaged with (Featherstone, 2004). The growth in attention by feminists to men's violent and abusive behaviour did little to support more positive or expansive constructions of men.

As we noted in Chapter 3, in the UK the last decade has seen both developments at the level of policy (the introduction of paid paternity leave is one example here) but also interesting developments in relation to services and practice. This appears very compatible with developments under the Clinton administrations in the US in the 1990s where a range of practice initiatives emerged encouraging 'active fatherhood', particularly targeted upon those who were poor and from minority ethnic backgrounds.

Burgess (2005) outlines some of the initiatives in the UK illustrating their scope. For example, some focus on young fathers, others on specific services for fathers and their sons, fathers and disabled children, specific communities such as African-Caribbean communities and topics such as supporting men and fathers to take care of their own health. Fathers Direct, a national information service on fatherhood, helps to build capacity in the field through training, consultancy and the provision of information aimed at fathers and services. Alongside the emergence of new initiatives and financial support for others, more mainstream services are being encouraged to reshape. In particular, health workers such as midwives are being encouraged to 'engage fathers', and maternity services more generally are being called upon to re-orient their services in a more 'father inclusive' way.

A literature of the 'how to' variety has emerged. Lloyd (2001) and Bartlett and Burgess (2005) offer practice guidelines on the following: the recruitment of fathers to projects, their retention, staffing issues and the organisational barriers and supports. Both these texts are based upon some limited research as well as 'practice wisdom'. The latter would seem to be important given that practice developments are still at a relatively early stage. More conventional academic research projects include Ghate et al.'s (2000) study of how family centres do or do not engage men and the barriers and obstacles men face. Daniel and Taylor (2001) have brought together literature that includes research findings on practice developments from a range of disciplines and countries in order to support health and social care practitioners seeking to engage fathers. The funding, since 1999, of Sure Start programmes has provided impetus for work on engaging fathers in early years settings and has been subject to evaluation (Lloyd et al., 2003). In the next section we draw on the above literature but recast it within the concerns of this book

Practising with fathers

Why do it?
As Featherstone (2004) has noted, practitioners in those sectors directly concerned with child neglect and abuse (often but not exclusively women) are often very concerned with exploring 'why' rather than concentrating on 'how' in relation to engaging fathers. This is partly because many of them are concerned with men who are posing difficulties for women and children in a variety of ways either through what they do (actual abuse) or don't do (neglect and lack of support). For the authors of this book, 'why' is a key question, given our commitment to advancing a gender-informed politics around men.

Stanley and Gamble (2005) have identified an explicit hierarchy of goals for their project around enhancing 'active fatherhood'. Their primary objective is to enhance fathers' involvement in order to improve children's experiences and outcomes. The secondary objective is to improve gender equity and the tertiary objective is to enable men to fulfil their own aspirations for their fathering role. While this may appear a sound pragmatic political strategy in a policy climate where outcomes for children are accorded central priority, we think it is unacceptable ethically and misconceived in that it is not located in concrete understandings of parental and partnering relationships and their dynamics. First, we reject the concept of a hierarchy and would argue that one set of considerations should not be assumed to trump another. We think it is very important that those who support father involvement locate it explicitly in a project that is critical of current gendered inequities, because not doing so runs the risk of supporting men who want to 'turn the clock back'. Moreover, we think Stanley and Gamble's hierarchy rests upon mistaken and misleading assumptions about being able to disentangle the needs and interests of children, women and men when in practice they are entangled in messy as well as beneficial ways. Good outcomes for children generally rest upon mothers and fathers being able to cooperate and the possibilities of such cooperation are surely jeopardised if attention is not paid to their concerns – or worse – their concerns are not recognised. Basically, father involvement cannot foster good outcomes for children if it rides roughshod over women's desires.

In our view, good practice rests upon engaging with the complexity of the relationships involved and developing mechanisms that allow for such complexity to be worked with and thought about, if not always resolved. It also involves engaging with diversity, fluidity and context.

Diversity

Diversity refers to diversity within the category 'fathers' but also, linked to that, is a recognition of the diversity of situations in which fathering practices can occur. Fathers who do not live with their children have received some research attention, but it is only more recently that services have developed to engage with them, such as the YMCA project outlined in Bartlett et al. (2006). The SKY project in Hackney, London, works with young fathers from minority ethnic backgrounds who may or may not be resident with their partners and who may need a considerable degree of support to work out mutually agreed roles and responsibilities in a context where mainstream services often view them through a lens of distrust, suspicion or neglect (Featherstone and White, 2006). Stepfathers can face many challenges, according to Brannen et al. (2000), and services need to be alert to how roles and responsibilities are worked out in the context of an array of often complex, competing and painful attachments and loyalties. Birth fathers whose children have been placed for adoption have also been a neglected group, and Clapton (2002) has both highlighted the issues faced by such fathers as well as explored the practice implications. Gay men, according to Mallon (2004), are increasingly choosing 'parenthood' and there has been some recognition within adoption and fostering services of this. Furthermore, gay and lesbian networks have sprung up in countries such as the UK and US to support those wishing to adopt or foster.

Fluidity (and/or ambivalence)

> The lack of a legitimate successor to the provider role and the maintenance of traditional gender roles in understanding contemporary gender relations can therefore be understood through a meaning system in which men are left with a dichotomised subjectivity of male-breadwinner, or ungendered egalitarianism. (Riley, 2003: 11)

In everyday life it would appear that there is considerable negotiation, often accompanied by considerable tension, between couples around the division of roles and responsibilities (Lewis, 2001). Men can find themselves negotiating an intermediate terrain which is neither that of male breadwinner nor ungendered egalitarian (see Featherstone and White, 2006). Moreover, Connell's work based in Australia suggests the need to understand that men can both wish to cooperate with the mothers of their children and undermine them. Practices need to be able to both recognise the negotiated terrain of much family life and to encourage the pursuit of respectful and non-violent or abusive possibilities. This is a difficulty in the current climate in the UK where many workers are either ill equipped or poorly supported in working with relationships (especially those between men and women). One practice method which holds some possibilities here is worth outlining. Family group conferences (FGCs) have emerged in the UK as a method of intervention in child welfare since the early 1990s.

Practice Example – Family group conferences (FGCs)

The origins of FGCs lie in Maori traditions and they were developed in New Zealand as a response to widespread concerns from within the Maori community about the disproportionately high numbers of their children being removed from their families and a sense that 'traditional' decision-making and problem-solving approaches were not being used to engage more positively with children's difficulties. The approach now appears to have been exported successfully to a range of different contexts such as the UK, USA, South Africa, Canada and Scandinavia. While its potential in relation to developing and supporting inclusive models of family (rather than normative and restrictive notions based upon a particular model) has been pointed out (Featherstone, 2004), it is with its potential for engaging fathers and men more generally with which we are concerned here. Holland et al. (2005: 69), in their study of such conferences, found that 'one encouraging development – from the point of view both of those who want to take pressure off women and of those who want to improve men's access to services – is the high incidence of men's attendance at conferences'. Clearly getting more men there may not always be desirable, but exploration of process issues in this

(Continued)

(Continued)

research suggested, for example, that fears of men dominating were not borne out for a variety of reasons, including the 'style' of the conference. While this aspect of their evaluation was small, there is increased interest in the UK in continuing to develop FGCs as a possibility for increasing men's participation in decision-making about their children and in encouraging men, women and children to develop more 'democratic' models of relating. (See Ferguson, 2004, for an extended discussion on the role of welfare workers in fostering such practices and the theoretical premises underpinning 'democratisation'.)

FGCs work within the arena of child welfare but there are concerns about their suitability for dealing with child protection issues. Here, even when men, including fathers, are the source of the problems faced by women and children they are not actively engaged with by practitioners (Scourfield, 2003). This often leaves women in the position of having to manage the consequences of abusive men's behaviour. Scourfield has argued for a reorienting of services but it must be acknowledged that this cannot be done without a reorienting of provision in a variety of ways. For example, domestic violence is increasingly recognised as an issue that impacts upon the safety and well-being of women and children in countries such as the UK and Canada (Davies and Krane, 2006). Research into practices by a range of professionals suggests that in the majority of cases women and their children either receive a perfunctory service and/or a punitive message that expects *mothers* to take responsibility for ending the violence because it is a child protection issue. Work with men on their behaviour is not carried out or even recognised as a priority unless they are among the minority who go through the criminal justice system (Featherstone and Peckover, 2007). Currently, however, there appear to be few services that work on violence prevention with men who self-refer. Furthermore, fathering has not been a core part of the curriculum of perpetrators' programmes (see Chapter 7 for a practice example from Norway, where men can self-refer and work on their violence in the context of being fathers).

In child protection services, the limited research which exists suggests that men who wish to care for children have to struggle to be seen as resources by professionals even in situations where mothers cannot look after children safely (Ashley et al., 2006). Fathers without parental responsibility (in the UK these were all unmarried fathers before 2003 and since 2003 those whose names are not on the child's birth certificate) seem to be particularly neglected by mainstream services, as are non-resident fathers generally.

A small but growing literature has emerged that suggests the need to critically interrogate the existing, if limited, research evidence on the prevalence of child maltreatment and the gendered issues in relation to causation and consequences. For example, although research on organisational culture in social work suggests that constructions of men as 'a threat' or as 'no use' are strongly entrenched (Scourfield, 2003), the evidence on prevalence of abuse points to a more complex picture (Cawson et al., 2000). While men predominate as sexual abusers, in Cawson et al.'s study fathers and stepfathers account for very few of these offenders. The same study found fathers to be responsible for 40 per cent of the physical abuse suffered by children. In contrast to well-established understandings of what constitutes 'neglectful mothering', the notion of the 'neglectful' father hardly exists and has been poorly researched, but there are ongoing attempts to explore the role of fathers as either risks or, in some cases, resources for children where mothers are neglectful (Taylor and Daniel, 2005). Men's involvement in domestic violence is by now well recognised as an issue in child protection, although there has been limited research on fathers, domestic violence and child protection.

As noted, Scourfield's (2003) research in a social work office found that there were few discourses around men which were positive. Furthermore, there was limited discourse around men's economic or cultural marginalisation despite the overwhelming evidence that those who come to the attention of services such as child protection services are poor, with substantial support needs in relation to physical and mental health (Ryan, 2000). There was some recognition from social workers in Scourfield's study that women from similar backgrounds were oppressed (though mainly by the men they lived with). It is possible to see these men as having been subject to the 'othering' processes described by Ferguson (2004) in his study of practices in the Republic of Ireland.

However, it is important to note here that few social work courses appear to offer training in this area. Furthermore, calls for mainstream services such as family centres or children's centres to develop services for fathers are often made by policy makers without adequate recognition of the issues that may emerge for what were often previously women-only spaces. How are safe spaces developed and fostered for those using such services to heal from and escape violent and abusive relationships with men? This relates to a further issue concerning the current female-dominated composition of the workforce. As Cameron et al. (1999) have noted from their research on the introduction of men into provisions such as nurseries, it is crucial that a process of engaging with women workers' fears, anxieties as well as hopes is undertaken. Moreover, discussions about what models of masculinity are being promoted are important.

Finally, alongside the organisational context, we suggest the importance of continuing to interrogate the policy context in which fatherhood initiatives are promoted. Abramovitz (2006), for example, notes that fatherhood initiatives in the US are increasingly located within an explicit 'marriage promotion' agenda. In the UK, exhortation to services to engage fathers needs to be interrogated in the context of what kinds of policies are in place to support constructions of fathers as providers of 'care' rather than solely of 'cash'. In the UK, the cash construction remains hegemonic in a 'long hours' and 'flexible' work culture. This may mean that services are working against the grain of demands such as work. As one of us found in an evaluation of a programme provided on a Sunday precisely in order to engage fathers who worked, the workers themselves can then experience their work/family life balance being badly disrupted (Bartlett et al., 2006). Clearly there are no easy answers here, particularly in the context of the growth in atypical hours worked by both parents, but it is important that such difficulties are clearly discussed and acknowledged. Are men who do not attend services reluctant fathers? Or insecure workers? Or both?

Conclusion

This chapter has traced some key themes from the research literature as well as highlighting differing theoretical perspectives. We have noted the need for vigilance in relation to reading men's claims as fathers as either progressive or reactionary and for careful exploration of what is being argued for and in what context. Furthermore, practice developments which seek to promote 'father involvement' cannot be read simply either. We have noted that there seems to be increased interest in some countries, such as the UK, in developing practices that 'engage fathers' and we extend these a qualified welcome, while suggesting the need for ongoing interrogation of why and how services are developed and delivered, in order that the needs of men, women and children are addressed and worked with in ways that foster 'democratic' practices.

Key texts

Ashley, C., Featherstone, B., Roskill, C., Ryan, M. and White, S. (2006) *Fathers Matter: Research Findings on Fathers and their Involvement with Social Care Services*, London: Family Rights Group.

This includes both up-to-date literature reviews and new empirical research.

Lamb, M.E. (ed.) (2004) *The Role of the Father in Child Development,* fourth edition, Chichester: Wiley.

The best introduction to relevant research from psychology.

Lupton, D. and Barclay, C. (1997) *Constructing Fatherhood: Discourses and Experiences*, London: Sage.

A qualitative sociological study based on interviews with new fathers in Australia. Grounded in post-structuralist and psychoanalytic theory.

7 Working with Abusive Men

Introduction

One of the most fundamental tensions in health and social care is that between care and control. This chapter will explore the area of work with men where the 'control' agenda is most significant (because the men's behaviour is most damaging to others), namely work with sexually abusive men and work with perpetrators of domestic violence. We will explore this area of practice by considering the models of work that are commonly implemented and demonstrate the connection between policy initiatives and practice. Even in this area of practice, however, one of the central themes of this book will emerge. We will emphasise both the special nature of work with abusive men *and* its commonalities with other approaches to work with men. Thus we will note the heterogeneity of men, even abusive men, who come from different cultures, sexual orientations and backgrounds.

Whereas a conscious political commitment is often only implicit in other kinds of work with men, in work with abusive men it is often explicit. As an area of practice therefore it situates itself on the *social engagement* end of the field. But as stated above, it shares a great deal with other aspects of men's work: it uses models outlined in Chapters 4 and 5 (in particular cognitive-behavioural approaches) and such work is predominantly undertaken in groups.

Working with sexually abusive men

Although there are many aspects to work with sex offenders – not least the breadth of the term and of the offences that come under it – one would expect a close connection between this work and that with perpetrators of domestic violence. Areas of similarity would be that both groups of men are acting outside the legal acceptability of behaviour and involve criminal justice responses. Both domestic violence and sexual abuse can be theoretically connected to patriarchy and men's abuse of power. In terms of the rehabilitation and treatment of offenders, both kinds of crime have traditionally been dominated by a groupwork intervention that claims to be effective.

However, curiously, here the similarities end. Ultimately this is because sex abuse work relies on the psychological presumption that sex abusers are psychologically deficient in some way from other men. In most texts on sexual abuse, some reference is made to theories that explain sexual abuse in terms of feminist perspectives, e.g., as connected both to the socialisation of men and to the use of sexual abuse as a method of control of women per se. Biggs et al. (1998: 25), for instance, comment that some writers: 'point out that the vast majority of sexual abuse is perpetrated by males mainly against females, and contend that it is intrinsic to a system of male dominance'.

However, such perspectives tend to function as an 'essential strand of the value system of those working with abusers' (Biggs et al., 1998: 25) rather than as an explanatory model. Instead, most treatment manuals and research rely upon a model in which the individual sex abuser is 'typologised' and his levels of 'fixation', 'social competence' and 'distorted cognitions' are mapped. In this way, cognitive-behavioural models have predominated in sexual abuse treatment services and have led to in-depth understandings of the 'cycle of offending'. Although most practitioners accept that men who rape adult women constitute a different group to men who sexually abuse children (Campbell, 1995), similar approaches to these men are adopted.

Policy in relation to sex abusers work

This predominance of a particular model for working with sexually abusive men is embedded within an overall policy arena in which control and risk are fundamental to thinking about this group of men. In the last ten years there have been rapid and increasing changes to the law to address the issue of sexually abusive men. Foremost has been the increasing use of 'registers' on which sexual offenders are placed (often for the duration of their lives). There have also been public campaigns for the introduction of 'Megan's Law' (or the British equivalent 'Sarah's Law') in the UK. This American legislation publicises the whereabouts of convicted paedophiles so that parents can take action to keep their children 'safe'. There has also been controversy about the length of sentences given to men who sexually abuse and there have been suggestions that proposed mental health legislation has been drafted to contain such 'dangerous offenders'.

Given this conflation of public interest and policy development, it is not surprising that work with this group of men is almost universally the territory of criminal justice practitioners. Of all the areas of working with men, working with sex abusers is the one where probation officers predominate. Mandeville-Norden and Beech (2004) comment that this is curious, as sexual crimes represent less than 1 per cent of all recorded crime (2004: 194) and less than 8 per cent of prison inmates are sex offenders (2001 figure), yet treatment of these men constitutes a significant part of probation services' activity. Furthermore, along with the regulation of various forms of offender programmes in the Probation Service in England and Wales, sexual offender work is accredited nationally, closely monitored and regulated via national assessors. Moreover, because this group of men are seen to be a high-risk group for women, children and in fact society in general, the literature on sexually abusing men is replete with various tools and manuals for the 'assessment of danger' (Campbell, 1995; Biggs et al., 1998; Calder, 2000). Once more it is evident that work with men becomes a site in which public policy drives practitioner interests.

Practice in work with sexually abusive men

As noted above, much research has been devoted to ascertaining how sexually abusive men differ from the general population of men. In summary, this research leads to the assumption that:

> sex offenders tend to have comparatively low levels of victim empathy ... deviant cognitions or beliefs about their victims [and] emotional loneliness and inadequate problem solving abilities. (Mandeville-Norden and Beech, 2004: 195)

With reference to men who sexually abuse children, their characteristics are described by these same authors as: 'a degree of cognitive distortion about children ... high levels of social inadequacy [and] lower levels of self-esteem' (2004: 196). This emphasis upon individual psychological features determines the treatment model adopted for this group of men. For instance, Beech (1998) has stated that unless treatment addresses the cognitions that children are sexual beings, that adult men have an entitlement to abuse them, that abuse causes no harm and that the abuser cannot control his urges, then treatment is unlikely to be successful.

On the other hand, Mandeville-Norden and Beech (2004) report that the evidence that rapists are a distinct group of men is less convincing. Indeed, one study compared rapists to non-rapists in prison and found the two groups to be very similar (Hudson and Ward, 1997). This finding of course points to practitioners needing to seek the specific individual adversities and interactional events that might have relevance to the individual rapist's actions.

Mandeville-Norden and Beech (2004) outline a history of work with sex offenders. What is immediately evident is that work with such men has been motivated by a desire to 'work out' the individual pathology of the abusers. Biggs et al. (1998) describe the 'models' that underpin treatment and assessment in this area of work. They accept that 'dominance' and 'power and control' theories have been put forward by feminists, but comment that 'empirical theories' have concentrated on 'sex offender typologies' linked to the 'cycle of offending' theory. Essentially, this perspective argues that men who sexually abuse either children or women have a 'different developmental pathway' from other men. Moreover, the variety of abusers can be differentiated into different 'degrees of sexual fixation'. This itself then connects to cycles of poor self-image, masturbatory 'compensation' and the committing of abuse.

The psychological perspective that informs this understanding inevitably leads to an emphasis on working with men on their 'cognitive distortions' in order to teach them to avoid repeating their abusive behaviour. For instance, one of these distortions might be that 'children like having sex with adults'. In the treatment of abusers, this cognition will be challenged by helping men think about being a child and perhaps by playing videotapes of children describing the effects abuse has had on them. In some groups, the men will go through role plays in which they are made to feel powerless and devalued, to help them connect with the child's experience.

Overwhelmingly, treatment for sex abusers is also in a groupwork format and also overwhelmingly it is cognitive-behavioural in focus. Mandeville-Norden and Beech reflect that earlier treatment programmes relied upon behavioural techniques such as aversion therapy. However, the rise of cognitive therapy altered this and as these kinds of programmes grew, the role of voluntary agencies in providing them faded away and they became the preserve of probation staff.

Proctor and Flaxington (1996) found that treatment programmes lasted on average for 80 hours with weekly sessions. Currently, almost all areas have such a programme: 177 programmes were reported in 1999 (Ford and Findlater, 1999). Probation service areas in England and Wales now adopt one of three possible programmes, all of which are largely similar but vary in length and structure. For instance, the West Midlands programme consists of three sections: an initial phase which lasts 50 hours, a more thorough section which lasts 190 hours (for 'high risk' offenders) and a relapse prevention module lasting another 50 hours. These programmes are designed to treat all sex offenders: rapists or child sex abusers.

Although there is controversy about the effectiveness of these programmes, which revolves around how effectiveness should be measured, various researchers claim that they 'work'. Alexander (1999) undertook a meta-analysis of outcomes from 79 studies (11,000 individuals) and found that treatment subjects had lower recidivism rates than others. Beech et al. (2002) compared outcomes for 52 offenders and similarly found lower rates of re-conviction, albeit these remained at 10 per cent (compared to 23 per cent).

What this discussion has highlighted is that there is a clear 'hegemonic' form of treatment for men who sexually abuse. This treatment has emerged with close reference to research findings and centres upon groupwork cognitive-behavioural principles. This has, however, not been without its critics. Vivian-Byrne (2004: 181) argued that 'it is premature' to be certain that this treatment is the best. She argues that more 'therapeutic' ways of working with this population have not been sufficiently tried or tested. To some degree, this view is confirmed by research undertaken by others, including Beech (Barker and Beech, 1993; Beech and Fordham, 1997), which indicated that the style and process of the groupwork format mattered in terms of the outcomes for men.

It could be argued that it is comforting for all of us to regard sexually abusive men as a distinct group. The search for 'cognitive distortions' in this group lets other men sleep secure that they are different and 'Other'. Yet the ideas about male sexuality described by Jukes (1993) imply that there is a quality within male sexuality that connects the masculine sexual urge to violence and abuse (see also Good and Sherrod, 1998). Others (e.g., Lisak, 1998) see the roots of sexual abuse within male socialisation, which restricts empathy and privileges power. This wider understanding of masculinity is not contained within the practice literature of working with sexually abusive men. It is, however, prevalent within the practice of working with men who are domestically abusive to which we now turn.

Interventions with men who perpetrate domestic violence

Programmes that work with men who perpetrate domestic violence emerged out of the women's refuge movement (La Violette, 2001) and out of the anti-sexist men's movement (Stoltenberg, 1989, 1993; Pease, 1997, 2000) in the 1970s and 1980s. During the next decade (1990s) some of these programmes were critiqued for being too 'therapeutic' (with implications that men's abusive behaviour was being excused) and too isolated from mainstream services (implying that they could not ensure the safety of women and children). These criticisms came hand-in-hand with a raised public profile of domestic violence within North America, the UK and Australasia, which led to more concerted attempts to prevent abuse. It also led to an interest in establishing effective and comparable programmes for abusive men. The mainstream feminist perspective, which interpreted the high rates of domestic violence as evidence of the patriarchal protection and socialisation of men, profoundly influenced this area of men's work.

Foremost of these pro-feminist approaches was what is now called the Duluth programme (Pence and Paymar, 1993). Significantly, this model is designed to be embedded within a *coordinated community response* (Shepard and Pence, 1999; Harwin et al., 1999) to domestic violence. The Duluth programme for men consists of a 26-week group format in which attention is given to the teaching tool of the Power and Control Wheel (Figure 7.1) and the Equality Wheel (Figure 7.2). The overall philosophy of the programme is one in which patriarchy is assumed. Pence and Paymar write that:

> Men are culturally prepared for their role of master of the home even though they must often physically enforce the 'right' to exercise this role. They are socialized to be dominant and women to be subordinate. (Pence and Paymar, 1993: 5)

Accordingly in a groupwork format, perpetrators are taught to review the Power and Control Wheel, describe what aspects of these methods they use to control their partners and then are taught to practise alternative behaviours from the Equality Wheel.

Programmes such as Duluth are also frequently described as cognitive-behavioural, although it is important to remember that there are other cognitive programmes (Russell, 1995). What this means is that within the pro-feminist perspective, Duluth practitioners also encourage the group members to verbalise the thoughts that justify their behaviour and then to challenge these thought processes. For instance, many abusive men will ascribe malicious intention to the actions of their partners and blame them for making the man feel useless or upset. This cognitive process will be challenged by encouraging men to empathise with their partners and recognise how they often force their partners to behave in the way they do. This cognitive-behavioural technology is underpinned by a clear feminist analysis in which the abusive man's definition of himself as a man is the focus of educational interventions.

Pence and Paymar (1993: 15) describe their work in this way:

> At the core of the curriculum is the attempt to structure a process by which each man can examine his actions in light of his concept of himself as a man. That examination demands a reflective process that distinguishes between what is in his nature and what is socially constructed. The things that are socially constructed

Figure 7.1   The Duluth Power and Control Wheel
Reproduced with permission of the Domestic Abuse Intervention Project.

can be changed. Each belief he holds can be traced back to his experiences in his family of origin, his neighbourhood, his peer group in school, his military service, his fraternities or other male groups, and to his exposure to the media and its countless images of what it means to be a man. These experiences shape his response to a basic question asked men in the groups over and over again: 'why do you want a woman in your life?'

In both North America and the UK these models of programme fitted the growing public demand for perpetrators of domestic violence to be challenged and changed.

Policy and domestic violence perpetrators in the UK

We have established that within the field of sexual offender treatment, a certain model of treatment has become 'hegemonic'. That is, a model of working

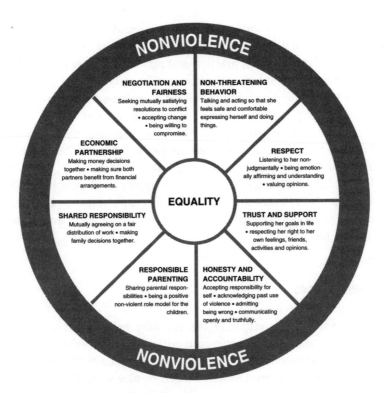

Figure 7.2   The Duluth Equality Wheel
Reproduced with permission of the Domestic Abuse Intervention Project.

with men has become both pre-eminent and almost unquestioned as the 'right' intervention. We have also demonstrated how policy has endorsed that hegemony. The same is also true within the field of domestic violence perpetrator work. Since the election of the 1997 Labour government, more resources have been devoted to domestic violence (Home Office, 1999a, 1999b, 2000). Thus there has been a growth in 'one-stop shop' services and of advocates for women (Robinson, 2003). There has been a growth in domestic violence specialist courts and in the use of multi-agency risk committees to manage repeat offenders of domestic violence (Robinson, 2004). These have led to a rise in successful prosecutions and better inter-agency communication. In terms of treatment for perpetrators, the Probation Service has followed the route of sex offenders, by a rolling out of accredited programmes for these men. These programmes represent the importation of the Duluth programme into the UK context – its groupwork component, that is, rather than the fully-fledged community intervention envisaged by the full Duluth model.

Similarly, practitioners within the field of perpetrator work have formalised their own professional organisation and created a charity called *Respect*, which lays down standards of 'good practice' and acts as a gateway for men to find help. Respect receives a substantial amount of its costs from the Home Office, which now funds a Respect helpline. Indeed, there is evidence that the Respect definition of 'good practice' of work with male perpetrators of domestic violence is being applied to voluntary and not mandated men. The current expectation is that, ultimately, all programmes will adopt a Respect/Duluth-style model and will be regulated in some way.

Although there is a greater variety of programmes for abusive men in North America, it is also relevant to note that many criminal justice agencies and, indeed, state governments also require 'standards' of any programme that they fund or refer men into.

Divergent voices

Just as there have been critics of the cognitive-behavioural model of sex offender treatment, there have also been critics of the pro-feminist cognitive-behavioural Duluth model. In the US, Mankowski et al. (2002) argue that both the therapeutic and the pro-feminist models involve some form of 'collateral damage' and 'unintended consequences' (p. 168). They emphasise the dilemma between 'punishing' abusive men and trying to 'help' them:

> In our experience, advocates and practitioners struggle alike with the question of whether batterers require therapeutic treatment to overcome a psychological problem or rather, directive re-education, and punishment to interrupt criminal behaviour. (Mankowski et al., 2002: 172)

Within this dilemma, they believe that the 'power and control' model of the Duluth approach fails to take into account the heterogeneity of male perpetrators, the frequent psychological difficulties many suffer from, and the experience of these men which is far from one of feeling 'powerful'. They further question the assumption of the Duluth model that abuse is 'intentional and a result of individual choice' (p. 171).

In the UK, Gadd (2004) has also questioned the Duluth approach to men who are abusive to their female partners. He comments that this approach misses 'the emotional dynamics that underpin men's abusive relationships' (p. 189). He also sees the hegemony of the model as connected to policy initiatives rather than to either practitioner wisdom or to research evidence:

The standardisation of interventions for domestic violence perpetrators … owes more to a series of political processes than it does to the research evidence. (Gadd, 2004: 189)

A similar point is made by Gelles in the USA:

Standardizing treatment programs before we know what works, for which men, under what circumstance, limits and eliminates the development of novel or innovative approaches to treating violent and abusive men. (Gelles, 2001: 18)

Gelles is suggesting that further research needs to be undertaken before the variety of programmes for men who are abusive to their female partners is restricted (see also Rees and Rivett, 2005). Indeed, worldwide, Duluth-style programmes fit into a multiplicity of approaches. Some of these approaches use therapeutic methods (Jenkins, 1990; Lee et al., 2003). Others rely on individual cognitive-behavioural treatment (Murphy and Eckhardt, 2005). Some preface their work with an understanding of psychological difficulties (Dutton, 1995; Dutton and Sonkin, 2003). In some areas, couple group treatment is used (Geffner and Mantooth, 2000) and is regarded as effective (Stith et al., 2002). Many of these authors have included some Duluth concepts into their manuals. They have adjusted the Duluth model to fit culturally diverse populations of men (Bepko et al., 1998). But they also include the teaching of issues such as 'relationship skills', 'emotional literacy', 'relapse prevention' and 'self-esteem training'. Such themes are 'out of place' in a model that assumes that male abusers are abusive only in order to control their partners.

Gelles's (2001) argument rests on a view that research has still not determined which form of treatment for domestically abusive men is most effective. We will therefore summarise this area of knowledge now.

The outcome evidence and perpetrator work

It is not possible for us to fully cover the literature studying the outcomes of the treatment of domestically abusive men in this book. Nor can we fully explore the complexities of this 'outcome' literature. For a full discussion, readers are referred to Gondolf (2002). What we can do is briefly mention useful findings. Thus two (Burton et al., 1998; Dobash et al., 2000) small-scale quasi-experimental studies carried out in the UK concluded that men who are abusive to their female partners can change if they join a treatment programme. Further, this change is more marked than no treatment interventions, e.g., 'probation supervision' (Dobash et al., 2000). Unfortunately, the numbers studied were small: the Dobash study had 51 men on a programme; Burton et al., 36.

However, meta-analysis has returned more equivocal findings. Babcock and La Taillade, for instance, comment that:

> Overall, batterers' treatment is related to a small reduction in recidivism of domestic violence. In addition, no intervention, psycho-educational groups, CBT groups or couples therapy have been shown to be differentially more effective than the other within the same sample. Furthermore, length of treatment does not seem to be clearly related to recidivism. (2000: 53)

More recently in a similar analysis Babcock et al. concluded that:

> Overall, effects due to treatment were in the small range, meaning that the current interventions have a minimal impact on reducing recidivism beyond the effect of being arrested ... there were no differences in effect sizes in comparing Duluth model vs CBT-type interventions. (Babcock et al., 2004: 1023)

However, these equivocal conclusions are tempered by the most long-term and well-designed study undertaken to date.

Gondolf (2002) evaluated four very different perpetrator programmes in the USA: in Pittsburgh, Dallas, Houston and Denver. His sample size was 840 men and their partners. The programme 'philosophy' and length varied between each site. Thus the Pittsburgh programme lasted 3 months and tended to adopt an 'instructional' approach. The Dallas programme lasted 3 months and adopted a 'discussion' approach (less structured). The Houston programme lasted 6 months and was the closest to a Duluth-style intervention. The Denver programme lasted 9 months and resembled a therapeutic-style group (called by Gondolf a 'process group'). The sample was followed up for four years and the rate of re-assault measured by adding partner reports to police reports.

Initially Gondolf found that there was a significant number of men who did re-assault their partners at both 15 months and 48 months. However, this re-assault rate reduced rather than increased over the period of study (implying that there might be a 'programme effect' long after the end of a programme). This meant that at 30 months 80 per cent of the men had been 'violence free'; and this rose to 90 per cent at 48 months. Moreover, as many men who re-assaulted were responsible for a number of re-assaults, 75 per cent of all the programme completers had not been violent in the last 2.5 years of the study. Gondolf summarises this research by saying that:

> The most encouraging finding is that the majority of men eventually do stop their violence, apparently for long periods of time. (Gondolf, 2002: 123)

Gondolf also sought to assess if these men had turned from physical to emotional abuse: a criticism often made against perpetrator programmes. Again, however, partner reports confirmed that 'more than a third of the men actually refrained from any abusive behaviour' rather than it 'escalating or intensifying' (p. 127). When Gondolf compared those men who completed which ever programme they joined, with those that 'dropped out' again he found the programme to have a significant value. 'Program completion', Gondolf writes, 'reduced the likelihood of re-assault by 44 to 64 percentage points' (p. 143).

Gondolf also had the opportunity to compare the results from the different programmes. He was able to compare longer programmes with shorter ones; he was able to compare Duluth-style ones with therapeutic ones. His conclusions were not what he expected:

My colleagues and I initially expected that intervention systems based on longer programs ... would have lower re-assault rates. We found at best only slight and weak evidence in support of the more comprehensive system. (p. 154)

Indeed, he found that programme philosophy also had little effect on outcomes:

We did find that court referrals, program formats, program duration, and additional services did not of themselves make for better outcomes. (p. 160)

What the research evidence therefore suggests is that perpetrator programmes do appear to work (on the whole and not for all abusers), but that model fidelity and programme length may not be the most important factors that determine success or failure. A recent qualitative study (Garfield, 2006) has suggested (like that of Beech and Fordham, 1997, in sex offender work) that the quality of the working relationship between facilitators and clients is a significant factor in understanding outcome rather than length or style of treatment.

Given these findings, it is also important to take into account that some programmes may be more effective with certain types of men. This nuance in treatment approaches was masked by the Duluth-style assumption that it was the commonalities of men which needed intervention, not individual men's unique difficulties/personalities. However, there has been substantial research to justify the view that all abusive men are *not* the same. Thus Gondolf (2002) found that some men in his sample had 'anti-social' disorders while others had mental health problems. Jacobson and Gottman (1998) found physiological differences within their sample of abusive men when they were angry. These physiological differences led them to believe that treatment was possible for some and not others. Gilchrist et al. (2003) in the UK studied offenders who were serving prison sentences for domestic violence crimes and also confirmed that some men were 'narcissistic' and others had 'borderline personalities'. In a community sample Hester et al. (2006) also found a heterogeneity rather than a commonality. This variety of domestically abusive men led Saunders (1996) to argue that the more emotionally 'damaged men' required a therapeutic intervention while the more anti-social men required a more Duluth-style intervention.

The research evidence therefore seems to suggest that perpetrator programmes should seek to address as many types of men as possible (including voluntary and mandated), use as many types of learning style as possible and also contain pro-feminist, cognitive-behavioural as well as therapeutic skills. Such services do exist (see practice example below). However, the field of services available to men who are abusive to their female partners remains dominated by the hegemony of the Duluth model. This is demonstrated in the Respect (2004) guideline document, which emphasises long-term treatment built on the power and control wheels and does not regard therapeutic competencies as essential for group facilitators.

Practice Example – Cardiff Domestic Violence Prevention Service (DVPS)

The Cardiff Domestic Violence Prevention Service (DVPS) (see Rivett and Rees, 2004) combines a pro-feminist approach with a therapeutic one. Its workers use skills and techniques from the systemic/family therapy tradition. For instance, men are encouraged to think for themselves and to challenge each other rather than this being the 'job' of the facilitators. Groups are 12 weeks long, not the standard 26 weeks of a Duluth programme. This is designed to meet the needs of voluntary men who are reticent to commit themselves to long-term treatment. Attention is given to helping the group 'form' so that men can begin to describe their abusive behaviour more fully. Various exercises are used to focus the men on the reason they are in the group. For instance, in initial stages, men are asked to talk to each other about what is stopping them change their lives around and what would be the benefits of doing so. In order to establish commonalities as well as differences, voluntary men are asked to talk to mandated men (Rees and Rivett, 2005). Men who have suffered abuse as children are asked to talk to men who haven't; men who have office jobs are asked to talk to manual workers; these exercises help create an atmosphere of trust and support. One therapeutic axiom that is adopted by facilitators is that no one will change if they are feeling forced, criticised or judged. Thus the internal resources and motivations of the men are encouraged and expressed. Sometimes this motivation comes from the men wanting a better life. Sometimes it comes from them wanting their children to have a better childhood than they did. Sometimes it comes from them being full of shame and regret for what they have done. Sometimes it comes from them fully believing that they love their partner and in wanting to make amends.

(Continued)

The DVPS takes referrals from mandated men and from voluntary men: one of the few in the UK to do this. It also works with men's partners, using the resources of a wider network to keep them safe. Furthermore, the DVPS also works with children who have witnessed domestic violence and it has a strong child protection framework. Because it combines these elements of domestic violence work, the men's group facilitators are kept close to the experience of women and children. Indeed, in team meetings the men's workers are seen to be accountable for safe practice to the other workers.

Domestic violence and diverse men

In the last decade, there has been an emerging literature and practice that recognises diversity between perpetrators of domestic violence. In particular, practice has developed to take account of minority ethnic cultures and the particular issues in same-sex violence. Carrillo and Tello (1998) have spearheaded new approaches to working with 'men of colour' in the United States. They assert that each community has its own 'identity, traditions, customs and healing practices' (p. xvi) which need to be understood and valued in treating men of colour who perpetrate domestic violence. In particular, a number of authors critique the use of the word 'equality' in the Power and Control wheel, arguing that the word 'respect' has a better cultural relevance for many communities. Tello (1998), for example, draws on Latino stories about balance and masculinity to help violent men reassess their lives. His ideas resonate with the mythopoetic movement's use of stories. Tong (1998) notes how the influence of racism impacts upon the lives of Asian-American men. He argues that traditional treatment approaches tend to undervalue the effect this has upon men and may interpret its discussion in a group as an 'excuse' for violence. On the contrary, he argues, a recognition of its effects is crucial in helping Asian-American men stop abuse and gain control of their lives.

O. Williams (1998: 83) argues that for African-American men who are abusive to their partners, what is required is a blending of 'conventional wisdom with an African-American male perspective'. Such a blending includes a recognition of the impact of racism, but it also calls upon culturally acceptable ways of healing. Included in this is an appropriate 'positive model' for African-Americans. This model is one which highlights men's ability to protect their families, not hurt them. Like Tello (1998) and Bepko et al. (1998), Williams uses a cultural definition of a 'good man' as a tool in working with African-American men who have been abusive. This echoes the point in Chapter 3 about working with marginalised men in South Africa – namely that white

Figure 7.3   The Duluth Lesbian/Gay Power and Control Wheel
Reproduced with permission of the Domestic Abuse Intervention Project.

Western pro-feminist models should not be seen as the automatic template for interventions, regardless of 'race' and class. Some traditional aspects of masculinity may have to be used as resources for intervention in pragmatic ways.

Gay violence has also received considerable attention in the last decade. Henderson (2003) demonstrated that levels of domestic violence in gay and lesbian relationships were similar to those in heterosexual ones. Walsh (1996), Fox (1999) and Leventhal and Lundy (1999) have all described ways of working with gay domestic violence. Similar to work with abusers from minority ethnic communities where the effect of racism is acknowledged, practitioners recognise the impact of homophobia both on the occurrence of domestic violence within gay relationships but also on the response of services to this violence (see Figure 7.3). It is also interesting to note that practitioners working with gay violence regard relationship dynamics as more significant than those working with heterosexual violence.

Practice Example – The 'Dyn' (Man) Project, Cardiff

The 'Dyn' Project was set up to work with men who are victims of domestic violence: gay and also heterosexual.

One case referred to the Dyn Project illustrates the similarities and difference between same-sex and heterosexual domestic abuse, which may confront a practitioner. Nathan was a gay man in his thirties. His relationship with his (male) partner had been emotionally and physically abusive. It bore evidence of many familiar risk factors; thus, the abuser exhibited controlling behaviour, jealousy and an alcohol problem. Physical violence was common, including attempted strangulation, which is a high risk indicator for potential homicide. The abuse also escalated towards the end of the relationship.

Yet the case manifested some of the unique issues for those in abusive same-sex relationships. Nathan found it difficult to seek help from professionals, because disclosing domestic abuse would require that he come out as a gay man. His housing association (which had a good reputation for responding effectively to abuse in heterosexual relationships) seemed unable to conceptualise the risks he faced because the abuse came from another man. Thus, they sought to evict him from his property for rent arrears and non-occupation. A cursory conversation with Nathan revealed he was too frightened of his former partner to return home, and that the rent arrears arose after he used his benefits to repair damage to the flat inflicted by his partner during an assault. Furthermore, while the police had attended numerous incidents, only a handful had ever been reported as domestic incidents.

The Dyn Project responded by facilitating a safety package that included target hardening of the property, alongside a more comprehensive response from the police and his housing association. Nathan also attended a group for gay men who had experienced domestic abuse. He benefited from the opportunity to meet other men in a similar position, and to develop his understanding of abuse, homophobia and heterosexism. Along with improving his confidence, he also began to think about his future plans and ultimately returned to work. Strikingly, none of this intervention was innovative. It should have been available to Nathan as of right, as someone who had experienced domestic abuse. Yet his sexuality constituted a barrier not of his own making, which we are all obliged to overcome.

Reproduced by kind permission from James Rowlands, former worker at the Dyn Project.

Working with fathers who are perpetrators of domestic violence

One of the more recent developments in working with abusive men has been that of engaging with men both as fathers and as perpetrators of domestic violence. These developments have been, to some extent, prompted by the emergence of fathers' projects as outlined in Chapter 7. Organisations such as Fathers Direct in the UK are engaging with domestic violence services to work out future developments.

Such developments have actually aroused a degree of controversy, as fathers' projects and domestic violence projects often have different emphases – one emphasising the 'father' identity and the other the 'perpetrator' identity. The latter approach is more likely to stress 'control' and the former 'support'. Dialogue continues on these issues, however.

This division (father/violent man) can also be evidenced in the question: can men who perpetrate domestic abuse be 'good fathers'? If the answer to this question is an unreserved 'No', then it follows that perpetrators should be separated from their children and treated for their abuse before being allowed to have contact with children. If, however, the answer is something like 'well no, but they may still be very important to their children', then it follows that services will seek to improve the father–child relationship while also ensuring that safety issues are addressed.

Guille (2004) has reviewed the evidence on abusive men as fathers. She comments that there 'is a lack of research directly addressing the father–child relationship in domestically violent families' (p. 130). She uses evidence that approximates the issue by first looking at research into the role of fathers when they are directly abusive to children and also when they are 'unavailable' due to alcohol abuse or divorce. Curiously, Guille reports significant research which suggests that fathers who are unavailable to their children pre-divorce become more connected post-divorce. Guille also studied the effects of witnessing domestic violence on children and evidence that perpetrators have multiple problems. Thus, she concludes that although perpetrators may not be 'good' fathers, their influence on the long-term development of their children should not be underestimated.

Bancroft and Silverman (2002) explore in more detail how the parenting practices of abusive men often involve their children in 'taking sides' over the abuse. They describe with great detail how domestic violence perpetrators undermine mothers. However, despite this catalogue of difficulties, they argue not for a blanket ban on contact but rather a careful assessment of the risks exposure to the abusive man would pose to the children. Their highest risk factor is that the man undermines the mother, interferes with her parenting, or uses contact to abuse her. They then note that some fathers may be authoritarian, rigid, inconsistent or neglectful as parents. In keeping with some other research, Bancroft and Silverman also note that some abusive men are physically, sexually and psychologically abusive and manipulative to their children. Saunders (2004) has noted that, of course, some children are killed during contact with a father who had previously been abusive to their mother.

The concept that fathers who are domestically violent need a 'dedicated intervention' has been taken forward in the 'Caring Dads' service running in London, Ontario (Kelly and Wolfe, 2004; Scott and Crooks, 2004). This programme combines a 'fatherhood' agenda with a 'perpetrator' agenda, although it certainly leans to the 'perpetrator' side. Scott and Crooks, for instance, state:

> The treatment needs of maltreating and at risk fathers are unique (...) based on the integration of parenting, child abuse, change promotion and batterer treatment. (2004: 95)

In Scott and Crooks (2004) this programme is outlined. It is a 17-week-long programme for fathers who have been targeted by child protection agencies as having both child abuse and domestic violence problems. Initially this programme works on the men's understandings and attitudes to children and fathering. A large issue here is psycho-educational: teaching men what to expect from children and encouraging a child-centred approach to parenting. This is then built on by helping the men realise that they are not being good fathers if they are abusive to the children's mother. In this part of the programme, the focus is on victim perspective and understanding 'What is abuse?' Last, the programme seeks to coach fathers into repairing the relationship they have with their children and enabling them to rebuild a positive fathering role.

Although the 'Caring Dads' programme does seek to broaden the perspective of the Duluth model, it still retains some of the features of that model. It provides a long intervention programme, it focuses on 'deficits' in masculinity and it asserts that such men need specialist intervention. Workers in family centres therefore may still see such a model as too distant from the men who regularly use their resources and therefore unlikely to be welcome to those men.

In Norway, a project working with fathers has recently been established within the already existing treatment and research centre, Alternative to Violence (ATV). According to Rakil (2006) the ATV models have a pro-feminist value base and the therapeutic work includes individual and group treatment. Their service to men who are fathers is embedded within a treatment programme for men who are violent to their partners. Men can self-refer and, indeed, approximately 60 per cent of their referrals are from men themselves. The model of treatment revolves around four phases the men are required to go through. The first phase explicitly focuses on the violence, the second on responsibility issues, the third on psychological connections between personal history and present use of violence, and the fourth on the harmful consequences of the violence. They have found that there is considerable work needed on getting the men to integrate the reality of their violence with their role as practising fathers. Overlooking the impact on the children is often an aspect of refusing to take responsibility.

ATV's experience suggests that interventions need to address:

- Men's perceptions of themselves as fathers;
- How the violence is affecting the father–child relationship;
- How the violence is affecting the mother–child relationship;
- How the child is affected on both a short- and long-term basis;
- The basic psychological needs of the child from a developmental perspective and how these needs are violated by the presence of violence. (Rakil, 2006:199)

While the programme has not yet been evaluated, experience of running the inputs is positive. Rakil does acknowledge the need for systematic evaluation as developments in the area of work with perpetrators as fathers are still fairly marginal to the field and no evidence base in relation to effectiveness has emerged.

Conclusion

This chapter has provided an overview of the treatment of men who perpetuate domestic violence and men who are sex abusers. It has argued – like the rest of the book – that men are not a homogenous group and therefore these areas of work need to address a variety of men. The chapter has also shown that, as in other areas of men's work, policy often leads, if not dictates, practice. In particular, the chapter has suggested that the field of services to men who abuse sexually or in domestic violence situations is not static: new areas of practice are developing and new methods for working with these men are emerging. We would argue that in these, of all areas of men's work, variety and innovation should continue.

Key texts

Calder, M. (2000) *A Complete Guide to Sex Abuse Assessments*, Lyme Regis: Russell House.

A thorough text which outlines a variety of relevant issues for working with sexual abusers.

Gondolf, E. (2002) *Batterer Intervention Systems*, Thousand Oaks, CA: Sage.

Based on the most extensive evaluation to date.

Pence, E. and Paymar, M. (1993) *Education Groups for Men Who Batter*, New York: Springer.

This is the original Duluth programme text, which outlines the philosophy and curriculum of the 26-week treatment programme.

8 Men's Physical Health and Disability

The next two chapters of the book focus on men's health. The first (Chapter 8) deals with physical aspects and the second (Chapter 9) with mental and emotional aspects. It was a pragmatic decision to organise the structure of the book in this way. It is not, of course, possible to sustain a clear and distinct separation between the two aspects of men's health. Physical health and disability have important implications for mental health. Equally, positive mental health may lead someone to keep fit and healthy. There is also, according to increasingly dominant voices from within medical research, some compelling evidence of the biological roots of some predispositions to mental illness. Physical and mental well-being therefore need to be considered together, but each requires more attention than a joint chapter of this book would allow, so we have decided to proceed with separate discussions.

The chapter starts with some introductory comments that situate the content in the context of the politics of gender and health. We then go on to explain how the *social* science of gender can illuminate our understanding and responses to physical illness and disability in men. It is worth emphasising at the outset that this chapter will not in any sense provide a medical overview. That is neither within our field of knowledge nor is it particularly relevant to a book that is concerned with the psycho-social location of men. The emphasis of the chapter is very much on the social context of men's health and its psychological implications. Since a chapter of about 7000 words can only do so much in terms of an overview, we select some specific gendered manifestations of physical illness and disability and some particularly vulnerable groups of men. We give an overview of social interventions that might be designed with men in mind and provide two more detailed specific examples of interventions (in the field of sexual health).

The politics of men's health

Second-wave feminism saw the women's movement challenging the traditional male dominance of medicine in the form of (mostly) male doctors and men as subjects for research studies. More recently, as with other areas of social life and social policy, we have seen a shift within social science to considerations of *gender* in health (Arber and Thomas, 2001) and also increasing attention being paid to 'men's health' specifically. As Sabo (2005) notes, there is now an array of activists and professionals working in the field of men's health.

Overviews of men's health typically include reference both to health problems that are specific to male biology and also to problems that are quite clearly connected to socially constructed patterns of gender identity and gender practices. So, for example, the second edition of Kirby et al.'s (2004) edited collection includes a few chapters on such biologically-specific issues as disease of the prostate and testicular cancer, alongside a much longer list of health problems that have at least some clear element of social causation, such as smoking-related illness, coronary heart disease and late diagnosis.

Where biology ends and society starts is of course unfathomable and we do not attempt a thorough discussion at this point. There are some initial comments that need to be made, however, in the context of a chapter on health. There are of course many blocks to reasoned conversations on this topic. Most social scientists and practitioners who consider themselves to be working broadly with a 'social model' of health and illness have encountered medical practitioners and researchers whose narrow focus on bodies and the medical gaze does not allow a serious consideration of social factors. Equally, there is a disciplinary arrogance from many sociologists in particular (not so much from frontline social workers in our experience), which refuses to countenance the role of biology. This is never more evident than in the contested field of gender studies, where to dare to suggest there might be biological predispositions according to sex triggers automatic accusations of essentialism or conservatism. Whether you feel beleaguered by biology or by anti-science sociology depends on your own history. We can point to the increasing power of genetics and biological explanations for problems that have previously been thought to be more psychological or sociological in origin (see Rose, 2001, on biopolitics). We can also reflect that despite scientific advances in understanding the role of genetics, many social scientists have not expanded their gaze at all to include any consideration of biology.

A pragmatic and reasonable approach has to be to acknowledge that men's bodies are naturally different in certain ways and are also socially constructed as different. We recognise of course that some social and cultural theorists have attempted to break down a distinction between socially constructed gender and 'natural' sex. However, there is – let's face it – an important concep-tual distinction between testicular cancer or Duchenne muscular dystrophy, which are specific to male biology, and injuries caused by industrial accidents in male-dominated manual labour, where the over-representation of men is entirely socially constructed. Kraemer (2000) argues that in responding to men's health problems we have to consider both biology and society. He notes that from the point of conception – that is, before social forces come into play – boys are more physically vulnerable in some respects than girls, as male foetuses are more at risk from impairment. He also notes that a whole range of social factors come into play from the point of birth that have a major influence on gendered experiences of illness.

As well as the politics of science, the question of what should be the appro-priate policy responses to men's health problems is contested. Sabo (2005) notes that much of the activity under the banner of 'men's health' is geared towards biomedical services for men and corporate targeting of health prod-ucts at men, and that some commentators have criticised these priorities. A gender relations approach has been recommended by Schofield et al. (2000). This approach argues that we cannot and should not consider men's health in isolation from the social circumstances of women and that differences between social groups of men are more significant than differences between sex groups. Connell (2000) notes that in fact 'no difference' is the main find-ing of a good proportion of Australian studies that have compared the health of men and women and that there is plenty of room for over-simplifications about the health hazard of the 'male role' to obfuscate more than they illu-minate our understanding of and our responses to health problems.

Generally relevant aspects of the gender order

One of the most significant social scientific insights into men's health prob-lems is the idea that there is a downside to dominance. There are aspects of the social construction of masculinity that are connected to men's historical dominance over women and also to ill health in men. Courtenay (2000) argues that a range of men's social practices, which have a causal link to health prob-lems, need to be understood in the context of the social construction of the 'stronger sex'. So, for example, men's historical dominance of the public sphere and primary involvement in employment can lead to work-related stress, which can contribute to coronary heart disease. The connection between irresponsibility, hedonism and masculinity means that physical health is in jeopardy from alcohol and drug misuse and risk-taking such as extreme sports and dangerous driving. The construction of men as strong, auto-nomous and independent might mean not recognising symptoms or seeking help.

New (2001) goes as far as to argue that men could be seen as 'oppressed' within the gender order – with oppression defined as systematic mistreatment – even when their historical dominance is taken into account, because of the problems that dominant models of masculinity cause for men. Although, as New argues, there are aspects of hegemonic masculinity which could be seen to have negative impacts on men who are in many respects also socially privileged, it is in fact in poor working-class men and minority ethnic men that the most severe health problems tend to be concentrated. This is particularly the case in relation to work. New notes that

> Overwork falls also on middle-class and upper-class men, although working-class men are assigned the dirtiest, most dangerous and exhausting jobs. Their bodies are treated as disposable. The masculine ideology of strength and endurance encourages men to accept and even take pride in these destructive effects, with serious implications for men's health. (New, 2001: 742)

On a global scale there is the stark reality of hard and dangerous physical labour for men, though of course women's health is also compromised in the poorest parts of the world. It is also the case that in the affluent Western world, many health outcomes for black and minority ethnic men are significantly poorer than for white men (Sabo, 2005). There is considerable variation in health status both within and between nations. An example of an interesting cross-national comparison is Hearn et al.'s paper (2002b), which notes that life expectancy of men in Europe ranges from 75 in Norway and Italy to only 60 in the Russian Federation. Another generally relevant aspect of the gender order is the social construction of the male body (see Watson, 2000). Ideas about bodily normativity (see Gerschick, 2005) in a given culture have an impact on what men do with their bodies – both men who conform to expected norms and those who do not, such as men with physical impairments. We refer later in the chapter to some specific issues to do with bodily normativity, such as the use of steroids and men's negotiation of disability and masculinity.

As noted above, various authors, including Schofield et al. (2000) and Sabo (2005), have noted that just as it is not helpful to only consider 'men' as a sex group and ignore differences between men, we also gain little by considering 'men's health' in isolation from women. There are important relational effects to take into account. Sabo gives the example of a man who is suffering from depression beating his wife and in turn causing her physical injury and trauma. He further makes connections between men's behaviour (and sexual health) and the global sex trade, with its devastating consequences for the health of women involved.

So, the most general message from social science must be that gender matters – gendered identities and gendered practices are bound up with health and illness – but that we cannot separate out 'men' as a sex group. We have to apply a relational approach, both in terms of the inter-relationship between men and women and in terms of the differences between men, especially class and ethnicity.

Masculinity, physical health and disability: some key issues

In this part of the chapter we have selected some key health issues where gendered practices are connected with poor outcomes in (some) men. We also discuss some issues with regard to disability. The list of issues below is of course not exhaustive. Our aim is simply to illustrate with rather more specific examples some of the general social factors summarised above. In places we comment on how policy is developing in response to recognised 'men's health' problems. We start the section by identifying some particularly vulnerable groups of men.

Vulnerable groups of men

We noted above the importance to health of intersecting social inequalities. The extent of the exposure of socially excluded young men to health risks leads Gary Barker (2005) to use the phrase 'dying to be men' in the title of his book. His book concentrates on young men in Brazil in particular and the constellation of an environment of extreme poverty and violence with aspirations to masculine dominance – what Connell (1995) describes as marginalised masculinity. While economically and socially successful men in the West can encounter health risks from the stress associated with their success and denial of weakness, there is a strong argument that health problems are in fact concentrated in poorer men.

In addition, there is a range of particular categories of men who could be seen as more vulnerable to physical health problems and physical impairment. Sabo (2005) mentions, among others, adolescent males, boys with ADHD, infertile men, male athletes, male caregivers, black and minority ethnic men and prisoners. (While there are some specific physical health issues for gay and bisexual men, the most obvious health inequalities relevant to sexual minorities are in the area of mental health, so we deal more substantially with gay and bisexual men in the next chapter.) McLeod and Bywaters (2000) set out a manifesto for social work to engage with health inequalities. Gender only really features in the book in relation to the oppression of women, which is part of the picture and perhaps a social and political priority, but is not the whole story. There is certainly potential for the general approach recommended by McLeod and Bywaters to be applied to work with men. In responding to men's health problems with social interventions it is vital that differences between men are understood and there is a real attempt to make interventions appropriate for the specific groups of men who are most affected.

Diet and coronary heart disease

Men are especially prone to coronary heart disease and this tendency is often linked to poor diets. Gendered cultural associations with food types vary considerably across cultural contexts and there is a well-developed anthropological literature on gendered food (see Counihan, 1999). In the West, whereas sweet foods have a stronger association with femininity – there is of course a complex and ambivalent relationship there – there is an association between some masculinities and fatty savoury foods. The British cooked breakfast is a good example of a meal that is associated with, among other things, manual (and manly) working-class labour and a hangover cure for men.

There are in fact particular risks of heart disease in working-class men. The UK New Labour government has made some attempt to combine gender and class dimensions in tackling men's ill health, stressing the difference between the social classes in male life expectancy (Department of Health, 1998). Working-class men have been especially targeted for some health promotion initiatives, via settings such as working men's clubs and sports clubs. Although targeted initiatives are broadly to be welcomed, as Scourfield and Drakeford (2002) have observed, some of the government rhetoric could be seen as implying that working-class men are themselves responsible for social inequalities in health because of their unhealthy lifestyles.

Not all commentators agree about the need for men to take more personal responsibility for their diets. Monaghan, in a controversial piece, notes that we live in a society where 'fat may as well be a four-letter word' (2005: 305). He sees government claims that two-thirds of men in Britain are obese as alarmist. He challenges the assumptions on which much policy is based, pointing out that in fact the science is contested and not all researchers agree on a link between obesity and excess mortality. He points out the danger of policy makers and professionals being 'blinded by fat' (p. 312) so that obesity becomes a target for individualistic interventions, rather than focusing efforts on social and economic marginalisation.

Although we should question the basis of simplistic policy assumptions, there is an issue with men and diet. Gough and Conner's (2006) qualitative research on barriers to healthy eating in men is interesting to note here. They report two main barriers to healthy eating in men. The first is a cynicism about healthy eating campaigns: a resistance to what were seen as confusing mixed messages and a reclaiming of personal choice in diet. Gough and Conner interpret these views in the context of dominant masculine ideologies of rationality and autonomy. The second barrier is a view that healthy food is less tasty, less filling and associated with a feminised 'fussiness'. The men spoke of eating a consciously healthy diet only after developing health problems associated with diet. Gough and Conner observe that their data reveal 'conventional masculinities which specify autonomous decision-making over obedience to authority, and plenitude and fulfillment over scarcity and self-denial' (p. 393). These cultural factors pose a major challenge to health promotion.

Sexual health

Men's sexual health is of course a very wide topic indeed, covering men's role in conception, sexually transmitted diseases and erectile dysfunction, among other issues. There has to be consideration of sexual diversity, but also of the historical association of hegemonic masculinity with sexual dominance and the enduring idea of innate male sexual 'drive'. As Plummer observes in the quotation below, the cultural significance of the penis is central to many aspects of men's sexuality. This cultural significance becomes deeply personal and embodied for individual men:

> there are worries of size when it is flaccid, worries of it not getting erect quickly enough, worries of it being too erect too often, worries of it not staying erect long enough, and severe worries of it not getting erect at all. Then there are problems of ejaculation – of coming too soon, too late, or not at all. Often, all of this is significant because men let it – or make it – define their masculinity. (Plummer, 2005: 179–180)

Along with the cultural emphasis on the penis goes a cultural prioritisation of penetrative sex, for heterosexual men in particular (though penetration also has [gendered] symbolic importance for many gay men). This is problematic in many ways, not least of which being heterosexual women's lack of satisfaction from the assumption that sex begins and ends with penetration. For men, there are many problems associated with the cultural centrality of the penis and penetrative sex. Many of the implications are for men's mental health. Potts et al. (2006) note the increased biomedicalisation of male sexuality since the advent of drugs such as Viagra (sildenafil citrate) and Cialis (tadalafil). The 'success stories' surrounding these drugs provide challenges for men with erectile difficulties who do not find a 'solution' that way. Potts et al. describe, however, ways in which their research participants – older men – were able to construct sexual alternatives to 'rock hard' erections and frequent penetration; non-penetrative alternatives which were often seen as 'better' sex than earlier in their lives.

Diversity among men is important to consider throughout the field of men's health, as noted several times in this chapter. There is potential for gay and bisexual men to experience sexual health inequalities. Gay and bisexual men continue to be the group at greatest risk of acquiring HIV (UK Gay Men's Health Network, 2004). In terms of the politics of men's health, the debates on the de-gaying and re-gaying of AIDS (see King, 1993) are worth noting. King explains how professionals and volunteers in the HIV field worked hard in the late 1980s and early 1990s to get across the message that anyone could contract HIV through unsafe practices and that it was unprotected sex or shared needles that posed risks rather than so-called 'high risk groups'. This was a conscious attempt at an anti-discriminatory strategy and was understandable in the context of homophobic discourse of gay men being to blame for HIV/AIDS. However, activists such as Gay Men Fighting AIDS set out to challenge this consensus among those working in care and prevention on the basis that by far the greatest number of people getting ill and dying were in fact gay men. These activists called for resources to be targeted on gay men as it was they who were at greatest risk. This debate illustrates both the inequalities between men in terms of sexual health and also the political complexity of interventions.

Practice Example – Sexual health promotion (from the UK)

First, we describe a project that originates in the work of FPA Cymru in South Wales on sexual health in young men. The programme is described and activities reproduced in Blake and Laxton (1998). As originally envisaged, groups for young men would be facilitated by youth and community workers, though they could in fact be instigated by a range of health and social welfare practitioners and in a range of different contexts. Group programmes could be based in youth clubs or in schools or potentially in contexts where a specific group of young people come together, such as young offenders being supervised in the community. The manual (Blake and Laxton, 1998) is geared towards professionals, though in fact this approach has also been used in South Wales within a peer education model whereby credible young people who are themselves at the same age and stage as group participants are trained to facilitate groups (see Shiner, 1999). The aim is to approach sexual health education in a different way from what is traditional. Rather than safer sex being seen as the responsibility of young women, relying on their assertiveness (after training) to say no to certain kinds of advances from men, the idea here is to encourage responsible sexual behaviour in young men. While the programmes are in theory accessible to all and certainly tackle issues of sexual diversity, the assumption is that heterosexual young men, usually thought to be beyond sexual education, are the main target of the intervention.

The *Strides* manual is an example of an extremely practical resource for practice, insofar as it includes examples of exercises that in many cases can literally be photocopied and used as they are. The manual is not prescriptive about content as the aim is for the young men to set the agenda, coming up with a list of issues they would like to discuss. As an example, on p. 20 of the manual there is a hypothetical eight-session programme for 16–17-year-olds. The topics of the eight sessions include building an agenda, sex and language, condoms, attitudes and values, being a man, supporting a friend and abortion. The manual then goes on to give many examples of actual exercises that can be used with young men to stimulate discussion. One example is the exercise 'What is a man?' (pp. 58–59). This involves participants in turn choosing a statement card and placing it on a continuum that ranges from 'acceptable' to 'unacceptable'. A similar exercise also features in Davidson (1990). In fact the Davidson book takes a similar approach to sexual health promotion in many respects. Some of the statement cards in the *Strides* manual relate to behaviours which are assumed to be traditional in terms of mainstream masculinity and some are non-traditional:

- to cry in public
- to not drink alcohol
- to not want to have sex
- to fancy other men
- to talk to friends about emotions
- to not play football
- to not use condoms
- to use a sexual health service
- to have female friends
- to have a sexual relationship
- to be a young father

This sexual health project cannot very straightforwardly be positioned within Messner's (1997) terrain of the politics of masculinity, largely because the exercises provided by Blake and Laxton are simply meant to prompt open discussion of sexuality, rather than to lead towards some kind of 'party line' that will be taken on board by participants. However, despite the role of the exercises being to open things up, rather than close them down, these are not somehow neutral and ideology-free. There is of course an implicit agenda in all youth work, whatever its practitioners might claim (see Hall

(Continued)

(Continued)

et al., 2000). It is clear from the introduction to the *Strides* manual that behind the ostensibly neutral exercises and session plans there are messages of anti-discrimination, such as respect for young women and acceptance of sexual diversity; practical health promotion teaching such as correct condom use and testicular self-examination; messages about men needing to be aware of emotion, and to give emotional support to others. Whilst the authors protest that 'young men are not a problem, they do not need to be changed' (Blake and Laxton, 1998: 10), in fact most of the discussion material does in fact aim towards change in mainstream young (heterosexual) British masculinity. Insofar as there is some recognition of the difficulties young men can face and also material which seeks to question inequalities between men and women, we would have to position the intervention roughly in-between Messner's two poles of the 'costs of masculinity' and the 'privileges of men'. There is some recognition of diversity between men, but this is not the project's prime focus.

Practice Example – Sexual health promotion (from South Africa)

Our second example of a sexual health intervention is from the global South. The Men as Partners programme (see Mehta et al., 2004; Engender Health, 2006) has operated in Pakistan, Nepal, Bolivia and South Africa. The programme has evolved so as to incorporate an understanding of 'the negative ways in which the unequal balance of power between men and women can play out' (Mehta et al., 2004: 90), so the aims would suggest a focus on the privileges of masculinity. That said, the approach to men has varied considerably according to local and national context and there is great concern both to start from a realistic point and to have objectives for change that are achievable, rather than idealistic. In Nepal, men of all ages have been trained as peer educators (a parallel with the work in South Wales described above). In Pakistan, where the basically patriarchal social structure makes engagement of men essential, in addition to adverts on rickshaws and enlisting of religious leaders, barbers have been trained to give information on reproductive health. Across the whole programme, there is training for service providers on their organisational and attitudinal barriers to engaging men, difficulties staff might face in working with men and clinical issues to do with men's sexual and reproductive health.

To focus in a bit more detail on this programme's work, the South African work described by Mehta et al. (2004) builds on the anti-apartheid movement's considerable history of male involvement in grass-roots organisations. Educational workshops have been run for men via trade unions, prisons, sports clubs, religious organisations and community halls. These workshops, often residential, are wide-ranging and structured around the overarching theme of the impact of gender roles on men's lives. Topics include parenting, sexual health, violence, the social impact of AIDS and men's potential for

(Continued)

improving quality of life in communities. As an illustration of how there is an ongoing emphasis on gender inequality, Mehta et al. note that an activity about HIV will explore the ways in which gender roles can increase the likelihood that men will engage in unsafe sex, or deter men from playing an active role in caring for and supporting those left chronically ill from AIDS (Mehta et al., 2004: 95).

Mehta et al. also note that over time there has been an increasing emphasis on the connections between gender and poverty. There is now recognition of the interaction of poverty and masculinity. When these authors note that poverty can undermine 'traditional male identities', leading to 'practices that can put both them and their partners at risk' (p. 95), the implication is a discourse of the masculine deficit (see Chapter 3), namely that men in poverty are denied traditional masculine privilege and this inevitably leads to social problems where men behave badly because of frustration at the lack of access to expected social and cultural resources.

Male cancer

As well as having some tendency to greater risk of cancers that affect both sexes (e.g., duodenal cancer and lung cancer) men are uniquely affected by prostate and testicular cancer. Clearly it is not helpful to emphasise too much the sex-specific nature of cancers. This can serve to direct attention away from other much more prevalent diseases in men and women (Nancarrow Clarke, 2004). However, given the cultural emphasis noted above on the centrality of male genitals to sexuality, there are some important psycho-social implications of these cancers and we briefly mention some relevant social research here.

In keeping with the study by Potts et al. reported above, other studies have found that traditional associations of male genitals with essentialised masculinity can coexist with discourse which resists this connection. Gurevich et al. (2004) interviewed men who had been treated for testicular cancer. A connection between testicular integrity and masculinity was simultaneously reinforced and disavowed by their research participants. They found the men to be constructing their illness as 'alternately inhibiting and enhancing masculinity and sexuality' so that, as the authors put it, 'disruption interpolates with potentiality' (p. 1600). Some of the men asked the question 'does it make me less of a man?' themselves during the interviews and most expected it to be asked by others, leading Gurevich et al. to conceptualise a discourse of 'precarious masculinity'. The men's ways of dealing with this included a discourse of anatomical superfluousness; the missing testicle being 'that little part down there' which does not affect your claim to manhood (p. 1603). Despite this disavowal, it is difficult to avoid the issue of anatomy in relation to gender/sex. The authors note that 'the preoccupation with the significance of the testicular to the masculine is always already present, even in the negation of the link' (p. 1603). Similarly, when Oliffe (2005) interviewed men about their experience of 'impotence' after treatment by prostatectomy, there was a general underlying assumption of phallocentric sex. However, there was a considerable diversity of strategies for redefining masculinity without the ability to achieve an erection and many of the men found that intimacy was achieved without penetrative sex.

There is, perhaps, some evidence for optimism from these qualitative studies – the ability of these men to conceive of intimacy with partners that does not rely on a hegemonic phallocentric model, although of course we do not hear in these studies from those men who are unwilling to discuss their circumstances with a researcher and might be experiencing greater difficulties to do with identity and intimacy. There is certainly need for emotional support for men with prostate or testicular cancer. It is a recurring theme within research on men's health that many men find it hard to look for help and support. Harrison et al.'s research (1995) found that men and women with cancer were equally likely to have confided a principal concern in others but men tended to use only one confidante while women typically made use of a fairly wide circle of family and friends, using a greater number of confidantes overall. Some success has been reported of the use of cancer support groups. For example, the Man to Man prostate cancer project in Florida found very high levels of satisfaction, though participants were mainly white and middle class (Coreil and Behal, 1999).

Substance misuse

Substance misuse could perhaps equally feature under the heading of mental health; often, problematic use of drugs or alcohol is accompanied by mental health problems or could be seen as *caused* by emotional difficulties that fall within the umbrella term of 'mental health'. However, we deal with the issue in this chapter because substance misuse can clearly also lead to physical health difficulties. We simply note here some important gendered cultural associations of drugs and alcohol insofar as they are relevant to social interventions with men.

Cultures of drugs and alcohol vary enormously across national and local context. So it is expected in Mediterranean countries, for example, that alcohol will be drunk by both sexes (though rather more by men) but generally in moderation. Alcohol is forbidden for Muslims, but Somali and Yemeni men are generally expected to take part in the communal chewing of khat, a stimulant that can produce feelings of euphoria, though the drug is illegal in the US, for example. There is enormous cultural variation here. It could be crudely claimed that some of the poorest countries of the world cultivate the raw materials for drugs that are used in some of the richest countries of the world, though disproportionately by the poorest people in these countries.

In large parts of the West there is an association between hedonistic excess with alcohol and certain masculinities. There are cultural age restrictions, insofar as boys below their mid teens and frail older men would not be expected to drink to excess, and also exceptions allowed for men whose religious faith prohibits this behaviour, but for most men, and especially most young men, an occasional or even fairly regular bout of binge drinking is expected. In some contexts, drinking to excess is associated with public spectacle, which can include violence (Tomsen, 1997). For marginalised men in particular there can be an association between substance misuse and crime against property or person (see Collison, 1996). In some gendered sub-cultures there can be acceptance and indeed expectation of the use of illegal drugs, including physically risky practices such as self-injecting. For all kinds of substances there can be an expectation of endurance, that you have to keep up with the boys. Not keeping up, not indulging in excess, is often feminised. So there is a very real sense in which health risks are associated with culturally authoritative ways of achieving manhood in many social contexts in many countries. Although gay sexuality is an aspect of what Connell (1995) calls 'subordinated masculinity', and not culturally authoritative, some continuity can be seen here. King and McKeown (2003) report high levels of alcohol and drug misuse among lesbian, gay and bisexual (LGB) people (especially young people). These authors associate this phenomenon with the dominance of pubs and clubs in LGB social life because there are few safe places to meet.

In many cultural contexts, men use drugs and alcohol as a means of coping with emotional difficulties where women are more likely to use other means of support, including talking to friends. We return to this theme in the next chapter when dealing with men's social capital. Furthermore, the use of drugs or alcohol as a coping mechanism can be gendered, as can be seen by Ettorre and Riska's (2001) research in Finland on users of tranquillisers such as benzodiazepines. They report that men saw themselves (and were seen by women) as using tranquillisers to cope with external stress in the public sphere such as work, whereas women were regarded as naturally emotional and susceptible to the problem of 'nerves' in relation to emotional labour, resulting in them feeling the need for the drugs.

There is an association between substance misuse and body modification. Klein (1993) documents the use of steroids by bodybuilders, as part of what he sees as a project to create a hyper-masculine body shape (note Monaghan's, 2001, very different interpretation of bodybuilding sub-culture). Monaghan et al. (2000) describe how 'steroid-using bodybuilders present themselves as radically different from "hedonistic" drug users' (paragraph 3.2) and tend to consciously distance themselves from those they see as 'junkies', including a general disapproval of Nubain, an opiate drug which has been associated with the bodybuilding scene.

Negotiating disability and masculinity

We should first note that the term 'disability' has been transformed by the 'social model', which sees the disablement coming from society's reaction to people with 'impairments'. According to the social model of disability it is the failure of non-disabled people to allow a wheelchair user into mainstream employment, education and social interaction that disables, rather than the physical impairment that means they need a wheelchair for help with mobility. Notwithstanding critiques of the social model and debates about it (Williams, 2001; Swain et al., 2004), it is a useful approach for understanding how the experience of physical disability can be socially gendered insofar as the emphasis lies with the societal reaction to the body rather than with the body itself.

The first thing to note is that, as Tom Shakespeare puts it,

> Much of what is traditionally associated with masculinity is in fact generative of impairment: fast cars, violence and war, excessive consumption, recklessness and risk, sport, and work, all contribute towards injury and illness. (Shakespeare, 1999: 57)

This is an important point, and health and social care professionals often encounter men who have become impaired as adults, for example through a road traffic accident, and are having to adjust to a disabled life. However, there is a risk that over-emphasising this insight could suggest that men bring impairments on themselves, or could even imply the view – so heavily criticised by the disability movement – that impairment is a personal tragedy.

A second point to note is that because many aspects of hegemonic masculinity are so closely associated with the body – ideal models include powerful sporting and military bodies – then a physically impaired man can potentially be feminised through his lack of participation in dominant bodily practices. For example, Shakespeare observes that central to popular filmic imagery of disabled men is the wheelchair-'bound' war veteran whose problems of coming to terms with his tragedy are 'crystallised in the context of impotency or sexual incapacity' (p. 50).

Of course, real disabled lives are much more complicated than the above comments suggest. There isn't one template of masculinity to which all disabled men aspire (and inevitably fail to conform to). For one thing, some men with physical impairments do in fact succeed in conventional masculine terms – perhaps in a successful career or sporting achievement. Also, there is considerable negotiation and contestation surrounding gender identities and gender practices (Shakespeare, 1999).

Gerschick and Miller (1995) have specifically studied the ways in which physically impaired men see themselves as men. They describe three dominant strategies. The first of these they call 'reformulation', which involves a negotiation and redefinition of masculinity according to the men's own terms, with a moulding together of traditional aspects and their current realities. The second strategy Gershick and Miller term 'reliance'. This involves working with very traditional notions of masculinity and of still attempting to meet these expectations. The third strategy they term 'rejection'. This entails the creation of alternative masculinities within oppositional sub-cultures. The first strategy – reformulation – was said to be successful insofar as these men were content with their situations. The second strategy of reliance on traditional notions of masculinity could lead to difficulties for the men, as the problems they face are ultimately located not within society but in their own impaired bodies that almost inevitably fail to conform to hegemonic masculine ideals. The third strategy leads to a radical rejection of conventional gender identity, with these men typically receiving support and affirmation through the alternative value system of the disability movement. There are perhaps lessons for health and social care professionals here in terms of understanding the gender identities available to disabled men and the kinds of support systems which might be most helpful.

Conclusion: an overview of interventions

Courtenay's (2003) review concludes that most health problems that can be seen as specific to men are modifiable because the causes are primarily social and behavioural rather than biologically innate. While we recognise the complex interaction between biological and psycho-social dimensions, as we noted at the start of this chapter, it is certainly true that the scope of the professional interventions we are addressing in this book is social and behavioural. We here briefly outline the main categories of intervention in relation to physical health and disability – both in terms of prevention and care. To take up again some concerns raised in Chapter 3, there are important questions to be asked about dedicated interventions with men: Which men are they aimed at? What messages do they give about masculinity? What implications do they have for women? It should be noted that there is relatively little evidence yet as to what works in health interventions for men. It is a relatively new policy and practice area and there has therefore been little research to date on the outcomes of different approaches.

The range of practice models reviewed in Chapters 4 and 5 can apply here. Community-based interventions will often be appropriate for health promotion. As noted above when discussing diet, the more proactive campaigns tend to try and reach men via traditional homo-social locations such as pubs and sports clubs. This is certainly a way to target a large number of men and possibly some of these will be men who are generally reluctant to present themselves to any kind of formal service for advice or treatment. It is a mistake, of course, to assume that reaching out to such locations will reach a diverse group of men. These institutions tend to have strong homogenising sub-cultures, which restrict the kinds of masculinities that would be welcome there. Some advertising campaigns have used quite traditional tough male images to attract the attention of reluctant men – for example, racing drivers and rock musicians. We should be aware that these images could be alienating for men who do not fit with these traditional stereotyped images.

Groupwork can be used for therapy, education and support. Some extended examples of education groups in the field of sexual health promotion were outlined earlier in this chapter. Face-to-face support groups have worked in some social contexts (see the examples earlier in the chapter of largely white middle-class cancer support groups and also gay men's groups in response to HIV). Online group support has mushroomed in recent years and some have claimed this to be particularly important for men who may feel more comfortable with a more distant form of communication as well as perhaps being more comfortable with technology. Broom's (2005) research on men coping with prostate cancer is interesting here. He supports the idea that men can be less inhibited online and can find intimacy easier through this medium than in face-to-face contact. However, he also observes that some men found computers problematic in this regard, and did not trust the honesty of online interactions.

Individual approaches may be appropriate for some people. For example, cognitive-behavioural or psycho-dynamic models might be appropriate for men who need individualised therapeutic programmes to help them with some aspect of behavioural change that is associated with their physical health. An example would be counselling for a problem drinker whose level of alcohol intake was causing serious risks to his bodily well-being (see Barber, 2002, on working with addicted individuals). This example of problem drinking, crossing as it does physical and mental health, leads nicely on to our next chapter, which focuses on men's mental health.

Key texts

Courtenay, W.H. (2000) 'Constructions of masculinity and their influence on men's well-being: a theory of gender and health', *Social Science and Medicine*, 50, 1385–1401.

A wide-ranging introduction to the topic by a key author in the field.

Kirby, R.S., Carson, C.C., Kirby, M.G. and Farah, R.N. (eds) (2004) *Men's Health,* second edition, London: Taylor & Francis.

An example of a textbook (there are several now on the market) that gives a summary of relevant clinical knowledge. This one is designed for primary care practitioners.

Sabo, D. (2005) 'The study of masculinities and men's health', in M. Kimmel, J. Hearn and R.W. Connell (eds) *Handbook of Studies on Men and Masculinities*, London: Sage, pp. 326–352.

An excellent and up-to-date overview of the topic which negotiates the politics of men's health very successfully.

9 Men's Mental Health

Introduction

As Coyle and Morgan-Sykes (1998) have noted with reference to their research on the media, an important dimension within popular discourse on contemporary gender relations is that of the 'crisis' in men's mental health. This discourse links the supposed increase in mental health problems in men – especially the increase in young men's suicides in the West – with social changes in the wake of second-wave feminism. We should note at the outset that we believe a critical distance is essential here and that a wholesale swallowing of crude simplifications about social and psychological trends can lead to interventions which are not helpful because they are not attuned to the subtleties of lived experience. Gendered mental health and illness is a complex psycho-social phenomenon that requires careful consideration.

Mental health is defined by the World Health Organisation as

a state of well-being in which the individual realizes his or her own abilities, can cope with the normal stresses of life, can work productively and fruitfully, and is able to make a contribution to his or her community. (WHO, 2001: 1)

This chapter discusses mental well-being as thus broadly defined, as well as some familiar manifestations of 'mental illness' or 'mental disorder'. Rather than being structured around diagnoses, most of the chapter is structured around aspects of socially constructed gender identities and gendered practices that have implications for men's mental health. This is not a gesture to distance ourselves from medical models of mental illness. In fact we would see a lot of potential for a bio-psycho-social model of mental illness, as originally outlined by Engel (1977; see also Pritchard, 2006, for an application of this model to mental health social work). Rather, we structure the chapter around social issues both because of the stated scope of this book and because there is a great deal of overlap between medical categories of mental disorder in terms of gendered social influences.

To begin with, we should summarise some of the key gender differences in prevalence of mental health problems. The survey of adult psychiatric morbidity in the UK conducted by Singleton et al. (2001) found the following key sex differences (bearing in mind various methodological caveats [see pp. 8ff. of their report]):

- All neurotic disorders except panic were more prevalent in women
- Personality disorders were more often found in men than in women
- The rates of probable psychotic disorder were slightly higher for men than for women
- The prevalence of hazardous drinking was higher among men than among women (with considerable variation by age)
- Use of illicit drugs was more common in men than women and within this group men were twice as likely as women to be assessed as drug dependent.

As for children, Green et al.'s (2005) survey found that, overall, boys were more likely to have a mental disorder than girls. Conduct disorders and hyperkinetic disorders (a similar category to ADHD) were particularly prevalent among boys in comparison with the rates for girls. The prevalence of emotional disorders, including anxiety and depression, was similar in boys and girls of school age.

The gendered nature of suicidal behaviour is well documented, with men more likely than women to kill themselves and women more likely to self-harm in ways that are not fatal. Suicide rates for men are much higher than for women across the Western world in general (Cantor, 2000), though on a global level there are exceptions, with China being the most notable one (Cheng and Lee, 2000). There has been considerable concern about the rising rate of suicide in younger men in many Western countries (see Gunnell et al., 2003, on trends in suicide rates in England and Wales). In fact the most recent figures for England show suicide rates in young men to be decreasing since 1998, although the gender gap in suicide rates is still largest in the 20–29 age group (NIMHE, 2006).

As noted repeatedly in the previous chapter in relation to physical health and disability, when we talk about men's mental health we emphatically do not mean that the mental health of all men is in jeopardy because of their sex. Some associations can in fact be made between male privilege (social, cultural, economic) and good mental health. For both men and women there are associations of poorer mental health and social class, with a disproportionate number of those with mental disorders having lower incomes, being unemployed and having fewer educational qualifications (Singleton et al., 2001). It seems that for suicide there may possibly be differential associations of sex and social class. Hawton et al. (2001) have found a significant association between area-based deprivation and suicide in men, though not in women. There is of course considerable global variation in understandings of and experience of mental health problems. There is also significant and complex variation within countries in terms of ethnicity (see for example Nazroo, 1997). For example, indigenous people have severe mental health problems in comparison with the white population in the United States, Canada, Australia and New Zealand and also higher rates of suicide (Hunter and Harvey, 2002).

It is important to avoid simplistic judgements about men's mental health. Various pitfalls abound. It was noted earlier in the book that there is a tendency across policy debates about men and social problems for a political polarisation where men are either regarded purely as victims or purely as perpetrators. Different lobbies within the policy arena tend to discuss men's mental health exclusively in terms of either one discourse or the other. So suicidal men tend to be constructed simply as social victims, although for some men, killing themselves is connected to control of others in some way (Scourfield, 2005). In contrast, one of the dominant messages within UK government policy on Mental Health Act reform is the danger posed by mentally ill men to public safety, obscuring both the non-violent behaviour of most men with mental health problems and the powerful connection between mainstream 'sane' masculinity and violence. As we have argued consistently in this book so far, in the field of gendered mental health there is a pressing need to consider both diversity and power relations. Not all men are the same, but neither are they all different. In analysing practice and in designing interventions in health care and social welfare we need to acknowledge the diversity of men and the diversity of men's mental health issues as well as the social–political dimension of masculinities and power.

A final observation to note by way of introduction to this chapter is that Singleton et al.'s (2001) British morbidity study also shows the considerable overlap between physical and mental health problems. This emphasises the point made in the previous chapter that the body–mind dualism reflected in our chapter structure, although a necessary pragmatic organisation of the book's material, is flawed in some respects.

Aspects of gender that affect men's mental health

There are arguably aspects of mental health that are relevant to being a man per se. There are, for example, essentialist psychoanalytical arguments about the impact of sex difference on object relations (see, for example, Jukes, 1994). There are also arguments about distinctive male biology – the idea of the 'male brain' (for example Baron-Cohen, 2004). We do not dwell on these universalist ideas here, but simply note they have been expressed. Rather we structure the chapter around aspects of men's socially constructed gendered identities and gendered practices, which have implications for some specific mental health problems in particular groups of men, as well as having broader implications for men more generally.

Dealing with emotion

The term 'emotional illiteracy' (Goleman, 1995) has been used to characterise the limited emotional repertoires that many men develop (Kindlon and Thompson, 2000). When we consider mental and emotional well-being, not only can having a limited emotional repertoire cause problems in relationships with others (and not just intimate others), but it also has the potential to cause profound tensions when situations arise that provoke emotional reactions that have not previously been encountered. It can lead to a failure to cope with a range of challenges, such as, for example, relationship breakdown. Of course, limited emotional repertoires are learned because they facilitate social dominance, so we should not simply interpret this phenomenon through a discourse of victimhood. Emotional distance enables men to stay focused on achievement in the public sphere. It allows competition to thrive.

It is not the case that men are prohibited from displaying emotion. There are social circumstances where an outward display of emotion is acceptable. In many cultural contexts it is expected that men would cry in extreme circumstances, such as in the immediate aftermath of bereavement. Although there is an association between certain forms of masculinity and emotional reserve, anger is a generally acceptable emotion for men in many situations. In fact some commentators have observed that it can often be the only socially acceptable emotion for men. The masculine 'emotional funnel' has been noted by Kilmartin (2005), among others. The funnel image describes how a wide range of emotions that are associated with vulnerability in men are converted into the narrow outlet of anger, as this is the only emotion that is culturally sanctioned.

A connected issue is that of the tendency for men to lack empathy. Baron-Cohen (2002) sees this is a natural state for men, on the basis of research which reveals profound differences between men's and women's brains in empathising and systematising. In terms of diagnoses, lack of empathy is an issue for personality disorders, autism and suicidal behaviour. Baron-Cohen sees the 'mind-blindness' of people with autism – an inability to appreciate that other people have a mental life – as one manifestation of what he calls the 'extreme male brain'. The traits that psychiatry uses to characterise 'personality disorder' include a lack of empathy. Recognising that this and other traits connected with personality disorder are not necessarily aberrations, but could be seen as consistent with aspects of hegemonic masculinity, Taylor (2006:

172) notes that Hare's commonly used checklist for psychopathy (a similar category to the newer label of 'dangerous and severe personality disorder') 'identifies traits consistent with patriarchal capitalist mores'. As for suicide, while most people who kill themselves are undoubtedly in extreme distress, they inevitably have to decide that the need to kill themselves overrides concern about the effect of their actions on those who are left behind. Hawton's (2000) review paper notes that having a child is a protective factor against suicide for women but not for men, for example. If a man is to succeed in hegemonic gender terms, he not only needs to develop a limited emotional range but also a distance from the emotions of others. Empathy is a challenge to aspects of hegemonic masculinity.

Asking for help

Gendered patterns of help-seeking are relevant to both physical and mental health. As Galdas et al. (2005) note in their review paper on the topic, although there is a well-known tendency for men not to seek professional help for physical and mental health problems, we should not make blanket assumptions about this phenomenon, since some studies on some specific illnesses have found no gender difference and there are also plenty of gaps in the evidence, especially in relation to diversity of masculinities. As for mental health more specifically, there is a wealth of evidence that women are more likely than men to ask for help in the face of mental and emotional problems (see for example Rickwood and Braithwaite, 1994; Boldero and Fallon, 1995) and have more positive attitudes towards asking for help (Cohen, 1999). Moreover, when men do seek help, they seem to do so as a result of a more negative perception of their mental health as well as having more severe mental health problems before they will access help sources (Albizu-Garciaa et al., 2001). The failure to seek help clearly needs to be understood in the context of the social construction of the 'stronger sex' (Courtenay, 2000). Autonomy is an important aspect of the ideology of hegemonic masculinity. A desire for autonomy can mean a failure to reach out and connect with others when you might need them and can also lead to problems in dealing with dependency. Perhaps men who experience mental health problems following relationship breakdown find it difficult to negotiate the tensions between the discourses of love/dependency and masculine autonomy.

Men's reluctance to seek help is not universal, however, and it is important to recognise the impact of the diversity of masculinities on help-seeking behaviour. For example, Greenland et al. (2007) found men with more traditionally feminine characteristics more likely to disclose distress. Zeldow and Greenberg (1980) measured the relationships between men's attitudes to women and help-seeking and found 'conservatives' more likely to seek a physician's advice for a physical problem and 'liberals' more negative towards physicians, whereas for use of psychotherapy the association with attitudes to women was reversed. Franks and Medforth (2005) studied young people's use of helplines and found some diversity of help-seeking according to ethnicity and sexuality. For example, the Muslim helpline they looked at had equal numbers of men and women callers. In addition, O'Brien et al.'s (2005) qualitative research found that the men they spoke to were willing to put aside their usual reluctance and seek professional help when it might help to preserve a valued aspect of masculinity, such as sexual performance.

It is clearly not the case that most men are socially unconnected to other men and women. Sixsmith and Boneham's (2002) qualitative research on men's social capital in relation to health is illuminating. The men they interviewed certainly did have social contacts, but they were less likely than women to participate in community institutions where they might get access to information on health and they did not tend to discuss health problems with other men. Where they did discuss health problems, this was usually with women they thought could be trusted not to ridicule them or to gossip. Given the greater reluctance of men to share emotional problems, Hawton (2000) calls into question the straightforward use of 'talking therapies' with men. Rather, he suggests that men may respond to more practical problem-solving techniques before talking is introduced (see also Chapter 5). Franks and Medforth (2005) note, however, that we should not assume action-oriented help is appropriate for all young men, since counselling as a first step may be more appropriate for young gay men wanting to come out, who may be nervous about confidentiality and trust.

Practice Example – Web-based suicide prevention for young men

The Campaign Against Living Miserably (CALM) website is specifically aimed at young men (see http://www.thecalmzone.net). The high quality design (with a choice of three 'skins') looks credible and the content is designed to appeal to young men as lads with fairly traditional attitudes and interests – features on sport and music for example. There is online live help every evening and a phone-line through the night. There is accessible written information and links on a range of issues that might cause distress. CALM is an example of an open-access service that aims to reach the kinds of young men who might be difficult to engage in counselling. It consciously targets what are thought to be mainstream interests in this group and does not have any transformational aims. Its approach has two possible pitfalls. The first is that it will not appeal to young men who

(Continued)

(Continued)

do not fit the mainstream youth culture niche created – no service can cater for everyone. The second is that, unfortunately, and perhaps as part of the effort to attract hard-to-reach men in distress, there are occasional indicators on the CALM website of antagonism towards some political advances for women – for example an article arguing that men are victims of the divorce system (CALM website as accessed in June 2006). The politics of masculinity are fraught and it is difficult to avoid offending some people whatever your approach. Our argument would be, however, that it is possible to appeal to traditional and pre- (or anti-) feminist men without either on the one hand preaching to them from the very start about their opinions and attitudes and thus alienating them or on the other hand reinforcing their suspicion of women by reproducing anti-feminist discourse.

Compulsory heterosexuality

An aspect of hegemonic masculinity which is connected to the issue of men's reluctance to engage with other men about emotional and psychological problems is that of compulsory heterosexuality (a term coined by Adrienne Rich, 1980). According to Connell (1995) and making allowances for global cultural variation (Herdt, 1981), gay sexual identity is most often socially subordinated within a hierarchy of masculinities. Kimmel (1994) argues that homophobia – fear of intimacy with other men – is the 'animating condition' (p. 135) of hegemonic masculinity in the USA.

The UK Gay Men's Health Network's report (2004) shows that it is in the domain of mental health, more than physical health, that health inequalities according to sexual identity can be found. King and McKeown's (2003) research found that although social support and physical health were found to be similar to those of heterosexuals, gay and bisexual men experienced higher levels of psychological distress, with bisexual men having higher levels of distress than gay men. Although there does not seem to be evidence of higher levels of major psychiatric illness in transgender adults, Bockting et al. (2006) note that there are specific issues of psycho-social stress for this group, including the experience of trans-phobia and poverty resulting from discrimination in employment. This is also a group historically under-served by health care services. The history of psychiatry is not a proud one of course in relation to sexual diversity. Taylor (2006: 152) notes that psychiatry has 'functioned historically as an instrument of hegemonic masculinity' and the pathologising of homosexuality is a clear example of this. Smith et al. (2004) spoke to men in the UK who had experienced a range of physiological and psychological interventions designed to change sexual orientation from the 1950s onwards and they catalogue the distressing effect these treatments had on most of these men.

There has been increasing concern expressed about suicide in lesbian, gay, bisexual and transgender (LGBT) populations in recent years. It is very difficult to know how many men who kill themselves are gay or bisexual, because we cannot expect same-sex relationships necessarily to be made public. However, some epidemiologists have found markedly higher levels of suicidal ideation in the gay and bisexual population than the heterosexual population (see, for example, Remafedi et al., 1998; Fergusson et al., 1999). Caution is needed against an alarmist approach that denies the pleasure experienced by LGBT men and women (Harwood and Rasmussen, 2004), but although there is indeed potential for the insensitive handling of gay suicidality to become pathologising, we would argue that this issue should be taken seriously. We would further argue that the elevated suicide risk for gay and bisexual men needs to be understood in the context of victimisation and psychological pressure in what is still arguably a context of compulsory heterosexuality.

Practice Example – Youth work with gay and bisexual men

PACE is a London-based lesbian and gay mental health and counselling project. Its services include advocacy, counselling, group-work, employment advice, youth work and training. OutZone is a youth service for gay and bisexual men and those who are unsure, which has a weekly group meeting on a Friday evening. It presents itself as offering an alternative social network to the commercial gay scene. The target age group is under-25s. The website (www.outzone.org) tells us that the average age of men attending the OutZone group meeting is 17–22, but there is no lower age limit. OutZone is not overtly about mental health, but the prevention of mental health problems and suicide is a key part of the rationale for setting up the service. There is clearly an assumption in providing the service that a social forum for young men who are gay or bisexual, or think they might be, which is outside of the pressure of the pub- and club-based scene, will provide an opportunity for support and the bolstering of self-esteem and threatened identities. One group member writes on the website, 'Before I came along to OutZone I felt powerless, nervous and unsure, but now I feel confident, calm and normal'. There is a deliberate strategy of running separate services for men and women. The website explains that 'our members have found that they are able to address gender specific issues more effectively and openly in single gender groups'.

Dominant constructions of heterosexuality are also deeply problematic for the mental health of men and women. Jukes (1994) argues that misogyny is an inevitable outcome of men's psychological development, because of processes bound up with the mother–son relationship. McLean (1996: 17) notes that femininity is simultaneously 'both intensely desirable and repulsive' to heterosexual men. The detailed case studies of young men discussed by McQueen and Henwood (2002) point to the significance of male–female dualism to psychological distress. These authors observe that the only alternative subject position to 'normal' masculinity is to be like a woman, which means being vulnerable and is therefore to be avoided. The male–female dualism itself could therefore be seen as creating distress.

Rationality

Objective rationality, unclouded by a complicating emotional dimension, has been associated with dominant ideas about masculinity since the Enlightenment (Seidler, 1994). As Scourfield (2005) observes, if we take Foucault's (1967) conceptualisation of mental illness as all about the regulation of rationality, and apply this more broadly to include 'newer' disorders, such as depression (as does Busfield, 1996), then diagnosed mental illness in men can be understood as subordinated masculinity, where rationality is hegemonic. Taylor's (2006) book is probably the first sociologically-oriented monograph specifically focused on men's mental health. He discusses in some detail the association between masculinity and rationality, ultimately arguing that mental breakdown can be seen as a positive challenge to this and other aspects of hegemony masculinity. Taylor's stance is anti-psychiatry. He is sympathetic with feminist and post-modernist critiques of the epistemology, scientific method and professional power on which psychiatry is based and he also critiques psychiatry from the position of a section of the mental health survivor movement.

There certainly are historical associations between rationality and hegemonic masculinity, but we do not want to imply a wholesale criticism of rationality on our part. We see an important role for medical science in helping people who suffer with mental ill health. It is important, however, to note how men who are seen as irrational might come to be stigmatised in part because of their sex and gendered assumptions about what kind of mental life is appropriate for men. The hegemony of rationality also has its part to play in men's denial of emotion and of reluctance to take part in talking therapies (Bennett, 1995). It is also the case that an over-emphasis on scientific epistemology means ruling out any consideration of the unconscious, which we would see as a crucial aspect of understanding men's mental health.

Control

There are issues here both of self-control and the desire to control others. To first consider control of others, there are important issues to note in connection with suicide in men. A very small minority of men who kill themselves do so after they have killed others, and there is also the phenomenon of suicide being used to threaten and punish in the context of relationship breakdown. There is some evidence from Polk (1994) of two types of murder-suicides: jealousy killings, which are primarily homicides, and 'depression plus control', where suicide is the primary aim but a woman's partner is murdered as the man's possession. Apart from murder-suicides, which are a very small proportion of all suicides, the other issue where control of others is central is the cases of men who kill themselves primarily as a punishment for someone else, more often than not a woman partner. It seems, however, that this issue of suicide as punishment is rather under-researched. There is general agreement from the quantitative research on suicide that men are more brittle to relationship breakdown than are women. The suicidal act may not be directly intended to itself have a controlling impact on an ex-partner, but the loss of control (or even loss of honour – see pp. 143–144) that comes with the end of the relationship may be too hard to bear for some men.

There is also the important issue of *self*-control to consider in relation to men's mental health. Although there are culturally acceptable exceptions, such as (in much, though not all, of the Western world) alcohol-fuelled hedonistic excess in young men, men in most cultures are generally expected to be experts in self-control. This means again that mental breakdown goes clearly against the hegemonic masculine norm if it is seen to involve loss of emotional and mental control. Even when in distress, a level of control is often expected of men. So there is, for example, a connection between masculinity and a 'decisive' 'successful' suicide, whereas a 'failed' suicide attempt is feminised and these cultural scripts affect how we respond to suicide, how deaths get interpreted by coroners and how potentially suicidal people think about what kinds of options are open to them (Canetto and Sakinofsky, 1998).

As noted above, Taylor (2006) argues that the vulnerability revealed in mental and emotional distress can disrupt hegemonic masculinity, and the tyranny of self-control is one of the targets in his sights:

> While it is important not to romanticise the torments (or ecstatic insights) of solitary madness, it seems that the experience of being in crisis can sometimes become an alchemical process during which the protective but distorting rigidity of masculinity is transmuted, and hegemonic habits abandoned. (Taylor, 2006: 158)

While noting Taylor's argument, it is also possible that aspects of hegemonic masculinity might be harnessed to aid recovery. Emslie et al. (2006) interviewed men with depression and focused on the gendered character of their talk about illness and recovery. They stress the heterogeneity of the men's strategies for recovery and in particular refute any blanket assumption that men with depression will not talk about it. The most common strategy for recovery they encountered was the incorporation of values from hegemonic masculinity into narratives, namely the importance of struggle for control, regaining strength and feeling responsible for others. Given how this strategy dominated their (admittedly small) sample, Emslie et al. note it is important for practitioners to be aware of and respond to it. They also note, however, the risks involved in such a strategy, since, for example, some men used the argument about responsibility for others to justify suicide on the grounds that their families would be 'better off without them' or they saw suicide as a way of regaining control. An approach of consciously and pragmatically using the values of hegemonic masculinity in therapy, but expanding them to incorporate more health-promoting and less traditionally masculine behaviour was outlined in Chapter 3 (pp. 35–36).

Violence and abuse

Violence and abusive behaviour are relevant to men both as perpetrators and as victims. Since Chapter 7 was devoted to the issue of violent and abusive men, we simply note at this point that men are far more often the perpetrators of violence of all kinds than are women. In some circumstances, in some sub-cultures or at particular stages of the life course, violence can be of central importance to a man's identity (see Barker, 2005, on gangs, for example). For young men whose response to social and economic disadvantage fits with the discursive practices that Connell (1995) labels as 'marginalised masculinity', aggressive behaviour may in fact be 'one of the few powerful subject positions available' (McQueen and Henwood, 2002: 1505).

Being victims of violence can also cause mental health problems in men of course. There is increasing knowledge now about not just women but also of men as sexual abuse survivors and the gendered dimension of their experience and appropriate service responses (Hooper and Warwick, 2006). To cite just one study, Walker et al. (2005) compared male victims of rape with a control group and found the victims of rape to have much poorer psychological functioning, lower self-worth and lower self-esteem. There were also suicide attempts associated with lack of treatment after the assault and the men reported avoidance of the incident. Mental health problems have been associated with the experience of war. On the one hand, war trauma is generally regarded as a gender-appropriate form of distress, as these men are seen to have endured a very tough masculine ordeal (e.g., US Vietnam veterans). However, when it is a sub-section of military men who become mentally ill, this group may be stigmatised and indeed feminised (e.g., British victims of shell-shock in World War I).

Violent and abusive men may themselves have poor mental health. Pritchard and King (2004) found a very high risk of suicide among perpetrators of intra- and extra-familial sexual abuse (25 and 78 times the general population suicide rate, respectively). The UK *National Confidential Inquiry into Suicide and Homicide by People with Mental Illness* (Appleby, 2001) reported that around a third of all perpetrators of homicide had a diagnosed mental disorder; the most common being alcohol dependence, drug dependence and personality disorder. However, as Taylor (2006) observes, medicalisation of violent men can serve to mitigate their behaviour, as if a diagnosis removes all responsibility for abusiveness.

Taylor further argues that although male violence and its impacts have to be taken seriously, mentally ill men tend to be unfairly labelled as necessarily dangerous. In fact he sees the undue linkage of madness and violence as oppressive to men in distress. He notes that it is black men in particular who are associated in media imagery with mentally disordered violence, further pathologising black masculinity. It is certainly true that the risk climate described by Rose involves a disproportionate association of black men among the mentally disordered 'predatory monsters' who threaten our 'seductive fantasies of ideal communities within which individuals and families are free to live an untroubled life of freedom' (Rose, 2002: 231).

Male honour

Although 'honour' is not a term strongly associated with Western modernity, there are some important points to be made here. We are taking 'honour' to mean the loss of the *status* and *regard* associated with hegemonic masculinity. One domain where loss of honour occurs is in relation to work. The breadwinner ethic is still strong, at least in the UK, despite shifting ideas about fatherhood: there is still a strong association between work and masculinity. Occupational problems seem to be a major factor in men's suicides in the West. As the systematic review by Platt and Hawton (2000) reveals, it is fairly clear that unemployment is linked to suicide risk in men.

More generally, there are indications from several studies that social comparison is an issue for men. Barber's (2001) analysis of mental health in seven countries shows that young men's suicide does not support a connection between suicide and 'absolute misery'. Indeed, higher rates of male suicide were associated with higher levels of psychological adjustment among the general adolescent population. Barber's interpretation is that men tend to make social comparisons with the situations of others by perceiving themselves to be not as happy as their peers. He proposes a 'relative misery' hypothesis where suicidality is related to upward social comparison which requires a level of psychological maladjustment and the perception that one is worse off than one's peers. This fits to some extent with Crawford and Prince's (1999) research showing that there is greater pressure placed on men who are still out of work when general employment levels are improving. These studies suggest perhaps the essentially competitive character of hegemonic masculinity. It is not only important to be successful in culturally approved ways, but also to see oneself as successful in relation to others. There has been considerable comment in recent years on happiness in a context of social inequality. Lane (2000) writes of the declining happiness in affluent Western countries, despite continual improvement in material quality of life. Lane argues that it is not money that makes people happy but relationships with friends and family. Given the historical importance of the breadwinner ethic to hegemonic masculinity, this is perhaps particularly relevant to men and to social interventions with men in distress.

Overview of interventions

Chapter 4 gave a general overview of therapeutic approaches to working with men as individuals. This range of approaches has been used to promote mental health in men. Men have historically dominated the talking therapies (Taylor, 2006) with many approaches having failed to question their in-built assumptions about gender, but critical approaches to gender identities and gendered practices have also evolved in recent years. Critics of cognitive therapy might claim that in reinforcing rationality its challenge to unhealthy aspects of hegemonic masculinity is limited. Nonetheless, as we see in the example below from Mahalik (2005), challenging cognitive distortions that lead to problems for men's mental health as well as problems for women and children has an important place within interventions. There are also examples of narrative (see McLean et al., 1996) and psychoanalytic approaches (see Frosh, 1994) that explicitly deal with masculinity.

Practice Example – Cognitive therapy for men

Mahalik (2005) describes cognitive therapeutic interventions with men which make masculinity explicit. Table 9.1 lists the strategies he recommends for moving men from modes of thinking which narrow down emotions and behaviour to expanded options that improve their own well-being and their relationships with others. The cognitive strategies as described by Mahalik tend to assume he is dealing with heterosexual clients, which to an extent limits their usefulness to a more diverse group of men. However, many of the points he makes about traditional notions of masculinity would arguably apply to the majority of men, regardless of sexual identity.

Table 9.1   Sample masculine-gender-related distortions and potential rational responses to nine masculinity injunctions

Masculine injunction	Masculine-gender-related cognitive distortion	Potential rational response
Winning	Winning isn't everything, it's the only thing	*History review*: Although it feels good to win I've lost a lot of friends and alienated a lot of people in the process. *Illogicalness*: Does it make any sense to have to win all the time when I can never relax and enjoy it? *Personal experiment*: Try to support other people in their efforts on the playing field or in the workplace and see how I feel about helping someone else instead of trying to beat him or her.
Emotional control	If I share my feelings with others, people will think I'm a sissy	*History review*: By controlling my emotions I protect myself from hurt, but I usually feel isolated and lonely. *Illogicalness*: Everybody has feelings. Does it make sense to ignore such an important part of myself? *Personal experiment*: As soon as I get home at night I'll try sharing some affection with my partner and children. After a couple of weeks, I'll see how they view me.
Risk taking	Taking dangerous risks helps me to prove myself	*History review*: Taking dangerous risks in the past has led to significant physical and financial costs. *Illogicalness*: Does it make sense to put the most important things in life (such as health) in jeopardy for no good reason? *Personal experiment*: Try out some pro-social risky behaviour that is challenging but doesn't risk life and limb (such as speaking out for a cause I believe in).
Violence	If you walk away from a fight you are a coward	*History review*: There certainly have been times in the past that I've been involved in violence and regretted it. *Illogicalness*: Does it make sense to risk jail because I'm angry at someone right now? *Personal experiment*: Talk to friends I respect who do not get into fights and check out how they deal with things when they're angry.

(Continued)

Table 9.1 *(Continued)*

Masculine injunction	Masculine-gender-related cognitive distortion	Potential rational response
Playboy	Without many sexual partners I won't feel fulfilled	*History review:* Although I feel excitement when I'm out at bars trying to seduce new partners, it becomes tiresome always trying to 'score'. *Illogicalness:* It does not make sense to be working so hard at maintaining my playboy image when I feel no real future, security or satisfaction in moving from one partner to another. *Personal experiment:* I might try staying with a partner who makes me feel good about myself and shares similar values, or try talking to people without trying to seduce them.
Self-reliance	Asking for help is a sign of failure	*History review:* I've helped others and not thought them inept. It has also saved me a lot of time, energy and frustration when I have gotten help in the past. *Illogicalness:* It is not practical to put such pressures on my time and energies to do everything myself. Also, it isolates me from my significant others (for example, partners and children). *Personal experiment:* Approach others whom I have some trust in to share the work. Work on some mutual tasks or chores. Approach others for help and see the effect that receiving help has on interpersonal and work effectiveness.
Primacy of work	Work must take priority over family and all other commitments or I'll never be successful	*History review:* I remember my father working all the time and feeling that I'd rather have him home more than have another car. *Illogicalness:* I try to take care of my family and be the good provider by working long hours, but is it worth it when I feel like a stranger with my significant others? *Personal experiment:* Leave work-related issues at work, especially on Friday evenings, and spend weekends with family activities. Set aside time for activities with significant others such as evening school events or special occasions.

(Continued)

Table 9.1 (Continued)

Masculine injunction	Masculine-gender-related cognitive distortion	Potential rational response
Disdain of homosexuals	I cannot be close to other men or people will think I am homosexual	*History review*: I shared chum experiences and friendships with childhood male friends and my family valued them. *Illogicalness*: It is not rational to view my close male friendships as being abnormal when they help and support me in times of need and crisis. *Personal experiment*: Try to remain rational about my male relationships and not to distort the warm feelings I might have for these important men in my life.
Physical toughness	I should always be tough as nails	*History review*: Sometimes it would have been better for me to have seen a doctor than to 'tough it out'. *Illogicalness*: Sure I don't want to cry over every bump and bruise, but does it make sense to have to take every physical blow that comes my way? *Personal experiment*: Try treating my body more carefully and see if it performs better for me.

Reproduced from Mahalik (2005: 224–227).

Various groupwork approaches (see Chapter 5) have also developed that make masculinity explicit and promote positive mental health. Men's groups have started up in day centres where women's groups have run for years, once it dawns on staff and service users that there are also gender issues to be discussed that have particular relevance for men. Taylor (2006) recommends 'critical life story research' as an approach that can be adapted for the promotion of men's mental health. This is avowedly action research, which involves participants telling their own stories and deconstructing their identities as men in the context of a men's group with a pro-feminist orientation (Taylor refers to the work of Jackson [1990] and Pease [2000]).

As for community interventions, there is a wide range of potential strategies that might have a positive impact on men's mental health. There is considerable potential, which is only just being recognised, for health promotion initiatives to be specifically targeted on men, although there is very little evidence yet on the effectiveness of such targeted initiatives (Harden et al., 2002). It might initially appear a common-sense assumption that any scheme focused on social and economic regeneration could have a positive impact on men's mental health. However, again very little is known about the effect of regeneration on mental health and what we do know does not immediately confirm an optimistic hypothesis (Huxley et al., 2004). Furthermore, the connection between economic position and mental health in men is equivocal, if the effect of unemployment on young men's mental health is worse where quality of life in the surrounding community is improving. The policy implication of this may not simply be the generation of more jobs, although full employment would probably improve mental health. There may also be an issue of men's priorities and expectations and a need to expand their options to include additional or alternative roles outside the formal labour market, such as caring for children or adult relatives.

Key texts

Good, G.E. and Brooks, G.R. (eds) *The New Handbook of Psychotherapy and Counseling with Men*, San Francisco: Jossey Bass.

Also recommended as key reading for Chapter 4, this is especially relevant to mental health, covering a wide range of theoretical orientations and different groups of men.

Pritchard, C. (2006) *Mental Health Social Work*, London: Routledge.

Has little to say specifically about men, but is an excellent guide to evidence-based practice in mental health within a bio-psycho-social model and therefore relevant to more than just social workers.

Taylor, B. (2006) *Responding to Men in Crisis. Masculinities, Distress and the Post-modern Political Landscape*, London: Routledge.

A theoretically sophisticated psycho-social analysis of mental and emotional distress in men, written by a 'survivor' of the mental health system.

10 Working with Boys and Young Men

Introduction

A range of anxieties are currently attached to boys and young men by a variety of constituencies: government, media and parents. Research with boys themselves suggests that many are well aware of how they are seen as problematic and resent this categorisation. Frosh et al. note that:

> sometimes this feeds into a vicious cycle in which they enact delinquencies as a way of expressing the anger which they feel: very frequently it is visible in an attitude of antagonism towards adults, who are seen as disparaging boys and favouring girls all the time. (2002: 260)

In this chapter we explore the differing theoretical traditions that have sought to understand boys and young men, paying particular attention to developments within the literature on masculinities. We interrogate the literature on 'risk', as this notion seems central to a variety of discussions about and practices with boys and young men. Finally, we address practice issues. A note about terminology and coverage: we recognise that there is a considerable and impressive literature on age and identity issues in relation to terms such as 'child', 'adolescent' and 'youth' (as well as 'risk', which is a key theme of this chapter). Therefore in this chapter we draw both on gender-specific material – how boys and young men are thought about and dealt with, particularly for policy and practice purposes – and also on theory and research that is not gender-specific but relates to childhood, youth, risk and social policy more generally. Where we deal with this non-gendered material we try to point out the more specific relevant issues for work with boys and young men.

Overview: biology, culture, diversity and multiplicity

Much of the theoretical analysis advanced in Chapter 2 is of relevance when considering how boys and young men are thought about and dealt with. For example, we have already noted the centrality to classical psychoanalysis of girls and boys developing a differentiated developmental trajectory. We will return to psychoanalytic approaches later in this section when considering contemporary developments in research on boys and masculinities. However, there are specific issues in relation to 'adolescence' and life transitions, which are the subject of an extensive literature, and we should make note of these at this point. Griffin (2004) notes the importance of Hall (1904), an early American psychologist who is credited with 'discovering adolescence'.

> The concept of 'adolescence' introduced a biological foundation to notions of age stages by constructing the shift away from childhood around the onset of puberty. However vague this moment of transition might be in practice (especially for boys), Hall's text clarified the representation of adolescence as a category which was biologically determined, shaped and driven by physiological imperatives that were profoundly sexual. His work provided a point of coalescence for emerging notions about young people and society in general, reflecting economic, political and ideological changes in Western societies at that time. (Griffin, 2004: 11)

While such notions of adolescence were seen by some as primarily a consequence of changes in class relations, Griffin notes that the 'discovery' of adolescence marked a key moment for gender, sexuality, 'race' and nationality, with the emerging ideology marking out a biologically determined norm of youthful behaviour and appearance which was male, white, Anglo, middle class and heterosexual.

Hall's identification of puberty as the defining moment of adolescence for young people provided a firm biological foundation for the influential model of adolescence as a period of 'storm and stress'. This model posited adolescence as a time of inevitable hormonal upheaval and stress, which required both a degree of freedom and the development of internal and external controls. It is argued that the legacy of arguments about the need for young people to have the freedom to discover their potential and the need for external and internal control still endures in professional discourses and practices (Sharland, 2006).

More generally, the work of Erikson (1968) on the life cycle has been influential, particularly in social work and child development studies. As Hockey and James (2004) note, while his model of eight stages of psychological development did encompass the entire life course, from birth through to death, the first six stages were argued to occur before the individual reached adulthood. It was 'as if, after childhood, change, growth and development ceased, that is until the onslaught wrought upon the physical body by entry into extreme old age' (Hockey and James, 2004: 36). However, they do point out the importance of recognising that many of the disciplines concerned with elaborating ideas on the life cycle originated in the late nineteenth century when only 5 per cent of the population were over 65. Despite very different demographic conditions pertaining today, the belief endures that the early years of a child's life are formative in establishing a stable identity.

The notion of clear and orderly transitions within the life cycle is strongly contested today, particularly in the context of recognising diversity in the category 'young people' or adolescents. Moreover, complex and uneven economic, cultural and policy developments render it deeply unhelpful to talk of clear and linear individual trajectories. These issues will be returned to throughout the chapter.

Developmental psychology has become the subject of considerable criticism during the past decade, particularly from sociologists who, according to Smart et al. (2001), have 'discovered' children. This literature, while particularly critical of developmental psychology, is also critical of sociological practices that render children invisibles: for example, research into family life which does not engage with children's perspectives and practices. Smart et al. (2001: 2, emphasis in original) claim that a new paradigm has emerged in which 'children are transformed from unfinished projects under adult control to fully social *persons* with the capacity to act, to interact and to influence the social world'. This new paradigm argues that childhood is socially constructed and not a natural or universal state arising from biology. There is, therefore, not one childhood but many: while age may be relevant, difference in terms of gender, ethnicity, culture, socio-economic status and so on becomes important. Moreover, the model of the 'embryonic child', which comes from developmental psychology, constructs children as 'weak, fragile, unstable, irrational, deficient and capricious in both mind and body' (Smart et al., 2001: 3) and operates with a stages notion of children's development which emphasises their potential rather than their being and justifies both constraint and control by adults so that the potential is appropriately realised.

There are many criticisms to be made of key claims from within this 'new' sociological paradigm (see, for example, Fawcett et al., 2004). However, for our purposes here it is important just to note that its emergence has been part of a growing movement towards research *with* children and young people rather than research *about* them. While there is a history of research with boys, particularly around schooling and masculinities, the emergence of a more child-centred research paradigm supports the expansion and widening of research with boys. Indeed, the ESRC Children 5–16 research programme, which was strongly rooted in this paradigm, facilitated very valuable research projects on a range of topics such as boys and masculinities and gender and help-seeking, which will be explored further below. Not only has there been a clear shift towards research with children and young people, but the growth in interest in children's rights has supported the development of practices that seek to include children and young people as participants in the development of policies and in their own care. It is also important to note that critiques of developmental psychology feed into a growing concern to interrogate received wisdom about children, childhood and child development within the literature directed at practitioners such as social workers (Taylor, 2004). This opens up possibilities within practice, as yet under-developed, for rethinking and unsettling accepted notions of what is normative development for both boys and girls.

In theorising and research in the field of youth studies there has been a longstanding engagement with youth, culture and identity, which in the UK particularly had its roots in the work of the Centre for Contemporary Cultural Studies, at the University of Birmingham in the 1970s, but which appears to have been influential in many countries. Shildrick and MacDonald (2006) offer an overview of this legacy but also of contemporary debates. Of interest is their argument that celebratory and post-modern theories have eclipsed previous concerns with exploring the role of social divisions and inequalities in young people's lives, but that such divisions and inequalities remain crucial. The research evidence offered below supports this argument.

As already indicated, there is now a considerable research literature into the 'making of boys into men'. While Connell (2000) argues that the school is probably not the key influence in the formation of masculinity for most men, considerable research has been done with boys in school in order to explore issues around masculinity/masculinities. Some (such as Mac AnGhaill, 1994) have been explicitly about the contribution of schooling to the 'making of men', while others are more concerned with taking the opportunity to talk to boys in school in relation to an under-explored area, such as emerging masculinities in early teenage years (Frosh et al., 2002).

Willis's 1977 study is recognised as a classic. It focused on white working-class young men making the transition from school to work. His description of an anti-school sub-culture has, over the years, been less engaged with than 'his more incidental but equally well observed description of a dominant form of youthful working-class masculinity at the time' (O'Donnell and Sharpe, 2000: 43). Willis argued that working-class boys became men by imitating the toughness, solidarity and physicality they associated with their fathers. Although it speaks of a time when jobs of a particular kind were available to working-class men, O'Donnell and Sharpe argue from their research that:

Toughness and posturing are common characteristics of this form of masculinity which remains an influential model of youthful 'laddishness' as we enter a new millennium, even though it has frequently become wholly detached from the culture of industrial manual labour in which it developed. (O'Donnell and Sharpe, 2000: 43)

O'Donnell and Sharpe (2000: 9–10), researching in London in the 1990s, situate their work specifically within the literature on masculinities that has emerged since Willis to explore how 15- and 16-year-old boys come to see themselves in relation to the 'gender order' of society – that is, to the structure and culture of gender inequality at the macro level. They also studied 'the gender regimes' in the schools to see how these affected boys' understandings of gender and masculinity. They identify multiple masculinities, with a key issue being the powerful role that ethnic identification, sometimes of a nationalist or neo-nationalist intensity, played in the way masculinities were articulated and expressed. While they noted the phenomena of 'borrowing' and 'imitation' and considered the possibility that these could evolve into ethnic or cultural hybridity, which could render racism redundant, that day seemed a long way off. A key point which will be returned to further in the section on practice is that there was a gap between the aims and cultures of schools and teachers and what was meaningful to some students, which did not necessarily lead to conflict but meant that teachers and, to some extent, other authority figures and students lived in different although overlapping worlds.

While O'Donnell and Sharpe's work falls within a mainstream sociological tradition of qualitative research, Frosh et al.'s research marks a departure and is in line with a growth of interest in combining social constructionist and psychoanalytic perspectives (see, for example, Jefferson, 1994, and Chapter 2 of this book). This interest arises from a concern to understand diversity between boys and men in terms of how they engage with discourses around masculinities, which for some obliges an engagement with psychoanalysis and the use of a particular research method and interpretive framework (Frosh et al., 2002). Their interviews were carried out in a 'clinical style', with a second interview being used to explore repetitions, contradictions and gaps. Analysis included reflections on process – including explorations of 'countertransference' aspects of the encounter. This approach marked a departure from the assumption of one unitary rational subject (interviewer) interviewing another (boy) in a transparent process where shared meanings are transferred in an unproblematic way.

What is of considerable interest in terms of our concerns is their finding about how well the boys were able to engage with the interviewer and the richness and depth of the accounts they could give. They ponder on this in the light of everyday assumptions about boys that suggest their inability to show psychological depth and sophistication. They suggest that many have very few encounters with people who really listen to them in an active, sympathetic and thoughtful way. We will return to this further in our section on practice.

In common with other research, Frosh et al. found the existence of multiple masculinities, with considerable policing of boys by other boys, particularly in relation to homosexuality. In line with a view of gender as relational and performative they also did research with girls both in order to avoid the 'over-gendering of boys' but also to explore how girls construct masculinities.

Currently, a wealth of research is being conducted on boys and young men that takes gender seriously. To give just a few examples of published papers, recent research has included studies of spirituality and masculinity in Australia (Engebretson, 2006); gender, young people's leisure and risk-taking behaviours in Scotland (Sweeting and West, 2003); and masculinities, femininities, car culture and auto theft in Canada (O'Connor and Kelly, 2006). As we suggested in Chapter 2, Connell's work on hegemonic masculinity has proved extremely influential and provides the theoretical frame for many of these studies. While summarising such diverse studies is problematic, it is worth observing that change, continuity, fixity and fluidity appear to be features of both young men's and women's lives today.

Alongside the above literature, less theoretically informed research has emerged in the last decades, often in response to particular concerns about boys and their 'troubles'. There is considerable information available in relation to gender and health that confirm concerns about significantly higher mortality rates for boys than girls alongside less apparent willingness to access services (see Chapters 8 and 9). There has been considerable attention paid to educational achievement in the UK, with the improvement in girls' performance at GCSE level. Such issues periodically engender a wave of popular angst in relation to what has become constructed as a crisis of boys' failures (often at specific times such as when examination results are announced). What does the research tell us about what is going on? O'Donnell and Sharpe note that the introduction in England and Wales of a compulsory national curriculum up to age 16 reduced but by no means removed gendered subject specialisation (this pattern of gendered subject specialisation has been central to gendered occupational segregation and inequality), which now tends to occur most sharply at A-level (exams taken at 18) and degree level. It has been middle-class men studying at post-compulsory education level that most benefit from the gendered pattern of subject specialisation and its consequences for career choice. Young working-class boys have been less likely than middle-class boys to remain in post-compulsory education and more likely than young women of all class origins to leave schools with poor qualifications – these boys are now major failures of the system and this must be understood in the context of changes in capitalism and technology. Those working-class boys who are academically successful can still reap the gender dividend from studying subjects associated with masculine rationality such as the natural sciences, computer studies or business studies.

In their research O'Donnell and Sharpe found an appreciation among the boys of the link between educational attainment and career achievement and of harsh economic realities, but, in practice, attitudes of indifference and antagonism to education persisted among white working-class boys. In terms of ethnicity there were considerable differences with boys of Indian and East Asian origins much more focused on developing career strategies than African-Caribbean boys.

Researchers differ on the extent to which boys perceive themselves to be discriminated against by teachers. The boys in O'Donnell and Sharpe's study did think that girls were treated more favourably than boys and that the boys were constructed as more troublesome, although the boys also saw their behaviour as actually being more troublesome. They did not see a significant amount of negative labelling occurring. By contrast, in Frosh et al.'s study, many of the boys expressed resentment about what they perceived to be teachers' preference for, and favouritism towards, girls, and this bias was perceived to be racialised, with black boys seen as more unfairly punished than white boys. Before moving away from this issue of educational attainment it is important to note that a zero-sum analysis is often presented – girls are doing better *and therefore* boys are doing worse. However, working-class boys have been doing badly for some time. There are clear patterns of disadvantage among minority ethnic groups. Furthermore, 50 per cent of girls do not achieve what is accepted as the standard for successful attainment at GCSE level (O'Donnell and Sharpe, 2000).

There is evidence in much of the research on boys that while there are multiple masculinities, boys police each other in relation to a favoured form of 'hegemonic masculinity', which actively militates against being seen as 'a swot'. The importance of exploring constructions of masculinity and interrogating them in the context of class and ethnicity is clear here. In particular, bodily practices, especially in the context of sport, seem central to many boys' constructions of masculinity.

In terms of patterns of child maltreatment, the most robust research evidence would suggest that gender differences are particularly significant in relation to sexual abuse, with known males disproportionately responsible for such maltreatment with victims predominantly – but by no means exclusively – girls (Cawson et al., 2000). Research into patterns of help-seeking for all forms of maltreatment indicates reluctance on the part of boys to seek out others either formally or informally (Featherstone and Evans, 2004). There is a general picture from research evidence that fathers tend not to be considered a strong source of support by either boys or girls. Boys in one study on bullying (Hallett et al., 2003) suggested that fathers could put unhelpful pressure on them 'not to be wimps'. In Frosh et al.'s study boys spoke poignantly about losses in their lives and either a poor or no relationship with their father was often an issue.

To summarise this overview, there has been a general move towards placing children's and young people's voices at the centre of research. This has co-incided with the growth of interest in research on masculinities. Theoretically, social constructionism has been very strongly represented but there is also an interest in combining social constructionist and psychoanalytic perspectives. In the next section we turn to explore writings from within a 'risk' paradigm that supplements the research evidence mentioned above and draws us into relevant policy arenas.

Being at risk and causing risks: theory and policy

The idea of 'youth at risk' appears to be central to current policy discourses and these in turn feed into professional practices. This is not new. Griffin's work over the years (2004) shows how central gendered and racialised mes-sages have been to 'representations of the young'; representations which have been profoundly influential at a range of levels, including policy making. Griffin suggests that in general young men, especially if they are working class and black, have been especially likely to be the focus of representations and policies that operate within a 'youth as trouble discourse' (that is, causing risks to others) and young women have been more likely to be dealt with under the 'youth in trouble' discourse (or youth *at* risk). However, of contemporary interest is a more general narrative of risk and uncertainty that Sharland (2006) interrogates in relation to notions of 'youth at risk'. While she does not employ a gendered analysis, her overview of more general discussions around risk offers a useful framework for us to integrate a gendered analysis.

Beck's book *Risk Society* (1992) continues to be seminal in discussions of risk. Beck argued that we are in a phase of modern society that could be termed 'reflexive modernisation', in which 'social, political, economic and individual risks increasingly tend to escape the institutions for monitoring and protection in society' (1992: 5). As Webb (2006) notes, in relation to social work, the concept of risk is connected to that of reflexivity because new anxieties about risks and the failure of experts and institutions to deal with them raise critical questions about current practices:

> The difficulties of building rule systems which can not only shape and control problems but enable their prediction is a symbol of our being in a risk society.

Unanticipated system failures combined with the public's persistent belief that governments should have anticipated them causes a spiralling of public fears about knowns and unknowns alike. (Webb, 2006: 2)

Politicians consistently construct themselves as controlling risks in a context of both widespread anxiety and scepticism and, as Sharland notes, currently appear particularly concerned to prevent young people from taking or being exposed to risks. The specific risks which Sharland identifies are, we would suggest, strongly linked to the imperatives of constructing a 'social investment state'. We will explain this notion of the social investment state briefly. In many Western countries the perceived challenges of globalisation have prompted a rethinking of the operation of the welfare state. In Canada and the UK currently it is argued that a 'social investment' state is being constructed (see Lister, 2006, for an overall exploration of this). A key aspect is that of investing in children, particularly in the early years, and there has been an expansion of early years' provision. While campaigners against child poverty have welcomed the interest in investing in children and the resources that have been attached to this approach, they have also expressed concerns about the following: the focus on children as 'becomings' rather than beings; the paid work-focused and future-oriented model of citizenship; the relative neglect of children who are not seen as such a good investment (e.g., children of asylum seekers); and the eclipse of parents' and in particular mothers' welfare (Lister, 2006: 315).

Fawcett et al. (2004) have suggested that the social investment state approach legitimates certain groups of children being seen as more worthy than others and justifies a focus on particular life stages. There is, for example, now a consensus supported by research that investing in children as early as possible through providing learning and play opportunities and support to their parents is key to countering future economic and social disadvantage. This does not mean that older children are forgotten but they appear much more likely to be demonised and criminalised. This is supported by the emergence of an influential research consensus that unchecked youthful or adolescent anti-social behaviour is the seedbed of a persistent criminal career. As Squires (2006) has outlined, this is partly what has fuelled the considerable policy focus on anti-social behaviour with the emergence of curfews, anti-social behaviour orders and child safety orders. While this is very apparent in parts of the UK at the point of writing, as Younge points out, such developments also emerged under President Clinton in the US in the mid-1990s (*The Guardian*, 12 June 2006).

The gendered implications of anti-social behaviour legislation have been noted by a number of writers. For example, a national study of social landlords' use of legal remedies to control anti-social behaviour revealed the punitive approach taken by both social landlords and the judicial system 'to women-headed households who fail to control boyfriends' and/or teenage sons' behaviour' (Hunter and Nixon, 2001: 395). Similarly, the national evaluation of parenting programmes developed under the Crime and Disorder Act 1998 found that the overwhelming majority of those who attended were mothers (over half of whom were lone mothers) and the children of concern were overwhelmingly boys (Ghate and Ramalla, 2002). In terms of understanding why boys and men may be behaving in such problematic ways, Rodger has argued that what he terms 'rising incivility' can be linked to a generalised reaction formation in the context of a crisis in masculinity in the post-Fordist economy (Rodger, 2006: 133). He suggests there is both an 'infantilist masculinism' and a 'protest masculinism' operating in contemporary youth cultures and gangs.

In relation to involvement in criminal activity more generally, Messerschmidt argues that

> one crucial way (not the only way) to understand the 'making of crime' by men is to analyze 'the making of masculinities'. Of course, men's resources for accomplishing masculinity vary depending on position within class, race, age, and gender relations. These differences are reflected in the salience of particular crimes available as resources for accomplishing masculinity. Accordingly, different crimes are chosen as means for doing masculinity and for distinguishing masculinities from each other in different social settings. (2005: 198)

McNeill (2006) reviews the research on the relationship between desistance from offending and transitions in young men's lives. He notes that earlier research had found that young women tended to stop offending quite abruptly as they left home, formed partnerships and had children, but that the processes for young men were much more elongated, gradual and intermittent. Young men were less likely to achieve independence and those that did leave home, formed partnerships and had children were no more likely to desist than those who did not. He notes that more recent studies have revised these conclusions, suggesting that similar processes of change do indeed occur for some men but that they seem to take longer to kick in; in other words, the assumption of responsibilities in and through intimate relationships and employment does make a difference, but this difference is more notable in men aged 25 years and over. However, it is not just about life changes but the meanings attached to them and, indeed, for McNeill desistance seems 'to reside somewhere in the interface between developing personal maturity, the changing social bonds associated with certain life transitions, and the individual subjective narrative constructions which people ... build around these key events and changes' (pp. 131–132). This will be returned to below in the section on practice as it suggests the importance of practices that can support and facilitate subjective constructions with particular implications for boys.

The other side of the 'risk literature' coin lies in the concerns of writers such as Beck (1992) and Giddens (1991) with how people 'life plan' in a risk society. Giddens has argued that in a post-traditional society the self has become a fluid and reflexive project no longer regulated by external structures and norms. This brings new freedoms and choices. Therapies are among the methodologies being used by people to 'life plan' in the context of such freedoms and choices. There have been ongoing debates within the social work literature about how helpful this type of analysis is in the face of structural inequalities and there have also been debates on whether social workers can facilitate 'life planning' (see Sharland, 2006). However, one does not have to accept Giddens' entire analysis to recognise that in terms of parenting and partnering patterns we are living in complex and changing times. External rules about marriage and gender roles are less invested in and, as Giddens (1992) suggests, boys and men appear less well equipped than girls and women to author their own narratives in a context of gender instability. There is some evidence from research to suggest a 'cultural lag' on the part of boys who appear less attuned than girls to the implications of changing gender and marital patterns for them. This is summed up well by the comments of one boy – Sam – in a study in London in the 1990s (Lees, 1999: 71): 'Sometimes feminism and women's equality is a load of rubbish but mostly it's just important for women. It's their choice really, what they do with their lives. Men have got a little bit to do with it but not much'.

In contemporary contexts the question 'who shall I be?' is inextricably linked with 'how shall I live?' Everyday life therefore becomes open to discussion and negotiation rather than being fixed. Intimate relations are central and are often the terrain for demands by women in relations to men's emotional behaviour (Ferguson, 2003; Featherstone, 2004). Women and girls, as the research on help-seeking suggests, seem more comfortable with and adept at using a range of therapeutic methodologies to 'life plan'. In contrast, recent research with young fathers from a variety of ages and ethnicities in London would suggest that men continue to struggle both to acknowledge and own their own emotionality and to engage in communication with the mothers of their children around emotions (Featherstone and White, 2006).

A further theoretical position on risk comes from the 'governmentality' literature. Based upon the ideas of Foucault, risk here exists not as some external reality but as 'a "calculative rationality" of governance through which particular groups or individuals may be identified as "at risk" or "high risk" and thereby observed, managed, disciplined' (Sharland, 2006: 255). This particular type of analysis is well-rehearsed across the social sciences (see, for example, Parton, 2006). It has been used to interrogate why youth is now constructed as by definition a risky category. Although often too imprecise in its treatment of risky categories, there are insights within this literature which are very helpful; for example, the way that neo-liberal governmentality can incite us to construct ourselves as at risk because of our own behaviour/choices. However, there are complex gender issues here – men and boys have appeared more likely to resist regulation and intervention by certain types of state agencies, such as social work, although arguably this has not always served them well in that their needs have gone unmet (Ferguson, 2003). Girls and mothers, particularly, are incorporated but in ways that mean they may possibly get some of their needs met, but that they are also subject to surveillance (and surveil themselves).

Policy developments in practice

According to Tucker (2004: 207), the climate for work with young people in much of the UK (particularly in the public sector) has changed so fundamentally that there is a need to understand not only the nature of that change, but also how it impacts upon professional work and the identities adopted by individuals and groups. A key issue has been the emergence of services that are targeted and subject to target-setting (Fawcett et al., 2004). Let us look at the youth service as an example. Historically, the youth service has been committed to universal practices (a commitment to work with all young people). Bradford (2005) documents its transformation in England in the last decade. He argues that there has been a fundamental shift from expressive to instrumental functions with traditional youth work seeing itself as having largely expressive purposes (emphasising the possibility of emotional engagement, seeing personal relationships as a 'good' in themselves and offering spaces in which young people can convey and work with their own and others' emotions):

> So-called 'modernisation' in UK public services has entailed a much more instrumental view and the attempt to achieve a 'functional authority' for youth work emphasising its capacity to achieve *particular* goals, a focus on task performance and a pre-occupation with effectiveness and efficiency. (Bradford, 2005: 64, italics in the original)

Bradford argues that youth work has moved into initiatives explicitly designed to manage specific groups of young people, particularly those thought to be at risk. In the social work field, Sharland (2006) argues that there is no generic social work with young people, but only work with young people who are attached to particular categories such as offenders or care leavers.

However, Bradford does argue that policy developments in youth work should be seen as part of another universalising process. The commitment to a pragmatic and technical approach constitutes a move to universal standards and increases the capacity for centralised accountability and control practices within youth work. As he himself recognises, this is impacting on much wider groups of workers than youth workers. There is an attempt more generally to prescribe, which has implications for professional knowledge. Corney (2004), too, reflects on the future of professional youth work education in Australia with the introduction of competency-based training.

As a counterpoint to this gloom there is a growth in interest in critical reflection and reflexivity (see White et al., 2006, for accounts from a range of countries including Germany, Australia, Malta and the UK). Within the field of youth offending, McNeill (2006) argues for the importance of relationships in promoting and sustaining desistance from offending. He suggests that young people conceptualise relationships both as a primary source of the distress they experience and as a key resource in the alleviation of their difficulties. The role of relationships in youthful desistance from offending is likely to be particularly significant, not least because the relational experiences of most young people involved in offending are characterised by disconnection and violation. It is vitally important to young people that they are treated by workers as ordinary human beings and not just as clients – and as whole people rather than as instances of some problem or disorder (McNeil, 2006: 133). As Frosh et al. note, this may be particularly important for boys who, in their experience, commonly experience a lack of 'recognition' as persons (see further discussion below). Particular categories of boys, for example those who become young fathers, can be seen as particularly problematic, although research with a small sample of such boys would suggest that taking on a fatherhood identity in the context of an intimate loving partnership can be central to eschewing former 'reckless' or 'irresponsible' identities (Reeves, 2006).

Practice around gender and masculinity issues

Currently, despite the rich store of theoretical and research literature, there appears to be a depressing lack of attention to gender in the policy and practice literature. For example, in a recent textbook on working with young people, a chapter on groupwork by Payne (2005) completely ignored gender issues in its exploration of content and process issues with a group of boys working on anger management issues. Many academic writings have concentrated on documenting and emphasising sexual violence by boys and men (see the practice example below) but far fewer have tackled the broader question of possibilities for transforming gender relations in mainstream health and social care practice with a wide range of young men.

Practice Example – Working with boys and young men who sexually abuse

Work with boys and young men who sexually abuse others in the UK has typified the divide outlined in this chapter between policies seeking to 'control' deviant groups of young men and ones seeking to view them as 'at risk'. Institutionally, this split is evident in the two sorts of agencies that work with such young people: youth offending teams and child protection services (often within the voluntary sector). Research has shown that this group of young people is heterogenous and diverse in terms of age, ethnicity and disability (Erooga and Masson, 2006). But the vast majority are male. Most treatment services recognise that perhaps half of all these young men have been abused themselves and further that their treatment should take into account developmental needs (e.g., most are still children). There are approximately 186 services for young people who have sexually abused others in the UK. The majority function under the youth offending team structure with children's voluntary organisations providing a substantial number of other services. Not all these services provide direct treatment: some offer assessment and consultation to mainstream statutory teams. Child welfare principles have been emphasised in policies which have made multi-agency collaboration essential (Youth Justice Board, 2004). Although these services emphasise that models designed for adult male sexual abusers cannot be made to 'fit' with this population, the two specialities actually have a lot in common. Thus, assessment formats (Beckett, 2006) consider risk factors such as family background, offending history and cognitive distortions. Treatment interventions have a cognitive-behavioural focus but are often 'softened' by a therapeutic approach combined with involvement of carers and family (Cherry and O'Shea, 2006; O'Callaghan et al., 2006). Curiously, despite the vast majority of perpetrators being male and the obvious links between sexual coercion and the gendered socialisation of boys (Messerschmidt, 2000, 2005), masculinity and masculine stereotypes of sexuality are rarely discussed in the practice literature as themes to be addressed in treatment, or at least not explicitly. However, as Hooper and Warwick (2006) report, there are lively debates about gender issues in many frontline services, including survivors' organisations. Also it may well be that aspects of dominant masculine socialisation are in fact implicitly being addressed in treatment even where they are not named as such.

It is important to note that in work with young men gender can be made explicit in potentially problematic ways. For example, the 'Dads and Lads' programme developed by the YMCA in the UK started from a premise that engaging men and their sons through the medium of football was important in itself but was also a way of encouraging more father involvement. It opened up practice possibilities, but was initially constructed within a frame that did not include any questioning of dominant forms of masculinity, even though the initiative was explicitly targeted at men and boys via a masculinised leisure activity. Indeed, Lloyd (2001) has argued that the early programmes seldom moved beyond a focus on football to discuss parenting issues. A recent evaluation of a second round of this programme would suggest considerable diversity in the activities being developed, including some more positive developments. For example, women and daughters have been involved in many locations and fathers are accessing programmes for a variety of reasons, including a desire to take on more childcare (Bartlett et al., 2006). In addition, an important and much needed resource is being offered to non-resident fathers in one location (see Chapter 6).

Perhaps not surprisingly there has long been interest in providing inputs to boys in schools. For example, the introduction of inputs on domestic violence in the education setting has become popular in recent years. Ellis's (2004) research on education initiatives found that 73 local authorities had programmes in operation in 2004. Frosh et al. are optimistic about the potential within the school setting for offering boys opportunities to discuss complex and difficult issues including those relating to gender, but they advocate for input which is steeped in a commitment to actively listening to boys and according them recognition:

> This kind of recognition is thought within some psychoanalytic theories to be a basic necessity for the emergence of psychological well-being ... that is, seriously acknowledging the existence of others as subjects is a crucial element in producing people who have confidence in their worth and their own capacity for thoughtfulness and positive relationships. (Frosh et al., 2002: 257)

They found that an aspect of their own research format which involved open group discussions with an adult other than a teacher worked well. It required patience to get past the teasing and 'cussing' but it seemed to allow new avenues for boys to think about redressing the distortions produced by the constraints of hegemonic masculinity. They suggest that this method could be used more widely and reflect on the merits or otherwise of boys-only groups. They suggest the importance of not reproducing self-fulfilling prophecies in relation to boys in groups, although they also acknowledge the difficulties that can arise, with boys continuing their policing of each other and reproducing versions of a 'cool' or 'hard' masculinity.

Frosh et al. challenge the tendency of projects to focus on football. As we first raised in Chapter 3 and have returned to at various points throughout the book, there are important debates about engaging boys and men who are alienated from traditional services via the pragmatic use of apparently dominant (working-class) masculine interests or by the manipulation, rather than fundamental challenge, of conventional masculine beliefs. The lure of involvement in sport may indeed be a useful pragmatic approach (see Chapter 3), though we should be aware of pitfalls. While a generally popular activity such as football can be attractive to many boys and can help them to bond on a certain level, Frosh et al. take the view that 'too much emphasis on what are taken to be "natural" boys' activities' can serve to reinforce a narrow definition of hegemonic masculinity and this 'makes the construction of alternatives more difficult' (Frosh et al., 2002: 261). There are obvious issues of exclusion for some disabled boys and those who do not wish to engage in football for a variety of reasons. Of course the same criticism – that not all will feel welcome – can be made of almost any approach to engaging clients, including the provision of traditional services which are arguably very unappealing to the majority.

Practice Example – Self-help groups for boys and young men

One practice development of interest has been in the area of supporting self-help groups for boys in particular circumstances. For example, Dadich (2006) argues from interviews with 28 young men who had experienced a mental health issue that self-help support groups can offer participants emotional and practical support; information on mental health matters; the opportunity to relate to the mental health experiences of others; inspiration and hope and strong social networks. Lloyd (2001) documents the development of a Young Fathers Group in Norfolk over a period of seven years. It emerged at the request of some young fathers who were attending a generic advice project for young people. An initial focus was on their needs as men rather than parents with fathering issues emerging for those who were not resident with their children and wanted more contact. Feelings about a lack of self-worth have been a recurrent theme in the group. The group has gone through a variety of phases with a core of five staying involved. It has at times functioned as a therapeutic group and, while this was uncomfortable, it helped the fathers become more respectful of each other. The group received funding at one point and produced a Fact Pack. This gave information on legal issues, services and facilities and the attendant publicity allowed spaces for the young men to challenge constructions of them as irresponsible and drew attention to how often they felt misunderstood and on the edge of their children's lives. Self-help groups may be of particular merit for young men given the findings outlined above of a disjuncture between young people and adults' worlds (O'Donnell and Sharpe, 2000).

Conclusion

This chapter has explored theorising about and research with boys and young men. A theme which appears to emerge is that many boys and young men construct their identities in contexts where they are aware that they are viewed as risky by a variety of constituencies. The chapter suggests that there are possibilities for research and welfare practices that engage with them around how they can re-author their lives in more progressive ways, but there are concerns about how gender-blind much of the literature directed at practitioners is.

Key texts

Frosh, S., Phoenix, A. and Pattman, R. (2002) *Young Masculinities*, Basingstoke: Palgrave.

Based on qualitative research with boys aged 11–14. Draws on ideas from social psychology, sociology and psychoanalysis.

Connolly, P. (2004) *Boys and Schooling in the Early Years*, London: Routledge Falmer.

A large number of books have been published in recent years on boys and schooling. We have picked out this example as it is written by one of the key researchers in this field and unlike most books it deals with early childhood (age 5–6).

Roche, J., Tucker, S., Thomson, R. and Flynn, R. (2004) *Youth in Society*, second edition, London: Sage/Open University Press.

An interesting attempt to look at young people's lives and experiences from a range of disciplines.

11 Working with Older Men

The world of 'old age' is a world of women.
(Phillips et al., 2006: 12)

While Phillips et al. capture a central feature of contemporary arrangements, they also acknowledge that key trends point to later life becoming less numerically dominated by women. Arber et al. (2003) note, for example, that while the expected increase for older women between 1981 and 2021 is only 28 per cent, the expected increase of older men over the same period is 60 per cent. Moreover, because of changes in divorce rates, a greater number of older men will be living on their own. Arber et al. (2003) have, therefore, called for greater research attention to be paid to older men and for a move away from the hitherto dominant emphasis on 'the feminisation of later life'.

In this chapter we explore relevant theoretical approaches, noting the neglect until recently of the study of masculinity (Calasanti, 2003). We explore themes from a more recent scholarship, which acknowledges the impact of changing demographics, marital and work patterns and gender relations and look particularly at areas such as the body, sexuality, social networks, care and diversity. In terms of looking at practice with older men, it has proved difficult to find a literature that focuses specifically on this area. However, Ruxton's (2006) review of services provided by a specific charity – Age Concern – and the wider research offer some useful pointers for practice.

Theories

Hareven (1986) has argued for the importance of recognising the socially constructed nature of knowledge about ageing, suggesting that chronological age has not always been the key distinction between life changes. During the early modern period, a distinction between the spheres of production and reproduction was not in place (Hockey and James, 2003). The emergence of a separate sphere of paid work instituted the major age-based form of social differentiation, with entry into and exit from work becoming key experiences in the life course by the end of the nineteenth century. However, Hockey and James suggest that the significance attached to paid work in many structurally-based historical accounts is unhelpful, as it offers a partial and overly simplified representation of the emergence of the modern life course and is hinged around men's full-time work histories. We will return to Hockey and James's perspective on the life course below. Suffice to say here that we think it important to recognise the social construction of knowledge about ageing and, indeed, contemporary demographic and cultural developments suggest that we are in complex times in relation to how ageing is experienced, constructed and reconstructed. However, as with figures in relation to child mortality, it is here that we encounter in its starkness some key features of global inequality in terms of life expectancy rates between different countries.

A key perspective to emerge from the social sciences has been that of the 'political economy of ageing' (see, for example, Phillipson, 1982). This work contests the construction of old age as an individual problem, with the impact of wider structures on individuals being ignored. Furthermore, it is argued that in Western society older people are seen as inherently problematic because they represent a 'drain' on resources to which they no longer contribute actively either as tax payers or as parents raising the next generation. This structural approach has been extremely important and has dovetailed with a growing interest in ageism. However, it is perhaps not surprising, given the theoretical currents within the social sciences documented in Chapter 2, that it has been critiqued, particularly by post-modernists and some feminists.

Hockey and James (2003), in developing their theory of the life course, argue that a fuller understanding of the process of ageing can be gained through connecting a number of factors that combine to construct each individual's experience. Each person belongs to a cohort, people who share similar experiences due to their membership of a group comprising people of similar age; additionally people can claim membership of other groups that are not dependent upon their age, such as gender. An individual experience of ageing is generated from an understanding of these various influences together with the specific psychological make-up of the individual. This perspective engages, therefore, with questions such as: Do women and men age differently? How does ageing intersect with gendered, sexualised identities? We will return to this when exploring research about the body. Alongside their concern to explore the complexity of identity, Hockey and James challenge the focus on production in earlier theories. Basically, in this earlier work, involvement in productive activity was seen as central to identity; ceasing to be involved in such activity was seen as a final state and those who were no longer involved were seen and saw themselves as illegitimate. However, Hockey and James stress the fluidity of work patterns today and the contemporary societal focus on consumption rather than just production and they explore how older people resist their construction as old through particular patterns of consumption.

While Hockey and James's work interrogates gender within a broader exploration of the fluidity and complexity of identities across the life course, others involved in empirical research with and on older people place gender centrally and it is within this work that research on and theorising about older men *as men* is increasingly to be found today. Arber et al. (2003) argue that changing gender roles and relationships in later life and the challenges to masculinity with advancing age are newly emerging areas in the study of gender and ageing. It is indeed the case that earlier feminist scholarship focused on women and there now appears to be a shift. Moreover, this newer work suggests that what is required is not only the interrogation of 'new' topics but also the need to move away from a 'female lens' in trying to make sense of older men's lives. Hitherto, it has been common to measure men against a dominant female script in relation to such issues as friendship (Phillips et al., 2006).

Changing relationships and gender roles: the implications for men and women

If we consider that the group of 'older people' can encompass those aged 60 and over today, it is clear that this represents enormous diversity and that we are comparing distinct age cohorts in which considerable changes in relation to family and labour market roles have occurred in most parts of the Western world. Certainly, the lives of women have changed considerably since the 1960s. Changes such as involvement in paid work have had least impact upon the oldest generation of older women (80+), who have tended to have experienced a very different life course to that of older men and to those women in their 60s.

The growth in divorce rates is strongly linked to changes in women's aspirations and life chances and again is reflected in what is happening to the 'younger old'. If we look at divorce, Borell and Karlsson (2003) note that issues that are central to family research more generally have not been in the mainstream of research on family life among older people. Life-long marital relationships have been assumed to be the norm and the focus of the studies has been on the 'developmental tasks' to be addressed following the contraction of the family (the 'empty nest syndrome' for example). While it continues to be the case that nearly three-quarters of older men are married and most remain married until they die, there are changes happening. Trends in Sweden indicate that since 1997 it has become more usual in the age group 65–69 to be a divorcee than to be a widow or widower. Moreover, Borrel and Karlsson note a trend towards 'living apart together' relationships among this group. While occasionally there has been research done on the impact of a child's divorce on their older parents, less has been done on older parents' own divorce experiences or the impact of divorce upon ageing and the differing gender implications. This is in stark contrast with the plethora of research there has been on the impact of parents' divorce on children and adolescence.

While divorce clearly has an impact on both sexes, given the focus of this book we will explore the specific issues for men. As Price and Ginn (2003) note, although generally men are much better off in retirement, divorced and separated men and women are at particularly high risk of poverty in later life. Their research suggests that there are very high rates of unemployment, irrespective of social class, among this group of men, which has a significant adverse effect on pension accumulation. Even for those in paid work, men's participation in third-tier pensions is markedly lower among the divorced and separated. While this might be in part because lower paid men are more likely to become divorced/separated, this lower level is probably also due to other calls on their income, such as maintenance payments, transfer of a house as part of the divorce settlement, or because of difficulties in coping.

Generally, researchers argue that it is crucial to treat marital status as an analytic variable when analysing men and women in later life (Arber et al., 2003). For example, older married men are the most advantaged group in terms of both material circumstances and social interaction with relatives, friends and neighbours. They report better health and fewer health-damaging behaviours than men who live alone. Married older women are also advantaged (but being married is a minority experience for older women, especially above the age of 75). The group most likely to lack social contact with relatives, friends and neighbours are divorced and never-married older men. We will return to this in a further section when exploring the research on social networks.

Aside from divorce, the key shift in men's and women's lives and therefore of consequence to relationships between them has been developments in relation to paid work. Much research has been carried out on women's involvement in paid work and the consequences for the division of domestic labour and caring in younger families (see Chapter 6). As Fairhurst (2003) notes, empirical research with older people has been largely concerned with connecting the economic sphere and marital relationships within a frame which saw the transition from work to retirement as a male one and appeared to suggest either that women feel their domestic space is encroached upon by men retiring or that new notions of masculinity may emerge as men renegotiate the division of domestic labour (see Cliff, 1993). However, Fairhurst notes that for some groups of young older women today, they have been at work themselves and thus domestic space takes on a different cast.

Fairhurst (2003) explored, with those between the ages of 40 and 69, issues in relation to identities and retirement. Her work is an attempt to empirically ground some of the analyses on 'new' identities and her findings suggest that health, financial status and who one mixes with are of greater salience to people in retirement than chronological age and that notions of masculinity and femininity are both complex and fluid. She suggests that '"his" and "her" retirement had no ontological status' (Fairhurst, 2003: 38). Basically, both men and women seemed able to engage with a range of activities irrespective of whether such activities were coded masculine or feminine. However, it is important to note the specificity of her age range (up to 69 only) and to note Hockey and James's (2003: 191) observation that 'traditional, modern and postmodern patterns of social organisation unfold in tandem'. While this quotation refers to work, it is equally applicable to retirement. Furthermore, it is important to recognise that early old age is a very particular time where leisure, money and physical and mental abilities often coincide for many in ways they have not done in the life course before. As we will explore further below, the body in particular becomes more significant in relation to how older people construct their identities, with often differing implications for men and women.

As already indicated above, recent work that is often not empirically grounded stresses the emergence of 'new' identities in middle and old age, linked to an emphasis on the possibility of new lifestyles through consumption. While some stress the liberating possibilities of leisure and consumption, others emphasise the importance of loneliness and poverty. It would appear, however, that the possibilities and constraints attached to ageing are gendered. For example, Ruxton (2006) notes that women are more likely to suffer social exclusion in terms of access to material goods, civic and cultural activities and financial products, whereas men are more likely to be excluded from social relationships.

Older men, bodies and sexuality

It is commonly understood that there is a double standard in relation to ageing and appearance, with women required to remain vigilant about their bodies and their appearance in ways that men are not. However, Fairhurst (1998), based upon her research with late middle-aged people, argues that both men and women strive to make the 'best of themselves' and to avoid accusations of 'mutton dressed as lamb'. Their children are important arbiters here, with chronologisation disrupted by the body in the sense that, as Hockey and James (2003) note, the same adults were once able to tell children what they should and should not wear.

While there may be a degree of fluidity in relation to appearance, as Fairhurst suggests, it is important to note that there continue to be double standards in relation to appearance and age which impact upon women particularly. However, a key issue for older men would appear to be the ability of their bodies to function sexually. Gott and Hinchcliff (2003) found ageing was more challenging to male sexual identity than female sexual identity and was bound up with the ability to perform. Generally sex remained important to quality of life until the point where people did not think they would have another sexual partner during their lifetime and could be termed 'sexually retired'. Men and women differed with regard to the factors precipitating a position of sexual retirement. For older men, experiencing erectile dysfunction or other health problems determined the adoption of a position of sexual retirement, whereas for older women widowhood was the key determinant in the adoption of such a position. The role of sex in decisions to remarry following widowhood has been explored and a gender difference in attitudes has been identified. Davidson (1999) found that 'not wanting sex' was a central reason for deciding *not* to remarry among some older widows. Whereas, 'not wanting sex' was not a reason advanced by older widowers who decided not to remarry. For some widows sex was seen as one of the 'marital duties' that, along with domestic chores, they had been freed from through widowhood. It is important to note Gott and Hinchcliff's (2003) observation that the notion of sex as a marital duty received considerable attention in the period when people in this age cohort were newly married and were bound up with specific concerns at that time about family size and the beginnings of concern about a rise in divorce rates. It is probable also that it is strongly related to norms about female sexual behaviour which have changed dramatically in recent decades. It will therefore be of considerable interest to see how the research evidence on this issue develops.

For older men, involvement or not in sexual activity is but one aspect of what is going on in relation to their bodies. Davidson and Arber (2004: 146) argue that 'although mediated by gender, ethnicity, class and geographical location, failing health is a virtual certainty at some point in old age'. They found from their research that there was a disjuncture between what the older men knew about subjective and objective health maintenance strategies and how they ultimately acted on this knowledge. They suggest that notions of independence and masculinity in health matters which have been identified in younger generations persist into older age. Moreover, as briefly mentioned above, marital status is crucial in relation to a range of health-related issues. Lone men were more likely to report poorer health than partnered men. Divorced men consistently report the poorest health across the age groups researched.

Ageing, social networks and men

We have already noted the advantaged position of older married men in relation to financial and social circumstances. Men living alone for whatever reason (bereavement, divorce, etc.) tend to have smaller networks and less weekly contact with kin and non-kin (De Jong Gierveld, 2003). Children comprise the highest source of weekly contacts but this does vary according to partner history for those older adults who live alone. De Jong Gierveld (2003) suggests that whereas widowers see children and children-in-law on a weekly basis, divorced men's contact is much more episodic and is linked to previous relationship history and the complexities and possible discontinuities of such relationships (see Chapter 6 on fathers). Ruxton (2006) suggests grandfathers are less likely to see grandchildren frequently if they are not living with a wife. Being the father of a divorced son especially decreases the likelihood of regular contact.

There are significant differences between older never-married men and women, with men having the highest loneliness scores and women the lowest, although after controlling for a range of variables including education, the differences, while still recognisable, are not as significant. Men's loneliness appears associated with a lack of an intimate bond with a female partner, whereas women appear to have a wider range of resources (see Tomassini et al., 2003).

Davidson et al. (2003) explored the social worlds of older men and found that not only are they likely to experience isolation and loneliness, but they often fail to frequent facilities designed to provide company or practical support. Their lack of engagement has been linked to the role women play in establishing and maintaining social networks. However, Davidson et al. do acknowledge the importance of engaging with how men and women 'do' friendship and recognise that we need to stop measuring men against a 'female norm' if we are to really appreciate their worlds and understandings. They note, for example, a small group of older never-married men who did not seek intimacy, did not report feeling deprived but 'did see themselves as different' from others insofar as they did not wish to seek out others either as intimates or more socially. Davidson et al. note the importance of acknowledging that some individuals may derive a sense of gendered self-identity precisely by conforming to gendered rules concerning emotion work.

One area that has received attention where men would appear not to conform to dominant gender discourses is in relation to caring and we will now explore this.

Who cares for whom and how?

Since the early 1980s there has been growing interest in and a growth in the literature on carers of older people (Phillips et al., 2006). Feminists were to the fore in highlighting the issues for women and the burden placed by caring upon women who were often caught between caring for children and their older parents with little recognition or state support. Indeed, it was argued that some policies, such as that of community care in the UK, relied upon women performing unpaid roles as carers. However, it has become increasingly recognised that who cares for whom is by no means straightforward now that research 'has disaggregated the type of carer, nature of care, gender and the situations faced by carers' (Phillips et al., 2006: 16). In the UK, the majority of carers under 65 are indeed women, with the most obvious gender difference in the 45–64 age range where 27 per cent of women compared with 19 per cent of men are carers. However, men are strongly represented in caring for women in older age. While numbers are indeed important, there is increasing qualitative research interest in issues which are germane to the concerns of this book and that are addressed by Calasanti (2003) in her explorations of how 'the intersections between gender and age relations shape manhood over the life course, particularly in old age' (p. 16). She takes unpaid spousal care work as a case study, in part because it is the only care relationship in which men and women perform similar amounts and also because she is concerned to address some key theoretical questions. For example, there has been a concern by researchers that men as carers have been ignored and she asks us to consider:

> To what extent are claims of ignoring men coming from a pro-feminist perspective that concerns the need to understand gender relations, versus an uneasiness that men are somehow being ignored or discriminated against, despite the fact that we know for the most part this is not the case. Further, if we accept that men have been *ignored* from the standpoint of being *subjects* of inquiry, how shall we go about filling the gap in our research. (Calasanti, 2003: 21, emphasis in original)

She suggests that we need to move away from a tendency in the debates to discuss which style of care (male or female) is better, towards exploring with those who are cared for what works for them.

Certainly in the literature on spousal care there have been a number of themes evident, as Calasanti suggests: male carers tend to be ignored, if not discriminated against; there has been a concern to evaluate different types of care and whether these are 'better' or 'worse', which has mapped onto discussions about differences between male and female care styles. What are less well rehearsed in the literature, however, are the implications of doing caring for 'doing' masculinity. The research evidence, for example, which suggests husbands are less distressed by caring for their demented wives than vice versa, in part because they feel useful and able and have a sense of accomplishment (Rose and Bruce, 1995) is of interest here. This research found that women did not take comfort or pride in their caring work, instead grieving for the lost relationship. What Rose and Bruce suggest is that men got more praise and recognition, although the tasks continued to be seen as feminine or gender neutral, never masculine. Their masculinity was not challenged, however; rather, they garnered admiration for doing women's work. This is supported by research from the US and Japan which confirms that husbands receive more praise and recognition for their caring than equivalent women, due to the perception in both cultures that it is more 'natural' for women to do this work (Calasanti, 2003). However, it will be of considerable interest to explore what happens as younger men age and particularly those who have been more involved with the care of their children. As Chapter 6 on fathers suggests, constructions of fatherhood have expanded considerably and the 'involved father' model has become openly and widely invested in even if there are uneven and complex tendencies apparent.

Diversity

As already indicated, while older people can be subsumed within a category which is marked by specific age-related concerns, their identities in relation to class, sexuality and ethnicity precede and intersect with such concerns. Indeed, in relation to ethnicity, Norman (1985) has highlighted that for many from ethnic minority groups in the UK, multiple experiences of exclusion and disadvantage are linked to oppression and discrimination. It is of course important to note diversity between ethnic and within ethnic groups in terms of differing patterns of migration, differing family structures and socio-economic circumstances. Currently, in the UK,

> Two-thirds of the black and ethnic population aged sixty and over are represented by black Caribbean and Indian communities and the remaining third are represented by black Africans, Chinese, Bangladeshis, Pakistanis and other groups. (Phillips et al., 2006: 15)

While research has been done on the issues facing Bangladeshi women and social support and ethnicity there seems to be little which focuses specifically on men and ethnicity in the UK. Indeed, even within Arber et al.'s (2003) groundbreaking work on masculinity and older men, there is only one reference in the index to 'race' and none to ethnicity. Calasanti, in that volume, when exploring spousal caring does suggest the need to attend to the intersections of age, gender and ethnicity and refers to preliminary work from the US with Puerto Rican, black and white men and women carers. This work suggests that although all groups report strain, they speak about it differently: 'for example, Whites note feelings of burden and, among women, anger; Puerto Rican women feel isolated; and Black and Puerto Rican men express frustration (Calderon and Tennstedt, 1998)' (Calasanti, 2003: 24).

As Gott (2005) notes, the vast majority of the sexuality and ageing literature assumes that older people are heterosexual and indeed very little has been written about how sexuality is understood and expressed in later life among gay, lesbian and bisexual older people. In the book *Sexuality, Sexual Health and Ageing*, Gott draws together some of the research which has been done and this is outlined in the section that follows.

Heaphy et al. (2003) have explored the attitudes and experiences of 266 older non-heterosexual men and women living in the UK. While couple relationships were valued highly, 41 per cent of women and 65 per cent of men lived alone. Ageing made it harder to meet a partner and the 'younger old' were more likely to be in a relationship. Moreover, while meanings attached to ageing and old age were found to be fluid, participants over 50 did refer to themselves as 'older'.

Rosenfeld's (1999) study from the US also explored age identity among older non-heterosexual adults. Rosenfeld suggests age is a significant issue because of how homosexuality has been reconstructed in the twentieth century.

> Crucially a shift is argued to have occurred in societal understandings of homosexuality from source of stigma to source of status from the late 1960s onwards, partly as a result of the 1969 Stonewall rebellion. Rosenfeld identifies that, contrary to previous expectation that lesbian and gay older men exclusively adopt the 'pre-Stonewall' discourse of homosexuality as a source of stigma, both discourses (…) are drawn upon to construct identity. This is explained by the fact that, although all of her participants grew up within the pre-gay liberation era, a distinction could be drawn between those who identified as gay at this time, and those who did so during the period of the liberation movement. (Gott, 2005: 83)

Gott, therefore, suggests that it is important to attend to differences in terms of experiences and attitudes and behaviours within age-defined cohorts of older non-heterosexual people.

In Heaphy et al.'s qualitative study, men seemed more likely than women to draw on gendered and heterosexual models to manage their relationship, although clearly gender sameness meant that there was a degree of negotiation in relation to roles and tasks. While women felt that having a non-heterosexual orientation could make you less conscious of ageing it was the reverse for men. Indeed Gott (2005) notes that it has often been said that gay men experience 'accelerated ageing', although research studies have proved inconclusive in this regard. Certainly in the gay male press there seems to be a premium placed upon youth and beauty and there is a sense that lesbians do seem to avoid to some degree at least the oppressiveness of such a focus (this seems to be in contrast not only to gay men but also heterosexual women). Of course such statements need to be treated with caution and certainly differing generations of lesbians, particularly those growing up in eras more removed from feminism and with greater earning power than previous generations of women, may prove no less immune to the pressures placed by ageing upon appearance and sexual attractiveness.

In the next section we further develop some of the themes covered in the chapter so far when we turn to look at practice issues.

Practice issues

Lymbery (2005: 1) comments on the paucity of literature on social work with older people in the British context, comparing it particularly with 'the veritable flood of books that focus on various aspects of social work with children'. He also notes that there is a limited critical edge to the literature with a lack of a more analytical focus and an emphasis on practice skills. Given his desire to provide a more analytic focus, it is perhaps surprising that his own discussion on gender is rather limited, particularly in relation to exploring men and masculinities. It reproduces rather dated evidence in relation to the preponderance of older women in the ageing population and refers primarily to the issues they may face. There is one reference to gendered expectations of behaviour which may also affect older men 'who may be given little opportunity to express their emotional responses to the losses of old age' (p. 23). Moreover, his discussion of gender in relation to practice is confined to a brief mention of the possible ways that the 'race' and gender of social worker and service user may affect the way in which communication takes place and the need for 'linguistic sensitivity' in order to avoid oppressive practice. While there is much in his very comprehensive book that is helpful to practitioners, the gender-neutral language employed throughout means the gendered implications of ageing do need to be drawn out by the reader.

Phillips et al. (2006) do acknowledge the changing demographic and marital patterns referred to in previous sections, but again follow Lymbery in developing a largely gender-neutral language in their also very comprehensive discussion on what good practice with older people might encompass.

In relation to health and health practices it also seems difficult to find either research or practice initiatives which engage explicitly with the issues for older men within the frame identified above. For example, the fascinating book by Watson (2000), *Male Bodies: Health, Culture and Identity*, is concerned with addressing the following questions: How do men perceive their bodies? How can empirical study of the body inform our understanding of the social world of men and what are the implications for public health? But it provides little for us to draw on in relation to men, ageing and public health. Davidson and Arber (2004), however, do look at this area and argue that while the customary approach to health improvement has been to target individuals, less attention has been paid to addressing the broad determinants of older men's health behaviours, which must include engaging with the social construction of masculinity. Their research has explored risk-taking behaviours and gender differences in treatment-seeking behaviours in relation to older men. We will explore these below.

Ruxton (2006) has done an interesting review of services provided by the charity Age Concern. This review was prompted by a desire to seek the views of men themselves on services and what the barriers were for men in using services. He was also concerned to explore specific projects which had successfully developed services and activities targeted at 'socially isolated' older men.

The barriers identified were at the societal/cultural and personal levels and were linked to features of service provision. His findings in relation to societal/cultural barriers mirror those of researchers into health and help-seeking. For health providers, a key issue is that, unlike women, some men have little or no ongoing contact with health professionals in their life course and, as Davidson and Arber (2004) note, it is therefore unlikely they will turn to health professionals as they age. According to their research, men considered going to the doctor 'as a sign of weakness' and they did not want to be seen to 'give in' to sickness:

> The men interviewed admitted to postponing making an appointment until they were very sick. They then have negative associations with the doctor, whom they see when they are in pain or feel very unwell and, importantly, who may give them bad news about their health. (Davidson and Arber, 2004: 146)

Ruxton, too, found older men were resistant to participating in Age Concern services because they perceived them as geared at those who need 'support' or those who are 'dependent' or 'incapable'. While such perceptions were particularly influential among the oldest men, they were widespread among all ages.

At a personal level the barriers identified suggested that the death of a spouse and the attendant emotional problems were important. Men over 80 tended to withdraw from social contacts and this was often linked to health and mobility issues (although these issues were factors across the category). The cost of attending groups could also be a factor. However, Ruxton did find that activities that resonated with older men's identities and appealed to their interests could overcome barriers and this will be returned to.

The nature of referral policies was a feature of service provision that emerged. Several staff interviewed suggested that where men were referred by agencies such as social services, doctors or other health care workers, they were more likely to attend. However, a lack of awareness of services, particularly among doctors, was a difficulty here. Equally, as suggested previously, activities seen as inappropriate ('feminised') were a barrier as has also been found in work with fathers (see Chapter 6).

Research has also been carried out on how health providers deal with sex and sexuality issues among older people. It suggests that there are barriers within health settings to discussing sexual issues with older patients, although these may be common to patients of all ages. The assumption of old age as 'asexual', however, can lead practitioners to assume that sexuality is less important or less relevant to older people, and this, as we noted earlier in the chapter, may have specific implications for older men (Gott, 2005).

In relation to sexuality, research suggests ignorance on the part of providers, heterosexist assumptions and homophobia in residential homes. Gott (2005) notes the experience of Roger, an older gay man who founded the Gay Carers Network after his partner developed dementia and moved into a residential care home:

> All the time people wanted to know why I was looking after David and who I was, so there was always the issue of needing to come out. Eventually I got to the point where I had no choice: I had a partner who couldn't talk, who was dependent upon me and who was showing me love. So if he showed me affection in public, I had to accept it. (quoted in Gott, 2005: 84)

Enabling practices with older men

In his review for Age Concern Ruxton did find evidence of 'enabling' factors and practices. For example, there were tentative indications of shifts in attitudes towards gender among men both in terms of taking on 'non-traditional' activities and doing friendship with other men differently. This suggests to Ruxton that over time it may become more 'normal' for men to be involved with services. Services that responded to men's need for contact and companionship and were warm, welcoming and did not cost too much did combat some men's isolation and this is very important given the research evidence on men's isolation. Being a certain kind of man (e.g., sensitive, a good listener and not too 'traditional') helped, although this may have posed tensions for men's own sense of being appropriately masculine.

Ruxton (2006) offers four practice examples of services attracting men, not because they necessarily offered a model for others but because they 'proved interesting fora for exploring some of the core issues facing older men, and for many of the men, they provided essential opportunities for friendship and mutual support' (p. 28). In terms of conclusions – which can be generalised only tentatively from these examples – they do echo those found in the literature on engaging fathers in family centres (Ghate et al., 2000): the existence of positive management and staff attitudes and policies to engaging with men; focused action on the part of the service such as targeted marketing, visiting men at home and ensuring protected space for activities for men. Again echoing the findings on services for fathers, it appears to be the attitudes of staff rather than their sex which matters in recruiting and sustaining male involvement. Specific activities, such as computer classes and digital camera projects, seemed successful (although there appear to be issues here in relation to the material resources available to particular groups of men). Those who came to learn about technology or for classes such as language courses tended to be more affluent, whereas less affluent men attended for more social reasons (although there were examples of such men attending courses also).

In terms of developing practices with older men in the coming years, the following broader points from the wider research literature would seem useful to bear in mind also:

- There are important differences and similarities in relation to age-specific cohorts within the category 'older men'.
- Social trends such as divorce rates and women's employment have implications for both the material and social experiences of men and women. For example, increasing rates of divorced older men who may or may not have relationships with their children is an issue.
- Men's retirement from paid work may be experienced differently by women who themselves have been in work and vice versa.
- Spousal caring may too take on a different cast as those who have been more involved in caring for their children get older.

Conclusion

This chapter has only scratched the surface of a subject that is fascinating but marginalised within both gerontology and gender studies; that of the circumstances and experiences of older men in a period where gender relations have come under considerable challenge. While many of those in older age have experienced particular gendered settlements based around the male breadwinner role, it would appear that the coming decades will see much change. It is important that the impact of demographic and cultural changes continues to be explored by researchers in order to map out the implications. In addition, as we have argued in this chapter, health and social care practitioners and the literature that directly addresses practice should take notice of such implications as a matter of some urgency.

Key texts

Arber, S., Davidson, K. and Ginn, J. (eds) (2003) *Gender and Ageing: Changing Roles and Relationships*, Maidenhead: Open University Press.

This is a comprehensive look at older men's lives and addresses areas such as poverty, divorce, health and caring.

Gott, M. (2005) *Sexuality, Sexual Health and Ageing*, Maidenhead: Open University Press.

A neglected area – this looks at gender and sexuality in relation to ageing and is both theoretical and applied in nature.

Ruxton, S. (2006) *Working with Older Men: A Review of Age Concern Services*, London: Age Concern.

A small research study into services provided by one charity but useful and important given the lack of research in this area and well located in the literature on masculinities.

12 Conclusion

As we indicated in the Introduction, this book could not have been written twenty years ago. That it can be now is due, in no small measure, to the challenges posed by women to every aspect of gender relations over the last decades. The response by men to such challenges has been explicitly explored in Chapter 3 in terms of organised and visible groups. But throughout the book (for example, in the chapters on fathers and young men) we find accounts from men and boys which suggest a complex picture of anger, pain, support and indifference. Clearly the book is about much more than men's responses to the challenges posed to and the changes in gender relations in the last decades, but it could be argued that these are its sub-text. Certainly, the emergence of feminist scholarship, as well as feminist political activities, has been central to the development of the body of literature which has been drawn on to inform the chapters.

While the book has been explicitly about men – and we hope that the usefulness and importance of this focus has been demonstrated throughout – we would argue that it is essential to recognise its broader location within, and its commitment to, a project that is concerned with understanding and transforming gender relations. We would suggest that it is within such a project that strong possibilities exist for advancing the welfare of women, men, boys and girls.

Understanding gender relations

We think the understanding of gender as relational is crucial as it obliges an understanding of how masculinities and femininities are constructed and operate over time and space. As Flax has noted, 'gender relations'

> is a category meant to capture a complex set of social relations. Gender both as an analytic category and a social process is relational. That is, gender relations are complex and unstable processes ... constituted by and through interrelated parts.

> These parts are interdependent, that is, each part can have no meaning or existence without the others. (1990: 44)

We do not suggest there is one theory that can capture the ongoing and complex nature and processes involved in sustaining and reproducing gender relations and, indeed, we explicitly distance ourselves from the search for one grand theory. We do, however, want to raise the importance of continuing to understand and think about how boys, girls, men and women come to perform their identities within systems which often continue to stress their differences and oppositional qualities. We think this is urgent as, in many parts of the Western world, complex and uneven changes have resulted in men who no longer know their 'place', women who feel unsupported and overburdened and boys who are exposed to a bewildering array of models of masculinity, some of which do not appear to equip them to negotiate the economic or emotional terrain of the future. For girls, in terms of both their present and future concerns, the consequences of all this may be at worst continued exposure to, or fear of, violence and abuse, and/or disappointment and a lack of support in the vital tasks connected with raising the next generation.

We would suggest that while there are 'winners' in the current post-modern mêlée that characterises gender relations, there are too many painful casualties to allow any room for complacency or indifference. We suggest that a crucial element of any project must involve understanding men and their 'goings on' as part of the problem and part of the solution. This glib formulation, of course, obscures as much as it opens up and this is sharply thrown into focus when we begin to think about the project of transformation.

Transforming gender relations

Just as we have steered away from adopting one single mode of understanding, we feel we cannot project one destination for our travels either. It is clear, though, that there are at least some things worth fighting for in the here and now, as well as in terms of ensuring a more hopeful future. It does seem imperative that we support and continue to develop practices at a range of levels which ensure that men's disproportionate involvement in violent and abusive practices becomes a thing of the past. While we recognise that gendered processes and belief systems are only part of much more wide-ranging processes in public and private spaces, there is enough evidence to suggest that much of what is encountered by practitioners in health and social care is to do with men's inability (for reasons which combine the psychic and the social) to invest in models of masculinity that promote respectful and non-objectifying practices. Action is needed, as we have indicated, at a range of levels to develop and support such investments for the sake of all concerned. Such action will involve controlling strategies as well as those which are supportive and continue well-rehearsed dilemmas about the role of control strategies with those who are impoverished and marginalised.

It is also important, we would suggest, that the material and cultural preconditions exist for offering men, women, boys and girls expanded and realistic possibilities to work in the paid labour force and take on caring responsibilities. As we have noted at various points throughout this book, these preconditions are not well developed in most countries. Until they are, it is difficult to assess many men's willingness to change or indeed some women's ability to let them.

Throughout this book we have also tried to highlight examples of practice interventions that variously seem to offer possibilities to boys and men to deal with contemporary difficulties and embrace new possibilities in relation to being 'men'. It is clear that much remains to be done, not only with men themselves, but also in offering interventions to men, women, boys and girls together to build 'democratic families'. For Ferguson (2001: 8) such families are those where: 'children are heard as well as seen and feel safe, women as well as men are treated with respect, and men as well as women are enabled to have expressive emotional lives and relationships'. It is with such hopes that we would wish this book to be associated, as well as with the associated practices: practices that recognise the importance of working with all concerned on what such hopes might look like and mean to them, and helping to make them happen. Such hopes do not translate easily into blueprints, however, but rather feed into the notion of a mosaic.

We offer this book in the hope that it supports and encourages those who work with men or want to do so within a project that recognises our interdependence in a world where interdependence is often misrecognised or devalued. Oppressive gender-based systems play a vital role in such misrecognition and devaluation and require challenging. Men have much to lose, gain and offer within such a project, but we would argue that their losses can become gains and their gains can become gifts, gifts that can enrich them, women and children.

References

Abramovitz, M. (2006) 'Welfare reform in the United States: gender, race and class matters', *Critical Social Policy*, 26(2): 336–365.

Albizu-Garciaa, C.E., Alegria, M., Freeman, D. and Vera, M. (2001) 'Gender and health services use for a mental health problem', *Social Science & Medicine*, 53(7): 865–878.

Alexander, M. (1999) 'Sexual offender treatment efficacy revisited', *Sexual Abuse: A Journal of Research and Treatment*, 19: 101–116.

Almeida, R. (1998) *Transformations of Gender and Race*. New York: Haworth Press.

Appleby, L. (2001) *Safety First: Five-year Report of the National Confidential Inquiry into Suicide and Homicide by People with Mental Illness*. Manchester: University of Manchester Department of Psychiatry.

Arber, S. and Thomas, H. (2001) 'From women's health to a gender analysis of health', in W.C. Cockerham (ed.) *Blackwell Companion to Medical Sociology*. Oxford: Blackwell, pp. 94–113.

Arber, S., Davidson, K. and Ginn, J. (2003) 'Changing approaches to gender and later life', in S. Arber, K. Davidson and J. Ginn (eds) *Gender and Ageing: Changing Roles and Relationships*. Maidenhead: Open University Press, pp. 1–15.

Arendell, T. (1995) *Fathers and Divorce*. Thousand Oaks, CA: Sage.

Ashley, C., Featherstone, B., Roskill, C., Ryan, M. and White, S. (2006) *Fathers Matter: Research Findings on Fathers and their Involvement with Social Care Services*. London: Family Rights Group.

Babcock, J. and La Taillade, J. (2000) 'Evaluating interventions for men who batter', in J. Vincent and E. Jouriles (eds) *Domestic Violence: Guidelines for Research Informed Practice*. London: Jessica Kingsley, pp. 37–77.

Babcock, J., Green, C. and Robie, C. (2004) 'Does batterers' treatment work? A meta-analytic review of domestic violence treatment', *Clinical Psychology Review*, 23: 1023–1053.

Bancroft, L. and Silverman, J. (2002) *The Batterer as Parent*. Thousand Oaks, CA: Sage.

Barber, J.G. (2001) 'Relative misery and youth suicide', *Australian and New Zealand Journal of Psychiatry*, 35: 49–57.

Barber, J. (2002) *Social Work with Addictions*. London: Palgrave.

Barker, G. (2005) *Dying to be Men: Youth, Masculinity and Social Exclusion*. London: Routledge.

Barker, M. and Beech, A. (1993) 'Sex offender treatment programmes: a critical look at the cognitive-behavioural approach', *Issues in Criminological and Legal Psychology*, 19: 37–42.

Baron-Cohen, S. (2002) 'The extreme male brain theory of autism', *Trends in Cognitive Sciences*, 6: 248–254.

Baron-Cohen, S. (2004) *The Essential Difference: Men, Women and the Extreme Male Brain*. London: Penguin.

Bartlett, D. and Burgess, A. (2005) *Working with Fathers: Six Steps Guide*. London: Fathers Direct.

Bartlett, D., Featherstone, B., Manby, M. and Jones, K. (2006) *Evaluation of YMCA 'Dads and Lads' programmes*, www.ymca.org.uk

Beck, U. (1992) *Risk Society: Towards a New Modernity*. London: Sage.

Beckett, R. (2006) 'Risk prediction, decision making and evaluation of adolescent sexual abusers', in M. Erooga and H. Masson (eds) *Children and Young People who Sexually Abuse Others*. London: Routledge, pp. 215–233.

Beech, A. (1998) 'A psychometric typology of child abusers', *International Journal of Offender Therapy and Comparative Criminology*, 42: 319–339.

Beech, A. and Fordham, A. (1997) 'Therapeutic climate of sexual offender treatment programs', *Sexual Abuse: A Journal of Research and Treatment*, 9: 219–237.

Beech, A. and Fisher, D. (2002) 'The rehabilitation of child sex offenders', *Australian Psychologist*, 37: 206–214.

Beech, A., Friendship, C., Erikson, M. and Hanson, R. (2002) 'The relationship between static and dynamic risk factors and reconviction in a sample of UK child abusers', *Sexual Abuse: A Journal of Research and Treatment*, 14: 155–167.

Benjamin, J. (1995) 'Sameness and difference: towards an "over-inclusive" theory of gender development', in A. Elliott and S. Frosh (eds) *Psychoanalysis in Contexts*. London: Routledge, pp. 106–123.

Bennett, M. (1995) 'Why don't men come to counselling? Some speculative theories', *Counselling*, November, pp. 310–313.

Bennun, I. (1989) 'Perceptions of the therapist in family therapy', *Journal of Family Therapy*, 11: 243–255.

Bepko, C., Almeida, R., Messineo, T. and Stevenson, Y. (1998) 'Evolving constructs of masculinity', in R. Almeida (1998) *Transformations of Gender and Race*. New York: Haworth Press.

Berg, B. and Rosenblum, N. (1977) 'Fathers in family therapy: a survey of family therapists', *Journal of Marriage and Family Counseling*, 3: 85–91.

Biggs, D., Doyle, P., Gooch, T. and Kennington, R. (1998) *Assessing Men Who Sexually Abuse*. London: Jessica Kingsley.

Blackie, S. and Clark, D. (1987) 'Men in marriage counselling', in C. Lewis and M. O'Brien (eds) *Reassessing Fatherhood: New Observations on Fathering and the Modern Family.* London: Sage, pp. 195–211.

Blake, S. and Laxton, J. (1998) *Strides: A Practical Guide to Sex and Relationships Education with Young Men.* London: Family Planning Association.

Bly, R. (1990) *Iron John.* Reading, MA: Addison-Wesley.

Bly, R. (1991) *Iron John.* Shaftesbury: Element Books.

Bockting, W., Knudson, G. and Goldberg, J.M. (2006) *Counselling and Mental Health Care of Transgender Adults and Loved Ones.* Vancouver: Vancouver Coastal Health.

Bograd, M. (ed.) (1991) *Feminist Approaches for Men in Family Therapy.* New York: Harrington Press.

Boldero, J. and Fallon, B. (1995) 'Adolescent help-seeking: what do they get help for and from whom?', *Journal of Adolescence,* 18(2): 193–209.

Borell, K. and Karlsson, S.G. (2003) 'Reconceptualizing intimacy and ageing: living apart together', in S. Arber, K. Davidson and J. Ginn (eds) *Gender and Ageing: Changing Roles and Relationships.* Maidenhead: Open University Press, pp. 47–63.

Bourgeois, L., Sabourin, S. and Wright, J. (1990) 'Predictive validity of therapeutic alliance in group marital therapy', *Journal of Consulting and Clinical Psychology,* 58: 608–613.

Bowl, R. (1985) *The Changing Nature of Masculinity.* Norwich: Social Work Monographs.

Bradford, S. (2005) 'Modernising youth work: from the universal to the particular and back again', in R. Harrison and C. Wise (eds) *Working with Young People.* London: Open University in association with Sage, pp. 55–70.

Bradshaw, J., Stimson, C., Skinner, A. and Williams, J. (1999) *Absent Fathers?* London: Routledge.

Braithwaite, J. and Daly, K. (1994) 'Masculinities, violence and communitarian control', in T. Newburn and E. Stanko (eds) *Just Boys Doing Business? Men, Masculinities and Crime.* London: Routledge.

Brannen, J., Heptinstall, E. and Bhopal, K. (2000) *Connecting Children: Care and Family Life in Later Childhood.* London: Routledge Falmer.

Broom, A. (2005) 'The eMale: prostate cancer, masculinity and online support as a challenge to medical expertise', *Journal of Sociology,* 41(1): 87–104.

Brown, L. (1996) 'Ethical concerns with sexual minority patients', in R. Cabaj and T. Stein (eds) *Textbook of Homosexuality and Mental Health.* Washington, DC: American Psychiatric Press.

Brown, T. (2006) 'Child abuse and domestic violence in the context of parental separation and divorce: new models of intervention', in C. Humphreys and N. Stanley (eds) *Domestic Violence: Directions for Good Practice.* London: Jessica Kingsley, pp. 155–168.

Brown-Standridge, M. and Piercy, F. (1988) 'Reality creation versus reality confirmation: a process study in marital therapy', *American Journal of Family Therapy*, 16: 195–215.

Buckley, K. and Young, K. (1996) 'Driving us crazy: motor projects and masculinity', in T. Newburn and G. Mair (eds) *Working with Men*. Lyme Regis: Russell House, pp. 49–67.

Burgess, A. (2005) 'Fathers and public services', in K. Stanley (ed.) *Daddy Dearest: Active Fatherhood and Public Policy*. London: Institute for Public Policy Research, pp. 57–65.

Burton, S., Regan, L. and Kelly, L. (1998) *Supporting Women and Challenging Men*. Bristol: Policy Press.

Busfield, J. (1996) *Men, Women and Madness*. London: Routledge.

Cabe, N. (1999) 'Abused boys and adolescents: out of the shadows', in A. Horne and M. Kiselica (eds) *Handbook of Counseling Boys and Adolescent Males*. Thousand Oaks, CA: Sage, pp. 199–216.

Calasanti, T. (2003) 'Masculinities and care work in old age', in S. Arber, K. Davidson and J. Ginn (eds) *Gender and Ageing: Changing Roles and Relationships*. Maidenhead: Open University Press, pp. 15–31.

Calder, M. (2000) *A Complete Guide to Sexual Abuse Assessments*. Lyme Regis: Russell House.

Cameron, C., Moss, P. and Owen, C. (1999) *Men in the Nursery*. London: Paul Chapman.

Campbell, B. (1993) *Goliath. Britain's Dangerous Places*. London: Methuen.

Campbell, J. (ed.) (1995) *Assessing Dangerousness: Violence by Sexual Offenders, Batterers, and Child Abusers*. Thousand Oaks, CA: Sage.

Campbell, T. (2002) 'Physical disorders', in D. Sprenkle (ed.) *Effectiveness Research in Marriage and Family Therapy*. Alexandria, VA: American Association of Marital and Family Therapy, pp. 311–338.

Canetto, S.S. and Sakinofsky, I. (1998) 'The gender paradox in suicide', *Suicide and Life-threatening Behavior*, 28(1): 1–23.

Cantor, C.H. (2000) 'Suicide in the Western world', in K. Hawton and K. van Heeringen (eds) *The International Handbook of Suicide and Attempted Suicide*. Chichester: Wiley, pp. 9–28.

Carrigan, T., Connell, R.W. and Lee, J. (1985) 'Towards a new sociology of masculinity', *Theory and Society*, 14(5): 551–604.

Carrillo, R. and Tello, J. (1998) *Family Violence and Men of Color*. New York: Springer.

Cauce, A., Domenech-Rodriguez, M., Paradise, M., Cochran, B., Munyi Shea, J., Srebnik, D. and Baydar, N. (2002) 'Cultural and contextual influences in mental health seeking', *Journal of Consulting and Clinical Psychology*, 70: 44–55.

Cavanagh, K. and Cree, V. (eds) (1996) *Working with Men*. London: Routledge.

Cawson, P., Wattam, C., Brooker, S. and Kelly, G. (2000) *Child Maltreatment in the United Kingdom: A Study of the Prevalence of Child Abuse and Neglect*. London: NSPCC.

Cheng, A.T.A and Lee, C.-S. (2000) 'Suicide in Asia and the Far East', in K. Hawton and K. van Heeringen (eds) *The International Handbook of Suicide and Attempted Suicide*. London: Wiley, pp. 29–48.

Cherry, J. and O'Shea, D. (2006) 'Therapeutic work with families of young people who sexually abuse', in M. Erooga and H. Masson (eds) *Children and Young People Who Sexually Abuse Others*. London: Routledge, pp. 200–214.

Chodorow, N. (1978) *The Reproduction of Mothering*. Berkeley, CA: University of California Press.

Christian, H. (1994) *The Making of an Anti-sexist Man*. London: Routledge.

Christie, A. (ed.) (2001) *Men and Social Work*. London: Palgrave Macmillan.

Christopherson, J., Furniss, T., O'Mahoney, B. and Peake, A. (1989) *Working with Sexually Abused Boys*. London: National Children's Bureau.

Clapton, G. (2002) *Birth Fathers and their Adoption Experiences*. London: Jessica Kingsley.

Clarke, L., Cooksey, E. and Verropolu, G. (1998) 'Fathers and absent fathers: sociodemographic similarities in Britain and the United States', *Demography*, 35(2): 217–228.

Clatterbaugh, K. (1990) *Contemporary Perspectives on Masculinity*. Boulder, CO: Westview Press.

Cleaver, F. (ed.) (2002) *Masculinities Matter! Men, Gender and Development*. London: Zed Books.

Cliff, D. (1993) '"Under the wife's feet": renegotiating gender divisions in early retirement', *Sociological Review*, 41: 30–53.

Cohen, B.Z. (1999) 'Measuring the willingness to seek help', *Journal of Social Service Research*, 26(1): 67–82.

Collison, M. (1996) 'In search of the high life: drugs, crime, masculinities and consumption', *British Journal of Criminology*, 36(3): 428–444.

Connell, R.W. (1995) *Masculinities*. Cambridge: Polity.

Connell, R.W. (1996) 'The politics of changing men', *Arena*, 6: 53–72.

Connell, R.W. (2000) *The Men and the Boys*. Cambridge: Polity.

Connell, R.W. (2002) 'On hegemonic masculinity and violence: a response to Jefferson and Hall', *Theoretical Criminology*, 6(1): 89–99.

Connell, R.W. and Messerschmidt, J.W. (2005) 'Hegemonic masculinity: rethinking the concept', *Gender and Society*, 19(6): 829–859.

Connell, R.W., Hearn, J. and Kimmel, M.S. (2005) 'Introduction', in M.S. Kimmel, J. Hearn and R.W. Connell (eds) *Handbook of Studies on Men and Masculinities*. Thousand Oaks, CA: Sage.

Coreil, J. and Behal, R. (1999) 'Man to man prostate cancer support groups', *Cancer Practice*, 7(3): 122–129.

Corney, T. (2004) 'Values versus competencies: implications for the future of professional youth work education', *Journal of Youth Studies*, 7(4): 513–527.

Counihan, C.M. (1999) *The Anthropology of Food and Body: Gender, Meaning and Power.* New York: Routledge.

Courtenay, W.H. (2000) 'Constructions of masculinity and their influence on men's well-being: a theory of gender and health', *Social Science & Medicine,* 50: 1385–1401.

Courtenay, W.H. (2003) 'Key determinants of the health and the well-being of men and boys', *International Journal of Men's Health,* 2(1): 1–30.

Cowburn, M. and Pengelly, H. (1999) 'Values and processes in groupwork with men', in J. Wild (ed.) *Working with Men for Change.* London: UCL Press, pp. 197–206.

Coyle, A. and Morgan-Sykes, C. (1998) 'Troubled men and threatening women: the construction of crisis in male mental health', *Feminism and Psychology,* 8(3): 263–284.

Crawford, M.J., and Prince, M. (1999) 'Increasing rates of suicide in young men in England during the 1980s: the importance of social context', *Social Science & Medicine,* 49: 1419–1423.

CROME (Critical Research on Men in Europe) (2004) *Men and Masculinities in Europe.* London: Whiting & Birch.

Crowder, A. (1995) *Opening the Door: A Treatment Model for Therapy with Male Survivors of Sexual Abuse.* New York: Brunner/Mazel.

Dadich, A. (2006) 'Self-help support groups: adding to the tool box of mental health care options for young men', *Youth Studies Australia,* 25(1): 33–41.

Daniel, B. and Taylor, J. (2001) *Engaging with Fathers: Practice Issues for Health and Social Care.* London: Jessica Kingsley.

Daniels, C.R. (ed.) (1998) *Lost Fathers: The Politics of Fatherlessness in America.* Basingstoke: Macmillan.

Dankoski, M., Penn, M., Carlson, T. and Hecker, L. (1998) 'What's in a name? A study of family therapists' use and acceptance of the feminist perspective', *American Journal of Family Therapy,* 26: 95–104.

David, D. and Brannon, R. (1976) *The Forty-nine Percent Majority: The Male Sex Role.* Reading, MA: Addison-Wesley.

Davidson, K. (1999) *Age and Widowhood: How Older Widows and Widowers Differently Realign their Lives.* Guildford: University of Surrey.

Davidson, K. and Arber, S. (2004) 'Older men: their health behaviours and partnership status', in A. Walker and C. Hagan Hennessy (eds) *Growing Older: Quality of Life in Old Age.* Maidenhead: Open University Press, pp. 127–149.

Davidson, K., Daly, T. and Arber, S. (2003) 'Exploring the social worlds of older men', in S. Arber, K. Davidson and J. Ginn (eds) *Gender and Ageing: Changing Roles and Relationships.* Maidenhead: Open University Press, pp. 168–186.

Davidson, N. (1990) *Boys Will Be ...? Sex Education and Young Men.* London: Bedford Square Press.

Davies, D. and Neal, N. (1996) *Pink Therapy: A Guide for Counselors Working with Lesbian, Gay and Bisexual Clients.* Buckingham: Open University Press.

Davies, L. and Krane, J. (2006) 'Collaborate with caution: protecting children, helping mothers', *Critical Social Policy,* 26(2): 412–426.

DAW (Division for the Advancement of Women) (2004) Commission on the Status of Women 48th Session, 'The role of men and boys in achieving gender equality', www.un.org/womenwatch/daw/csw/csw48/Thematic1.html (accessed February 2006).

Day Sclater, S. and Yates, C. (1999) 'The psycho-politics of post-divorce parenting', in A. Bainham, S. Day Sclater and M. Richards (eds) *What is a Parent? A Socio-legal Analysis.* Oxford: Hart Publishing, pp. 271–295.

De Jong Gierveld, J. (2003) 'Social networks and social well-being of older men and women living alone', in S. Arber, K. Davidson and J. Ginn (eds) *Gender and Ageing: Changing Roles and Relationships.* Maidenhead: Open University Press, pp. 95–111.

Delamont, S. (2001) *Changing Women, Unchanged Men?* Buckingham: Open University Press.

Delphy, C. (1984) *Close to Home: A Materialist Analysis of Women's Oppression,* translated and edited by D. Leonard. London: Hutchinson.

Dennis, N. and Erdos, G. (1992) *Families Without Fatherhood.* London: IEA Health and Welfare Unit.

Department of Health (1998) 'Poor men die youngest', press release 98/175, 11 May.

Dienhart, A. (2001) 'Engaging men in family therapy: does the gender of the therapist make a difference?', *Journal of Family Therapy,* 23: 21–45.

Dienhart, A. and Avis, J. (1994) 'Engaging men in family therapy: an exploratory Delphi study', *Journal of Marital and Family Therapy,* 20: 397–417.

Dobash, R., Dobash, R., Cavanagh, K. and Lewis, R. (2000) *Changing Violent Men.* Thousand Oaks, CA: Sage.

Dougherty, P. (1993) 'Caverns of rage: exploring a gender-conscious alternative to feminism', *Family Therapy Networker,* March/April.

Douglas, T. (2000) *Basic Groupwork.* London: Routledge.

Dutton, D. (1995) *The Batterer: A Psychological Profile.* New York: Basic Books.

Dutton, D. and Sonkin, D. (eds) (2003) *Intimate Violence: Contemporary Treatment Innovations.* New York: Haworth Press.

Edwards, T. (2005) 'Queering the pitch? Gay masculinities', in M. Kimmel, J. Hearn and R.W. Connell (eds) *Handbook of Studies on Men and Masculinities.* Thousand Oaks, CA: Sage, pp. 51–69.

Ellis, J. (2004) *Preventing Violence against Women and Girls: A Study of Educational Programmes.* London: Womankind.

Emslie, C., Ridge, D., Ziebland, S. and Hunt, K. (2006) 'Men's accounts of depression: Reconstructing or resisting hegemonic masculinity?', *Social Science & Medicine,* 62: 2246–2257.

Engebretson, K. (2006) 'Identity, masculinity and spirituality: a study of Australian teenage boys', *Journal of Youth Studies*, 9(1): 91–110.

Engel, G.L. (1977) 'The need for a new medical model: a challenge for biomedicine', *Science*, 196(4286): 129–136.

Engender Health (2006) Working with men website, www.engenderhealth.org/ia/wwm/ (accessed May 2006).

Erickson, B. (1993) *Helping Men Change: The Role of the Female Therapist.* Newbury Park, CA: Sage.

Erikson, E. (1968) *Identity, Youth and Crisis.* New York: Norton.

Erooga, M. and Masson, H. (2006) 'Children and young people with sexually harmful or abusive behaviours: underpinning knowledge, principles, approaches and service provision', in M. Erooga and H. Masson (eds) *Children and Young People Who Sexually Abuse Others.* London: Routledge, pp. 3–17.

Esping-Andersen, G. (1990) *The Three Worlds of Welfare Capitalism.* Cambridge: Polity.

Etherington, K. (1995) *Adult Male Survivors of Childhood Sexual Abuse.* London: Pitman.

Ettorre, E. and Riska, E. (2001) 'Long-term users of psychotropic drugs: embodying masculinized stress and feminized nerves', *Substance Use and Misuse*, 36, 9 & 10: 1187–1211.

Evans, C. (2006) *Genetic Counseling: A Psychological Approach.* New York: Cambridge University Press.

Fairhurst, E. (1998) '"Growing old gracefully" as opposed to "mutton dressed as lamb": the social construction of recognising older women', in S. Nettleton and J. Watson (eds) *The Body in Everyday Life.* London: Routledge, pp. 258–276.

Fairhurst, E. (2003) 'New identities in ageing: perspectives on age, gender and life after work', in S. Arber, K. Davidson and J. Ginn (eds) *Gender and Ageing: Changing Roles and Relationships.* Maidenhead: Open University Press, pp. 31–47.

Faludi, S. (1999) *Stiffed: The Betrayal of the American Man.* London: Chatto & Windus.

Fawcett, B., Featherstone, B. and Goddard, J. (2004) *Contemporary Child Care Policy and Practice.* Basingstoke: Palgrave.

Featherstone, B. (2004) *Family Life and Family Support: A Feminist Analysis.* Basingstoke: Palgrave.

Featherstone, B. (2006) 'Fathers and their discontents: what's a feminist to do?', paper presented at Conference on Identities, Sexualities and Diversities, University of Bradford and the Feminist and Women's Studies Association, University of Bradford, 13–14 July.

Featherstone, B. and Evans, H. (2004) *Children Experiencing Maltreatment: Who Do They Turn To?* London: NSPCC.

Featherstone, B. and White, S. (2006) 'Dads talk about their lives and services', in C. Ashley, B. Featherstone, C. Roskill, M. Ryan and S. White (eds) *Fathers*

Matter: Research Findings on Fathers and Their Involvement with Social Care Services. London: Family Rights Group.

Featherstone, B. and Peckover, S. (2007) 'Letting them get away with it: fathers, domestic violence and child welfare', *Critical Social Policy*, 27(2): 181–203.

Ferguson, H. (2001) 'Promoting child protection, healing and welfare: the case for developing best practice', *Child and Family Social Work*, 6(1): 1–13.

Ferguson, H. (2003) 'Welfare, social exclusion and reflexivity: the case for woman and child protection', *Journal of Social Policy*, 32: 199–217.

Ferguson, H. (2004) *Protecting Children in Time*. Basingstoke: Palgrave.

Fergusson, D.M.L., Horwood, J. and Beautrais, A.L. (1999) 'Is sexual orientation related to mental health problems and suicidality in young people?', *Archives of General Psychiatry*, 56(10): 876–880.

Fitzclarence, L. and Hickey, C. (2001) 'Real footballers don't eat quiche: old narratives in new times', *Men and Masculinities*, 4(2): 118–139.

Flax, J. (1990) 'Postmodernism and gender relations in feminist theory', in L. Nicholson (ed.) *Feminism/Postmodernism*. London: Routledge, pp. 19–39.

Flouri, E. (2005) *Fathering and Child Outcomes*. Chichester: Wiley.

Fook, J. (2002) *Social Work: Critical Theory and Practice*. London: Sage.

Ford, H. and Findlater, D. (1999) *Community Based Interventions with Sex Offenders Organised by the Probation Service: A Survey of Current Practice*. Report for ACOP Work with Sex Offenders Committee. London: Probation Service.

Foucault, M. (1967) *Madness and Civilisation. A History of Insanity in the Age of Reason*. London: Tavistock.

Fox, L. (1999) 'Couples therapy for gay and lesbian couples with a history of domestic violence', in J. McClennen and J. Gunther (eds) *A Professional's Guide to Understanding Gay and Lesbian Domestic Violence*. New York: Edwin Mellen Press, pp. 107–126.

Franks, M. and Medforth, R. (2005) 'Young helpline callers and difference: exploring gender, ethnicity and sexuality in helpline access and provision', *Child and Family Social Work*, 10: 77–85.

Fraser, N. and Nicholson, L. (1990) 'Introduction', in N. Fraser and L. Nicholson (eds) *Feminism/Postmodernism*. London: Routledge, pp. 1–19.

Freudenberger, H. (1990) 'Therapists as men and men as therapists', *Psychotherapy*, 27: 340–343.

Friedlander, M., Escudero, V. and Heatherington, L. (2006) *Therapeutic Alliance in Couple and Family Therapy*. Washington, DC: American Psychological Association.

Friedman, R. (1994) 'Psychodynamic group therapy for male survivors of sexual abuse', *Group*, 18: 225–234.

Frosh, S. (1987) *The Politics of Psychoanalysis*. London: Macmillan.

Frosh, S. (1994) *Sexual Difference. Masculinity and Psychoanalysis*. London: Routledge.

Frosh, S. (1997) 'Fathers' ambivalence (too)', in W. Hollway and B. Featherstone (eds) *Mothering and Ambivalence*. London: Routledge, pp. 37–54.

Frosh, S., Phoenix, A. and Pattman, R. (2002) *Young Masculinities*. Basingstoke: Palgrave.

Furrow, J. (2001) 'Tools for the trade: clinical interventions with fathers in family therapy', in J. Fagan and A. Hawkins (eds) *Clinical and Educational Interventions with Fathers*. New York: Haworth Press.

Gadd, D. (2004) 'Evidence led or policy led evidence? Cognitive-behavioural programmes for men who are violent towards women', *Criminal Justice*, 4: 173–197.

Galdas, P.M., Cheater, F. and Marshall, P. (2005) 'Men and help-seeking behaviour: literature review', *Journal of Advanced Nursing*, 49(6): 616–623.

Gardiner, D. and Nesbit, D. (1996) 'Cognitive-behavioural groupwork with male offenders', in T. Newburn and G. Mair (eds) *Working with Men*. Lyme Regis: Russell House.

Garfield, S. (2006) 'Minding the gap: the therapeutic alliance in domestic abuse intervention groups', unpublished PhD thesis, University College London.

Gartner, R. (1999) *Betrayed as Boys: Psychodynamic Treatment of Sexually Abused Men*. New York: Guilford.

Geffner, R. and Mantooth, C. (2000) *Ending Spouse/Partner Abuse: A Psychoeducational Approach for Individuals and Couples*. New York: Springer Publishing Co.

Gelles, R. (2001) 'Standards for men who batter? Not yet', in R. Geffner and A. Rosenbaum (eds) *Domestic Violence Offenders: Current Interventions, Research, and Implications for Policies and Standards*. New York: Haworth Press.

Gerschick, T.J. (2005) 'Masculinity and degrees of bodily normativity in Western culture', in M. Kimmel, J. Hearn and R.W. Connell (eds) *Handbook of Studies on Men and Masculinities*. Thousand Oaks, CA: Sage, pp. 267–378.

Gerschick, T. and Miller, A.S. (1995) 'Coming to terms', in D. Sabo and D. Gordon (eds) *Men's Health and Illness*. Thousand Oaks, CA: Sage, pp. 183–204.

Ghate, D. and Ramalla, M. (2002) *Positive Parenting: The National Evaluation of the Youth Justice Board's Parenting Programme*. London: Youth Justice Board.

Ghate, D., Shaw, C. and Hazel, N. (2000) *Fathers and Family Centres: Engaging Fathers in Preventive Services*. London: Policy Research Bureau/Joseph Rowntree.

Giddens, A. (1991) *Modernity and Self-identity*. Cambridge: Polity.

Giddens, A. (1992) *The Transformation of Intimacy*. Cambridge: Polity.

Giddens, A. (1998) *The Third Way*. Cambridge: Polity.

Gilchrist, E., Johnson, R., Takriti, R., Weston, S., Beech, A. and Kebbell, M. (2003) *Domestic Violence Offenders: Characteristics and Offending Related Needs*. Home Office Findings 217. London: Home Office.

Gilmore, D. (1990) *Manhood in the Making: Cultural Concepts of Masculinity*. New Haven, CT: Yale University Press.

Goldner, V. (1991) 'Sex, power and gender: a feminist systemic analysis of the politics of passion', *Journal of Family Therapy*, 3(1–2): 63–83.

Goleman, D. (1995) *Emotional Intelligence*. New York: Bantam.

Gondolf, E. (2002) *Batterer Interventions Systems*. Thousand Oaks, CA: Sage.

Good, G. and Sherrod, N. (1998) 'Men's resolution of nonrelational sex across the lifespan', in R. Levant and G. Brooks (eds) *Men and Sex: New Psychological Perspectives*. New York: Wiley, pp. 1–13.

Good, G.E. and Brooks, G.R. (eds) (2005) *The New Handbook of Psychotherapy and Counseling with Men*. San Francisco: Jossey Bass.

Gordon, B. and Allen, J. (1990) 'Helping men in couple relationships', in R. Meth and R. Pasick (eds) *Men in Therapy*. New York: Guilford, pp. 181–208.

Gott, M. (2005) *Sexuality, Sexual Health and Ageing*. Maidenhead: Open University Press.

Gott, M. and Hinchcliff, S. (2003) 'Sex and ageing: a gendered issue', in S. Arber, K. Davidson and J. Ginn (eds) *Gender and Ageing: Changing Roles and Relationships*. Maidenhead: Open University Press, pp. 63–79.

Gough, B. and Conner, M.T. (2006) 'Barriers to healthy eating amongst men: a qualitative analysis', *Social Science & Medicine*, 62(2): 387–395.

Green, H., McGinnity, A., Meltzer, H., Ford, T. and Goodman, R. (2005) *Mental Health of Children and Young People in Great Britain 2004*. London: The Stationery Office.

Greenland, K., Scourfield, J., Smalley, N., Prior, L. and Scourfield, J. (2007) 'Theoretical antecedents of distress disclosure in a community sample of young people'. Unpublished paper, Cardiff School of Social Sciences.

Greenson, R. (1993) 'Dis-identifying from the mother: its special importance for the boy', in D. Breen (ed.) *The Gender Conundrum*. London: Routledge, pp. 258–264.

Griffin, C. (2004) 'Representations of the young', in J. Roche, S. Tucker, R. Thomson and R. Flynn (eds) *Youth in Society*, second edition. London: Sage, pp. 10–19.

Grubman-Black, S. (1990) *Broken Boys/Mended Men: Recovery for Childhood Sexual Abuse*. Blue Ridge Summit: TAB Books.

Guarnaschelli, J. (1994) 'Men's support groups and the men's movement: their role for men and for women', *Group*, 18: 197–211.

Guille, L. (2004) 'Men who batter and their children: an integrated review', *Aggression and Violent Behavior*, 9: 129–163.

Gunnell, D., Middleton, N., Whitley, E., Dorling, D. and Frankel, S. (2003) 'Why are suicide rates rising in young men but falling in the elderly? A time-series analysis of trends in England and Wales 1950–1998', *Social Science & Medicine*, 57: 595–611.

Gurevich, M., Bishop, S., Bower, J., Malka, M. and Nyhof-Young, J. (2004) '(Dis)embodying gender and sexuality in testicular cancer', *Social Science & Medicine*, 58(9): 1597–1607.

Gutmann, M.C. and Vigoya, M.V. (2005) 'Masculinities in Latin America', in M. Kimmel, J. Hearn and R.W. Connell (eds) *Handbook of Studies on Men and Masculinities*. Thousand Oaks, CA: Sage, pp. 114–129.

Halderman, D. (2005) 'Psychotherapy with gay and bisexual men', in G.E. Good and G.R. Brooks (eds) *The New Handbook of Psychotherapy and Counseling with Men*. San Francisco: Jossey Bass, pp. 369–383.

Hall, G.S. (1904) *Adolescence: Its Psychology and its Relation to Physiology, Anthropology, Sociology, Sex, Crime, Religion and Education*. New York: D. Appleton.

Hall, T., Williamson, H. and Coffey, A. (2000) 'Young people, citizenship and the third way: a role for the youth service?', *Journal of Youth Studies*, 3(4): 461–472.

Hallett, C., Murray, C. and Punch, S. (2003) 'Young people and welfare: negotiating pathways', in C. Hallett and A. Prout (eds) *Hearing the Voices of Children: Social Policy for a New Century*. London: Routledge Falmer.

Harden, A., Sutcliffe, K. and Lempert, T. (2002) 'A scoping exercise for a review of the effectiveness of health promotion interventions of relevance to suicide prevention in young men (aged 19–34)', The Evidence for Policy and Practice Information and Co-ordinating Centre, University of London Institute of Education.

Hareven, T.K. (1986) 'Historical changes in the construction of the life course', in M. Kohli and J.W. Meyer (eds) Social Structure and Social Construction of Life Stages (Proceedings), *Human Development*, 29: 145–180.

Harne, L. (2004) 'Childcare, violence and fathering – are violent fathers who look after their children likely to be less abusive?', in R. Klein and B. Wallner (eds) *Gender, Conflict and Violence*. Vienna: Studien-Verlag.

Harrison, C. (2006) 'Damned if you do and damned if you don't? The contradictions between public and private law', in C. Humphreys and N. Stanley (eds) *Domestic Violence and Child Protection: Directions for Good Practice*. London: Jessica Kingsley, pp. 137–155.

Harrison, J., Maguire, P. and Pitceathly, C. (1995) 'Confiding in crisis: gender differences in patterns of confiding among cancer patients', *Social Science & Medicine*, 41(9): 1255–1260.

Harwin, N., Hague, G. and Malos, E. (eds) (1999) *The Multi-agency Approach to Domestic Violence*. London: Whiting & Birch.

Harwood, V. and Rasmussen, M.L. (2004) 'Problematising gender and sexual identities', paper delivered at Cardiff School of Social Sciences, 10 February.

Hawton, K. (2000) 'Sex and suicide: gender differences in suicidal behaviour', *British Journal of Psychiatry*, 177: 484–485.

Hawton, K., Harriss, L., Hodder, K., Simkin, S. and Gunnell, D. (2001) 'The influence of the economic and social environment on deliberate self-harm and suicide: an ecological and person-based study', *Psychological Medicine*, 31(5): 827–836.

Heaphy, B., Yip, A. and Thompson, D. (2003) *Lesbian, Gay and Bisexual Lives over 50*. Nottingham: York House Publications.

Hearn, J. (1996) 'Is masculinity dead? A critique of the concept of masculinity/masculinities', in M. Mac AnGhaill (ed.) *Understanding Masculinities*. Buckingham: Open University Press.

Hearn, J. (2004) 'From hegemonic masculinity to the hegemony of men', *Feminist Theory*, 5(1): 49–72.

Hearn, J. and Pringle, K. (2006) 'Men, masculinities and children: some European perspectives', *Critical Social Policy*, 26(2): 365–389.

Hearn, J., Pringle, K., Müller, U., Oleksy, E., Lattu, E., Tallberg, T., Chernova, J., Ferguson, H., Holter, Ø., Kolga, V., Novikova, I., Ventimiglia, C. and Olsvik, E. (2002a) 'Critical studies on men in ten European countries (3): the state of law and policy', *Men and Masculinities*, 5(2): 192–217.

Hearn, J., Pringle, K., Müller, U., Oleksy, E., Lattu, E., Chernova, J., Ferguson, H., Holter, O., Kolga, V. and Novikova, I. (2002b) 'Critical studies on men in ten European countries (2): the state of statistical information', *Men and Masculinities*, 5(1): 5–31.

Henderson, L. (2003) *Prevalence of Domestic Violence Among Lesbians and Gay Men*. London: Sigma Research.

Herdt, G. (1981) *Guardians of the Flutes, Volume 1: Idioms of Masculinity*. Chicago: Chicago University Press.

Hester, M., Westmarland, N., Gangoli, G., Wilkinson, M., O'Kelly, C., Kent, A. and Diamond, A. (2006) *Domestic Violence Perpetrators: Identifying Needs to Inform Early Intervention*. Bristol: University of Bristol in association with the Northern Rock Foundation and Home Office.

Hobson, B. (ed.) (2002) *Making Men into Fathers. Men, Masculinities and the Social Politics of Fatherhood*. Cambridge: Cambridge University Press.

Hockey, J. and James, A. (2003) *Social Identities across the Life Course*. Basingstoke: Palgrave.

Holland, S. and Scourfield, J. (2000) 'Managing marginalised masculinities: men and probation', *Journal of Gender Studies*, 9(2): 199–211.

Holland, S., Scourfield, J., O'Neill, S. and Pithouse, A. (2005) 'Democratising the family and the state? The case of family group conferences', *Journal of Social Policy*, 34(1): 59–77.

Hollway, W. (1997) 'The maternal bed', in W. Hollway and B. Featherstone (eds) *Mothering and Ambivalence*. London: Routledge, pp. 54–80.

Home Office (1999a) *Living Without Fear*. London: Women's Unit.

Home Office (1999b) *Breaking the Chain*. London: Home Office.

Home Office (2000) *Reducing Domestic Violence: What Works?* London: Policing and Reducing Crime Unit.

Hooper, C.-A. and Warwick, I. (2006) 'Gender and the politics of service provision for adults with a history of childhood sexual abuse', *Critical Social Policy*, 26: 467–479.

Hudson, S. and Ward, T. (1997) 'Rape: psychopathology and theory', in D. Laws and W. O'Donohue (eds) *Sexual Deviance: Theory, Assessment and Treatment.* New York: Guilford, pp. 332–355.

Hunter, C. and Nixon, J. (2001) 'Taking the blame and losing the home: women and anti-social behaviour', *Journal of Social Welfare and Family Law*, 23(4): 395–410.

Hunter, E. and Harvey, D. (2002) 'Indigenous suicide in Australia, New Zealand, Canada and the United States', *Emergency Medicine*, 14: 14–23.

Hunter, M. (2006) 'Fathers without *amandla*: Zulu-speaking men and fatherhood', in L. Richter and R. Morrell (eds) *Baba: Men and Fatherhood in South Africa.* Cape Town: HSRC Press, pp. 99–107.

Huxley, P., Evans, S., Leese, M., Gately, C., Rogers, A., Thomas, R. and Robson, B. (2004) 'Urban regeneration and mental health', *Social Psychiatry and Psychiatric Epidemiology*, 39(4): 280–285.

Irigaray, L. (1982) *Je, Tu, Nous: Towards a Culture of Difference*, trans. A. Martin. London: Routledge.

Jackson, C. (ed.) (2001) *Men at Work: Labour, Masculinities, Development.* London: Frank Cass.

Jackson, D. (1990) *Unmasking Masculinity.* London: Unwin Hyman.

Jacobs, M. (1988) *Psychodynamic Counselling in Action.* London: Sage.

Jacobson, N. and Gottman, J. (1998) *When Men Batter Women.* New York: Simon & Schuster.

Jefferson, T. (1994) 'Theorising masculine subjectivity', in T. Newburn and E.A. Stanko (eds) *Just Boys Doing Business? Men, Masculinities and Crime.* London: Routledge, pp. 10–32.

Jefferson, T. (2002) 'Subordinating hegemonic masculinity', *Theoretical Criminology*, 6(1): 63–88.

Jenkins, A. (1990) *Invitations to Responsibility.* Adelaide: Dulwich Centre Publications.

Johnson, D. (1999) *Father Presence Matters: A Review of the Literature.* National University of Pennsylvania, National Centre on Fathers and Families.

Johnson, L., Wright, D. and Ketring, S. (2002) 'The therapeutic alliance in home-based family therapy', *Journal of Marital and Family Therapy*, 28: 93–102.

Johnson, S. (2002) 'Marital problems', in D. Sprenkle (ed.) *Effectiveness Research in Marriage and Family Therapy.* Alexandria, VA: American, Association of Marital and Family Therapy, pp. 163–190.

Johnson, T. and Colucci, P. (1999) 'Lesbians, gay men and the family life cycle', in B. Carter and M. McGoldrick (eds) *The Exparded Family Life Cycle.* Boston, MA: Allyn and Bacon, pp. 88–105.

Jukes, A. (1993) 'Violence, helplessness, vulnerability and male sexuality', *Free Association*, 4: 25–43.

Jukes, A. (1994) *Why Men Hate Women.* London: Free Association Books.

Kaufman, M. (2006) *The AIM Framework: A Report Prepared for UNICEF*, www.michaelkaufman.com

Kelly, T. and Wolfe, D. (2004) 'Advancing change with maltreating fathers', *Clinical Psychology: Science and Practice*, 11: 116–119.

Killick, S. (2006) *Emotional Literacy*. London: Paul Chapman.

Kilmartin, C. (2005) 'Depression in men: communication, diagnosis and therapy', *Journal of Men's Health and Gender*, 2(1): 95–99.

Kimmel, M. (1994) 'Masculinity as homophobia: fear, shame and silence in the construction of gender identity', in H. Brod and M. Kaufman (eds) *Theorizing Masculinities*. Thousand Oaks, CA: Sage, pp. 119–141.

Kindlon, D. and Thompson, M. (2000) *Raising Cain: Protecting the Emotional Life of Boys*. New York: Ballantine.

King, E. (1993) *Safety in Numbers. Safer Sex and Gay Men*. London: Cassell.

King, M. and McKeown, E. (2003) *Mental Health and Social Wellbeing of Gay Men, Lesbians and Bisexuals in England and Wales*. London: Mind.

Kirby, R.S., Carson, C.C., Kirby, M.G. and Farah, R.N. (eds) (2004) *Men's Health*, second edition. London: Taylor & Francis.

Klein, A. (1993) *Little Big Men: Bodybuilding Subculture and Gender Construction*. Albany: University of New York Press.

Kraemer, S. (2000) 'The fragile male', *British Medical Journal*, 321: 23–30.

Kupers, T. (1993) *Revisioning Men's Lives*. New York: Guilford.

La Violette, A. (2001) 'Batterers' treatment: observations from the trenches', in R. Geffner and A. Rosenbaum (eds) *Domestic Violence Offenders: Current Interventions, Research, and Implications for Policies and Standards*. New York: Haworth Press, pp. 45–56.

Lamb, M.E. (ed.) (2004) *The Role of the Father in Child Development*, fourth edition. Chichester: Wiley.

Lamb, M.E. and Lewis, C. (2004) 'The development and significance of father–child relationships in two-parent families', in M.E. Lamb (ed.) *The Role of the Father in Child Development*, fourth edition. Chichester: Wiley, pp. 272–307.

Lamb, M.E. and Tamis-Lemonda, C.S. (2004) 'The role of the father: an introduction', in M.E. Lamb (ed.) *The Role of the Father in Child Development*, fourth edition. Chichester: Wiley, pp. 1–37.

Lane, R. (2000) *The Loss of Happiness in Market Democracies*. New Haven, CT: Yale University Press.

Lee, M., Sebold, J. and Uken, A. (2003) *Solution Focused Treatment of Domestic Violence Offenders*. New York: Oxford University Press.

Lees, S. (1999) 'Will boys be left on the shelf?', in G. Jagger and C. Wright (eds) *Changing Family Values*. London: Routledge, pp. 59–72.

Levant, R. and Pollack, W. (1995) *A New Psychology of Men*. New York: Basic Books.

Leventhal, B. and Lundy, S. (1999) *Same-sex Domestic Violence: Strategies for Change*. Thousand Oaks, CA: Sage.

Lewis, J. (1992) 'Women and late-nineteenth-century social work', in C. Smart (ed.) *Regulating Womanhood, Historical Essays on Marriage, Motherhood and Sexuality.* London: Routledge, pp. 78–100.

Lewis, J. (2001) *The End of Marriage? Individualism and Intimate Relations.* Cheltenham: Edward Elgar.

Lewis, J. (2002) 'The problem of fathers: policy and behaviour in Britain', in B. Hobson (ed.) *Making Men into Fathers. Men, Masculinities and the Social Politics of Fatherhood.* Cambridge: Cambridge University Press, pp. 125–150.

Lingard, B. (2003) 'Where to in gender policy in education after recuperative masculinity politics?', *International Journal of Inclusive Education*, 7(1): 33–56.

Lisak, D. (1998) 'Male gender socialization and the perpetration of sexual abuse', in R. Levant and G. Brooks (eds) *Men and Sex: New Psychological Perspectives.* New York: Wiley, pp. 156–180.

Lister, R. (2003) *Citizenship: Feminist Perspectives.* Basingstoke: Palgrave.

Lister, R. (2006) 'Children (but not women) first: New Labour, child welfare and gender', *Critical Social Policy*, 26(2): 315–336.

Lloyd, N., O'Brien, M. and Lewis, C. (2003) *Fathers in Sure Start Local Programmes,* www.ness.bbk.ac.uk (accessed 1 September 2003)

Lloyd, T. (2001) *What Works with Fathers?* London: Working with Men.

Lupton, D. and Barclay, L. (1997) *Constructing Fatherhood: Discourses and Experiences.* London: Sage.

Lymbery, M. (2005) *Social Work with Older People: Context, Policy and Practice.* London: Sage.

Mac AnGhaill, M. (1994) *The Making of Men: Masculinities, Sexualities and Schooling.* Buckingham: Open University Press.

Mahalik, J.R. (2005) 'Cognitive therapy for men', in G.E. Good and G.R. Brooks (eds) *The New Handbook of Psychotherapy and Counseling with Men.* San Francisco: Jossey Bass, pp. 217–233.

Malley, M. and Tasker, F. (2004) 'Significant and other: systemic family therapists on lesbian and gay men', *Journal of Family Therapy*, 26: 193–212.

Mallon, G.P. (2004) *Gay Men Choosing Parenthood.* New York: Columbia University Press.

Mandeville-Norden, R. and Beech, A. (2004) 'Community-based treatment of sex offenders', *Journal of Sexual Aggression*, 10: 193–214.

Mankowski, E., Haaken, J. and Silvergleid, C. (2002) 'Collateral damage: an analysis of the achievements and unintended consequences of batterer intervention programs and discourse', *Journal of Family Violence*, 17: 167–184.

Marsiglio, W. and Pleck, J. (2005) 'Fatherhood and masculinities', in M. Kimmel, J. Hearn and R.W. Connell (eds) *Handbook of Studies on Men and Masculinities.* Thousand Oaks, CA: Sage, pp. 249–250.

McLean, C. (1996) 'The politics of men's pain', in C. McLean, M. Carey and C. White (eds) *Men's Ways of Being.* Boulder, CO: Westview Press, pp. 12–28.

McLean, C., Carey, M. and White, C. (eds) (1996) *Men's Ways of Being*. Boulder, CO: Westview Press.

McLeod, E. and Bywaters, P. (2000) *Social Work, Health and Equality*. London: Routledge.

McMahon, A. (1999) *Taking Care of Men: Sexual Politics in the Public Mind*. Cambridge: Cambridge University Press.

McNeill, F. (2006) 'Community supervision: context and relationships matter', in B. Goldson and J. Muncie (eds) *Youth Crime and Justice*. London: Sage, pp. 125–139.

McQueen, C. and Henwood, K. (2002) 'Young men in "crisis": attending to the language of teenage boys' distress', *Social Science & Medicine*, 55: 1493–1509.

Meade, M. (1993) *Men and the Water of Life: Initiation and the Tempering of Men*. San Francisco, CA: Harper.

Mehta, M., Peacock, D. and Bernal, L. (2004) 'Men as partners: lessons learned from engaging men in clinics and communities', in S. Ruxton (ed.) *Gender Equality and Men. Learning from Practice*. Oxford: Oxfam GB, pp. 89–100.

Messerschmidt, J. (1993) *Masculinities and Crime: Critique and Reconceptualisation of Theory*. Lanham, MD: Rowman & Littlefield.

Messerschmidt, J. (2000) 'Becoming "real men": adolescent masculinity challenges and sexual violence', *Men and Masculinities*, 2(3): 286–307.

Messerschmidt, J.W. (2005) 'Men, masculinities and crime', in M. Kimmel, J. Hearn and R.W. Connell (eds) *Handbook of Studies on Men and Masculinities*. Thousand Oaks, CA: Sage, pp. 196–213.

Messner, M. (1997) *The Politics of Masculinity*. Newbury Park, CA: Sage.

Mitchell, J. (1974) *Psychoanalysis and Feminism*. Harmondsworth: Penguin.

Monaghan, L.F. (2001) *Bodybuilding, Drugs and Risk*. New York: Routledge.

Monaghan, L.F. (2005) 'Discussion piece: a critical take on the obesity debate', *Social Theory and Health*, 3: 302–314.

Monaghan, L., Bloor, M., Dobash, R.P. and Dobash, R.E. (2000) 'Drug-taking, "risk boundaries" and social identity: bodybuilders' talk about Ephedrine and Nubain', *Sociological Research Online*, 5(2): http://www.socresonline.org.uk/5/2/monaghan.html

Morrell, R. (2005) 'Sport, violence and masculinities in three Durban secondary schools', paper delivered to the Childhoods 2005 conference at the University of Oslo, Norway.

Morrell, R. (2006) 'Fathers, fatherhood and masculinity in South Africa', in L. Richter and R. Morrell (eds) *Baba: Men and Fatherhood in South Africa*. Cape Town: HSRC Press, pp. 13–25.

Murphy, C. and Eckhart, C. (2005) *Treating the Abusive Partner*. New York: Guilford.

Murphy, K. (1996) '"Men and offending" groups', in T. Newburn and G. Mair (eds) *Working with Men*. Lyme Regis: Russell House.

Murray, C. (1990) *The Emerging British Underclass*. London: IEA.

Nancarrow Clarke, J. (2004) 'A comparison of breast, testicular and prostate cancer in mass print media (1996–2001)', *Social Science & Medicine*, 59(3): 541–551.

National Institute for Mental Health in England (NIMHE) (2006) *National Suicide Prevention Strategy for England: Annual Report on Progress 2005*. Leeds: NIMHE.

Nazroo, J. (1997) *Ethnicity and Mental Health*. London: Policy Studies Institute.

New, C. (2001) 'Oppressed and oppressors? The systematic mistreatment of men', *Sociology*, 35(3): 729–748.

Newburn, T. and Mair, G. (eds) (1996) *Working with Men*. Lyme Regis: Russell House.

Norman, A. (1985) *Triple Jeopardy: Growing Old in a Second Homeland*. London: Centre for Policy on Ageing.

Nyman, A. and Svensson, B. (1995) *Boys: Sexual Abuse and Treatment*. London: Jessica Kingsley.

O'Brien, M. (1988) 'Men and fathers in therapy', *Journal of Family Therapy*, 10: 109–123.

O'Brien, M. and Shemilt, I. (2003) *Working Fathers: Earning and Caring*. London: Equal Opportunities Commission.

O'Brien, R., Hunt, K. and Hart, G. (2005) '"It's caveman stuff, but that is to a certain extent how guys still operate": men's accounts of masculinity and help seeking', *Social Science & Medicine*, 61(3): 503–516.

O'Callaghan, D., Quayle, J. and Print, B. (2006) 'Working in groups with young men who have sexually abused others', in M. Erooga and H. Masson (eds) *Children and Young People Who Sexually Abuse Others*. London: Routledge, pp. 145–173.

O'Connor, C. and Kelly, K. (2006) 'Auto theft and youth culture: a nexus of masculinities, femininities and car culture', *Journal of Youth Studies*, 9(3): 247–267.

O'Donnell, M. and Sharpe, S. (2000) *Uncertain Masculinities: Youth, Ethnicity and Class in Contemporary Britain*. London: Routledge.

Oakley, A. (2003) *Gender on Planet Earth*. Cambridge: Polity.

Oliffe, J. (2005) 'Constructions of masculinity following prostatectomy-induced impotence', *Social Science & Medicine*, 60(10): 2249–2259.

Padesky, C. (1995) *Mind over Mood: Cognitive Treatment Therapy Manual for Clients*. New York: Guilford.

Papp, P. (1988) 'The godfather', *Family Therapy Networker*, May/June.

Parton, N. (2006) *Safeguarding Childhood: Early Intervention and Surveillance in a Late-modern Society*. Basingstoke: Palgrave.

Payne, M. (2005) 'Working with groups', in R. Harrison and C. Wise (eds) *Working with Young People*. London: Sage/Open University, pp. 122–142.

Pease, B. (1997) *Men and Sexual Politics.* Adelaide: Dulwich Centre Publications.

Pease, B. (2000) *Recreating Men. Postmodern Masculinity Politics.* London: Sage.

Pease, B. (2002) '(Re)constructing men's interests', *Men and Masculinities,* 5: 165–177.

Pease, B. and Camilleri, P. (eds) (2001) *Working with Men in the Human Services.* Sydney: Allen & Unwin.

Pence, E. and Paymar, M. (1993) *Education Groups for Men Who Batter.* New York: Springer.

Phillips, J., Ray, M. and Marshall, M. (2006) *Social Work with Older People,* fourth edition. Basingstoke: Palgrave.

Phillipson, C. (1982) *Capitalism and the Construction of Old Age.* London: Macmillan.

Philpot, C. (2005) 'Family therapy for men', in G.E. Good and G.R. Brooks (eds) *The New Handbook of Psychotherapy and Counseling with Men.* San Francisco, CA: Jossey Bass, pp. 278–288.

Pinsof, W. and Catherall, D. (1986) 'The integrative psychotherapy alliance', *Journal of Marital and Family Therapy,* 12: 137–151.

Platt, S. and Hawton, K. (2000) 'Suicidal behaviour and the labour market', in K. Hawton and K. van Heeringen (eds) *The International Handbook of Suicide and Attempted Suicide.* London: Wiley, pp. 309–384.

Plummer, K. (2005) 'Male sexualities', in M. Kimmel, J. Hearn and R.W. Connell (eds) *Handbook of Studies on Men and Masculinities.* Thousand Oaks, CA: Sage, pp. 178–195.

Pocock, D. (1995) 'Searching for a better story: harnessing modern and postmodern positions in family therapy', *Journal of Family Therapy,* 17: 149–174.

Polk, K. (1994) *When Men Kill. Scenarios of Masculine Violence.* Cambridge: Cambridge University Press.

Popenoe, D. (1998) 'Life without father', in C.R. Daniels (ed.) *Lost Fathers: The Politics of Fatherlessness in America.* Basingstoke: Macmillan, pp. 33–51.

Postner, R., Guttman, H., Sigal, J., Epstein, N. and Rakoff, V. (1971) 'Process and outcome in conjoint family therapy', *Family Process,* 10: 451–474.

Potts, A., Grace, V.M., Vares, T. and Gavey, N. (2006) '"Sex for life"? Men's counterstories on "erectile dysfunction", male sexuality and ageing', *Sociology of Health and Illness,* 28(3): 306–329.

Price, D. and Ginn, J. (2003) 'Sharing the crust? Gender, partnership status and inequalities in partnership status', in S. Arber, K. Davidson and J. Ginn (eds) *Gender and Ageing: Changing Roles and Relationships.* Maidenhead: Open University Press, pp. 127–148.

Pringle, K. (1995) *Men, Masculinities and Social Welfare.* London: UCL Press.

Pritchard, C. (2006) *Mental Health Social Work.* London: Routledge.

Pritchard, C. and King, E. (2004) 'A comparison of child-sex-abuse-related and mental-disorder-related suicide in a six-year cohort of regional suicides: the importance of the child protection–psychiatric interface', *British Journal of Social Work,* 34(2): 181–198.

Proctor, E. and Flaxington, F. (1996) *Community Based Interventions with Sex Offenders Organized by the Probation Service: A Survey of Current Practice*. Report for ACOP Work with Sex Offenders Committee. London: Probation Service.

Rabinowitz, F. (2005) 'Group therapy for men', in G. Good and G. Brooks (eds) *The New Handbook of Psychotherapy and Counseling with Men*. San Francisco, CA: Jossey Bass, pp. 264–277.

Rabinowitz, F. and Cochran, S. (1987) 'Counselling men in groups', in M. Scher, M. Stevens, G. Good and G. Eichenfield (eds) *Handbook of Counseling and Psychotherapy with Men*. Newbury Park, CA: Sage, pp. 51–67.

Rakil, M. (2006) 'Are men who use violence against their partners and children good enough fathers? The need for an integrated child perspective in treatment work with men', in C. Humphreys and N. Stanley (eds) *Domestic Violence and Child Protection: Directions for Good Practice*. London: Jessica Kingsley, pp. 190–203.

Rampage, C. (2001) 'Marriage in the 20th century: a feminist perspective', *Family Process*, 41: 261–268.

Real, T. (1997) *I Don't Want to Talk About It*. New York: Scribner's.

Rees, A. and Rivett, M. (2005) '"Let a hundred flowers bloom, let a hundred schools of thought contend": towards a variety in programmes for perpetrators of domestic violence', *Probation Journal*, 52: 277–288.

Reeves, J. (2006) '"You've got to keep your head on": a study of the stories male service users tell about the transition to fatherhood', unpublished PhD thesis, Open University.

Remafedi, G., French, S., Story, M., Resnick, M. and Blum, R. (1998) 'The relationship between suicide risk and sexual orientation: results of a population-based study', *American Journal of Public Health*, 88(1): 57–60.

Respect (2004) *Statement of Principles and Minimum Standards of Practice for Domestic Violence Perpetrator Programmes and Associated Women's Services*. London: Respect.

Rich, A. (1980) 'Compulsory heterosexuality and lesbian existence', *Signs: Journal of Women in Culture and Society*, 5(4): 631–660.

Richter, L. and Morrell, R. (eds) (2006) *Baba: Men and Fatherhood in South Africa*. Cape Town: HSRC Press.

Rickwood, D.J. and Braithwaite, V.A. (1994) 'Social psychological factors affecting help seeking for emotional problems', *Social Science & Medicine*, 39(4): 563–572.

Riley, S. (2003) 'The management of the traditional male role: a discourse analysis of the constructions and functions of provision', *Journal of Gender Studies*, 12(2): 99–113.

Ritter, K. and Terndrup, A. (2002) *Handbook of Affirmative Psychotherapy with Lesbians and Gay Men*. New York: Guilford.

Rivett, M. and Street, E. (2003) *Family Therapy in Focus*. London: Sage.

Rivett, M. and Rees, A. (2004) 'Dancing on a razor's edge: systemic groupwork with batterers', *Journal of Family Therapy*, 26: 142–162.

Robbins, M., Turner, C., Alexander, J. and Perez, G. (2003) 'Alliance and dropout in family therapy for adolescents with behaviour problems: individual and systemic effects', *Journal of Family Psychology*, 17: 534–544.

Robinson, A. (2003) *Cardiff Women's Safety Unit: Final Evaluation*. Cardiff: Cardiff University.

Robinson, A. (2004) *Domestic Violence MARACs for Very High Risk Victims in Cardiff: A Process and Outcome Evaluation*. Cardiff: Cardiff University.

Rodger, J. (2006) 'Antisocial families and withholding welfare support', *Critical Social Policy*, 26(1): 121–143.

Rose, H. and Bruce, E. (1995) 'Mutual care but differential esteem: caring between older couples', in S. Arber and J. Ginn (eds) *Connecting Gender and Ageing*. Buckingham: Open University Press, pp. 114–129.

Rose, N. (2001) 'The politics of life itself', *Theory, Culture & Society*, 18(6): 1–30.

Rose, N. (2002) 'At risk of madness', in T. Baker and J. Simon (eds) *Embracing Risk*. Chicago: University of Chicago Press, pp. 209–237.

Rosenfeld, D. (1999) 'Identity work among lesbian and gay elderly', *Journal of Ageing Studies*, 13: 121–144.

Roth, A. and Fonagy, P. (2005) *What Works for Whom? A Critical Review of Psychotherapy Research*. New York: Guilford.

Rowan, J. (1997) *Healing the Male Psyche: Therapy as Initiation*. London: Routledge.

Rowe, C. and Liddle, H. (2002) 'Substance abuse', in D. Sprenkle (ed.) *Effectiveness Research in Marriage and Family Therapy*. Alexandria, VA: American Association of Marital and Family Therapy.

Russell, M.N. (1995) *Confronting Abusive Beliefs*. Thousand Oaks, CA: Sage.

Ruxton, S. (2004) *Gender Equality and Men: Learning from Practice*. Oxford: Oxfam.

Ruxton, S. (2006) *Working with Older Men: A Review of Age Concern Services*. London: Age Concern.

Ryan, M. (2000) *Working with Fathers*. Abingdon: Radcliffe Medical Press.

Sabo, D. (2005) 'The study of masculinities and men's health', in M. Kimmel, J. Hearn and R.W. Connell (eds) *Handbook of Studies on Men and Masculinities*. Thousand Oaks, CA: Sage, pp. 326–352.

Safran, J. and Muran, J. (2000) *Negotiating the Therapeutic Alliance*. New York: Guilford.

Saunders, D. (1996) 'Feminist-cognitive-behavioural and process psychodynamic treatments for men who batter: interaction of abuser traits and treatment models', *Violence and Victims*, 11: 393–413.

Saunders, H. (2004) *Twenty-nine Child Homsicides: Lessons Still to be Learnt on Domestic Violence and Child Protection*. London: Women's Aid.

Scher, M., Stevens, M., Good, G. and Eichenfield, G. (1987) *Handbook of Counselling and Psychotherapy with Men*. Newbury Park, CA: Sage.

Schlachet, P. (1994) 'Editor's note', *Group*, 18: 194–195.

Schofield, T., Connell, R.W., Walker, L., Wood, J.F. and Butland, D.L. (2000) 'Understanding men's health and illness: a gender-relations approach to policy, research, and practice', *Journal of American College Health*, 48(6): 247–256.

Scott, K. and Crooks, C. (2004) 'Effecting change in maltreating fathers: critical principles for intervention planning', *Clinical Psychology: Science and Practice*, 11: 95–111.

Scourfield, J. (2003) *Gender and Child Protection*. London: Palgrave Macmillan.

Scourfield, J. (2005) 'Suicidal masculinities', *Sociological Research On-line*, 10(2): www.socresonline.org.uk/10/2/.html

Scourfield, J. and Dobash, R.P. (1999) 'Programmes for violent men: recent developments in the UK', *Howard Journal of Criminal Justice*, 38(2): 128–143.

Scourfield, J. and Drakeford, M. (2002) 'New Labour and the "problem of men"', *Critical Social Policy*, 22(4): 619–640.

Segal, L. (1987) *Is the Future Female? Troubled Thoughts on Contemporary Feminism*. London: Virago.

Segal, L. (1990) *Slow Motion. Changing Masculinities, Changing Men*. London: Virago.

Seidler, V. (1994) *Unreasonable Men, Masculinity and Social Theory*. London: Routledge.

Seidler, V. (2006) *Transforming Masculinities: Men, Culture, Bodies, Power, Sex and Love*. London: Routledge.

Senior, P. and Woodhead, D. (eds) (1992) *Gender, Crime and Probation Practice*. Sheffield: PAVIC.

Shakespeare, T. (1999) 'When is a man not a man? When he's disabled', in J. Wild (ed.) *Working with Men for Change*. London: UCL Press, pp. 47–58.

Sharland, E. (2006) 'Young people, risk taking and risk making: some thoughts for social work', *British Journal of Social Work*, 36: 247–265.

Shepard, M. and Pence, E. (1999) *Co-ordinating Community Responses to Domestic Violence: Lessons from Duluth and Beyond*. Thousand Oaks, CA: Sage.

Shildrick, T. and MacDonald, R. (2006) 'In defence of subculture: young people, leisure and social divisions', *Journal of Youth Studies*, 9(2): 125–140.

Shiner, M. (1999) 'Defining peer education', *Journal of Adolescence*, 22(4): 555–566.

Singleton, N., Bumpstead, R., O'Brien, M., Lee, A. and Meltzer, H. (2001) *Psychiatric Morbidity Among Adults Living in Private Households*. London: The Stationery Office.

Sixsmith, J. and Boneham, M. (2002) 'Men and masculinities: accounts of health and social capital', in C. Swann and A. Morgan (eds) *Social Capital for Health. Insights from Qualitative Research*. London: Health Development Agency, pp. 47–60.

Smalley, N., Scourfield, J. and Greenland, K. (2005) 'Young people, gender and suicide: a review of research on the social context', *Journal of Social Work*, 5(2): 133–154.

Smalley, N., Scourfield, J., Greenland, K. and Prior, L. (2004) 'Services for suicidal young people: qualitative research on lay and professional perspectives', *Youth and Policy*, 83: 1–18.

Smart, C. (2004) 'Equal shares: rights for fathers or recognition for children?', *Critical Social Policy*, 24: 484–503.

Smart, C., Neale, B. and Wade, A. (2001) *The Changing Experience of Childhood: Families and Divorce*. Cambridge: Polity.

Smith, G., Bartlett, A. and King, M. (2004) 'Treatments of homosexuality in Britain since the 1950s, an oral history: the experience of patients', *British Medical Journal*, 328: 427–429.

Spiegal, J. (2003) *Sexual Abuse of Males*. New York: Brunner-Routledge.

Squires, P. (2006) 'New Labour and the politics of antisocial behaviour', *Critical Social Policy*, 26(1): 144–168.

Stacey, J. (1998) 'Dada-ism in the 1990s: Getting past baby talk about fatherlessness', in C.R. Daniels (ed.) *Lost Fathers: The Politics of Fatherlessness in America*. Basingstoke: Macmillan, pp. 51–85.

Stanley, K. and Gamble, C. (2005) 'Introduction: fathers and policy', in K. Stanley (ed.) *Daddy Dearest? Active Fatherhood and Public Policy*. London: Institute for Public Policy Research, pp. 1–16.

Stith, S., Rosen, K. and MacCollum, E. (2002) 'Domestic violence', in D. Sprenkle (ed.) *Effectiveness Research in Marriage and Family Therapy*. Alexandria, VA: American Association of Marital and Family Therapy.

Stoltenberg, J. (1989) *Refusing to Be a Man*. New York: Meridian.

Stoltenberg, J. (1993) *The End of Manhood*. London: UCL Press.

Stratford, J. (1998) 'Women and men in conversation: a consideration of therapists' interruptions in therapeutic discourse', *Journal of Family Therapy*, 20: 383–394.

Swain, J., French, S., Thomas, C. and Barnes, C. (eds) (2004) *Disabling Barriers, Enabling Environments*, second edition. London: Sage.

Sweeting, H. and West, P. (2003) 'Young people's leisure and risk taking behaviours: changes in gender patterning in the west of Scotland during the 1990s', *Journal of Youth Studies*, 6(4): 391–412.

Sweetman, C. (2001) *Men's Involvement in Gender and Development Policy and Practice: Beyond Rhetoric*. Oxford: Oxfam GB.

Symonds, B. and Horvath, A. (2004) 'Optimizing the alliance in couple therapy', *Family Process*, 43: 443–455.

Taylor, B. (2006) *Responding to Men in Crisis. Masculinities, Distress and the Postmodern Political Landscape*. London: Routledge.

Taylor, C. (2004) 'Underpinning knowledge for child care practice: reconsidering child development theory', *Child and Family Social Work*, 9(3): 225–235.

Taylor, C. and White, S. (2000) *Practising Reflexivity in Health and Welfare: Making Knowledge*. Buckingham: Open University Press.

Taylor, J. and Daniel, B. (eds) (2005) *Child Neglect: Practice Issues for Health and Social Care.* London: Jessica Kingsley.

Tello, J. (1998) 'El Hombre Noble Buscando Balance: the noble man searching for balance', in R. Carrillo and J. Tello (eds) *Family Violence and Men of Color.* New York: Springer, pp. 31–52.

Tomassini, C., Glaser, K. and Askham, J. (2003) 'Getting by without a spouse: living arrangements and support of older people in Italy and Britain', in S. Arber, K. Davidson and J. Ginn (eds) *Gender and Ageing: Changing Roles and Relationships.* Maidenhead: Open University Press, pp. 111–127.

Tomsen, S. (1997) 'A top night: social protest, masculinity and the culture of drinking violence', *British Journal of Criminology,* 37(1): 90–102.

Tong, B. (1998) 'Asian-American domestic violence: a critical psychohistorical perspective', in R. Carrillo and J. Tello (eds) *Family Violence and Men of Color.* New York: Springer, pp. 114–127.

Treadway, D. (1988) 'Walking the tightrope', *Family Therapy Networker,* May/June.

Tucker, S. (2004) 'Youth working: professional identities given, received or contested', in J. Roche, S. Tucker, R. Thomson and R. Flynn (eds) *Youth in Society,* second edition. London: Open University in association with Sage, pp. 81–90.

Tucker, S. (2005) 'The sum of the parts: exploring youth working identities', in R. Harrison and C. Wise (eds) *Working with Young People.* London: Sage/Open University Press, pp. 204–213.

UK Gay Men's Health Network (2004) *Sexual Exclusion. Homophobia and Health Inequalities: A Review.* London: Health First.

Vivian-Byrne, S. (2004) 'Changing people's minds', *Journal of Sexual Aggression,* 10: 181–192.

Walker, J., Archer, J. and Davies, M. (2005) 'Effects of male rape on psychological functioning', *British Journal of Clinical Psychology,* 44(3): 445–451.

Walsh, F. (1996) 'Partner abuse', in D. Davies and N. Neal (eds) *Pink Therapy: A Guide for Counsellors Working with Lesbian, Gay and Bisexual Clients.* Buckingham: Open University Press, pp. 188–198.

Watson, J. (2000) *Male Bodies: Health, Culture and Identity.* Buckingham: Open University Press.

Webb, S. (2006) *Social Work in a Risk Society.* Basingstoke: Palgrave.

Weingarten, K. (1995) *Cultural Resistance: Challenging Beliefs About Men, Women and Therapy.* New York: Harrington Press.

Werner-Wilson, R., Price, S., Zimmerman, T. and Murphy, M. (1997) 'Client gender as a process variable in marriage and family therapy: are women clients interrupted more than men clients?', *Journal of Family Psychology,* 11: 373–377.

White, S., Fook, J. and Gardner, F. (2006) *Critical Reflection in Health and Social Care.* Buckingham: Open University Press.

Whitehead, S. (2002) *Men and Masculinities*. Cambridge: Polity.

WHO (World Health Organisation) (2001) *Strengthening Mental Health Promotion*. Geneva: World Health Organisation (Fact sheet no. 220).

Wild, J. (ed.) (1999) *Working with Men for Change*. London: UCL Press.

Wilkins, P. (1997) *Personal and Professional Development for Counsellors*. London: Sage.

Williams, F. (1998) 'Troubled masculinities in social policy discourses: fatherhood', in J. Popay, J. Hearn and J. Edwards (eds) *Men, Gender Divisions and Welfare*. London: Routledge, pp. 63–101.

Williams, G. (2001) 'Theorising disability', in G. Albrecht, K. Seelman and M. Bury (eds) *Handbook of Disability Studies*. Thousand Oaks, CA: Sage, pp. 123–144.

Williams, O. (1998) 'Healing and confronting the African American male who batters', in R. Carrillo and J. Tello (eds) *Family Violence and Men of Color*. New York: Springer, pp. 74–94.

Willis, P. (1977) *Learning to Labour: How Working Class Kids Get Working Class Jobs*. Aldershot: Saxon House.

Younge, G. (2006) 'Young people's protests are easy to mock. But ignore them at your peril', *The Guardian*, 12 June.

Youth Justice Board (2004) *Key Elements of Effective Practice: Young People Who Sexually Abuse*. London: Youth Justice Board.

Zeldow, P.B. and Greenberg, R.P. (1980) 'Who goes where: sex-role differences in psychological and medical help-seeking', *Journal of Personality Assessment*, 44(4): 433–435.

Index

Index